From Sit-Ins to SNCC

UNIVERSITY PRESS OF FLORIDA

Florida A&M University, Tallahassee
Florida Atlantic University, Boca Raton
Florida Gulf Coast University, Ft. Myers
Florida International University, Miami
Florida State University, Tallahassee
New College of Florida, Sarasota
University of Central Florida, Orlando
University of Florida, Gainesville
University of North Florida, Jacksonville
University of South Florida, Tampa
University of West Florida, Pensacola

From Sit-Ins to SNCC

The Student Civil Rights Movement in the 1960s

Edited by Iwan Morgan and Philip Davies

University Press of Florida

Gainesville · Tallahassee · Tampa · Boca Raton
Pensacola · Orlando · Miami · Jacksonville · Ft. Myers · Sarasota

This book may be available in an electronic edition.

First cloth printing, 2012
First paperback printing, 2013

Library of Congress Cataloging-in-Publication Data
From sit-ins to SNCC : the student civil rights movement in the 1960s /
edited by Iwan Morgan and Philip Davies.
p. cm.
Includes bibliographical references and index.
ISBN 978-0-8130-4151-3 (cloth)
ISBN 978-0-8130-4959-5 (pbk.)
1. Student Nonviolent Coordinating Committee (U.S.) 2. Civil rights
demonstrations—United States. 3. College students—Political activity—
History. 4. Civil rights movements—History. 5. United States—Race
relations—History—20th century. I. Morgan, Iwan W. II. Davies, Philip,
1948-
E185.61.F917 2012
323.1196′073—dc23
2012009911

University Press of Florida
15 Northwest 15th Street
Gainesville, FL 32611-2079
http://www.upf.com

Contents

Contents

Preface

The student sit-ins to challenge segregated lunch counters in the early 1960s were, in civil rights activist Ella Baker's famous phrase, "bigger than a hamburger." The wave of protests that rapidly developed in the wake of the first demonstration in Greensboro, North Carolina, on February 1, 1960, and the consequent formation of the Student Nonviolent Coordinating Committee (SNCC) in April to provide organizational support for peaceful direct action had fundamental significance for the achievement of the civil rights revolution of the 1960s. SNCC, or "Snick," as it was known, would be at the forefront of the black freedom struggle until internal dissension and ruthless repression brought about its collapse in the early 1970s.

The student-centered movement for African American civil rights that began in 1960 may not have swept aside all vestiges of racial inequality but it had a major role in destroying the public segregation and black disenfranchisement that were the hallmarks of the South's Jim Crow system. Accordingly, there were celebratory events to mark the transformative significance of this new activism in the fiftieth anniversary year since its emergence. These included the opening of the International Civil Rights Center and Museum on the former site of the Woolworth store in Greensboro, where the first sit-in took place, and a conference attended by many SNCC veterans at Shaw University, where the organization was first launched. On the other side of the Atlantic there was also recognition of the profound importance of the new protest movement that emerged in 1960. A conference, co-organized by the British Library's Eccles Centre for American Studies and the Institute for the Study of the Americas (part of the University of London's School of Advanced Study), marked the half-century anniversary not only of the sit-ins but also the formation and subsequent development of SNCC. This collection of essays written by conference participants is the outcome of that event.

Our book has no claim to be a comprehensive history of the student-centered civil rights movement that was born in Greensboro and underwent significant evolution in line with SNCC's changes in outlook over the decade that followed. Instead, it examines selected aspects of this movement to cast light on its complex substance, development, and significance. Insofar as possible, as the title of this book indicates, the contributors keep their lens focused on the student movement in pursuit of African American civil rights. As SNCC developed, of course, the full-time staff that it employed at its headquarters and on its field projects ceased to be students. This was particularly the case after voter registration superseded anti-segregation direct action as the organization's primary focus from the latter part of 1962 onward. Nevertheless, we feel justified in our effort to assess SNCC in its later phases of development as part of the student civil rights movement from which it had emerged. However much the organization underwent change in the 1960s, it retained two fundamental characteristics associated with its early history. First, in contrast to longer-established civil rights bodies, it was an organization primarily built upon on the support of young activists. Second, it continued to embody the belief of the mass sit-in protesters that ordinary people without significant resources and specialized skills could be decisive in effecting social and political change.

This collection is not a history of leaders but of innovative grassroots protest and new organizational development in support of the African American freedom struggle in the world's most powerful democracy. The key themes emphasize the nature and dynamics of student civil rights activism, the impact of direct action on the white South, the internal culture of SNCC, and the ideological evolution of this organization from the biracial optimism of 1960 to a pessimistic view of America and what it represented. The international influence of a movement that captured the imagination of the world in the 1960s also comes under review, in relationship both to SNCC's changing attitudes on the Cold War and the development of racial equality protest in other countries, most notably the United Kingdom. Finally, the epilogue considers to what extent the goals of the civil rights movement remain unfulfilled at a time when there is an African American in the White House and what are the prospects of further advancement toward racial equality in early-twenty-first-century America.

To help place in context the evolution of the movement spawned by the sit-in demonstrations, Iwan Morgan analyzes the nature of student civil rights protest in its seminal year in "The New Movement: The Student Sit-Ins in 1960." This explores how African American college students broke free from the constraints of time, place, and family to launch a new movement that adopted innovative tactics of peaceful mass direct action, established its independence from the longer established civil rights organizations, considered youthful blacks to have more potential for boldness than older ones in challenging Jim Crow, and was more interested in action than philosophy. It also examines the early belief of the youthful protesters that they would gain access to the material promise of American life through the overthrow of Jim Crow and their related conviction about the democratic justification of the U.S. cause in the Cold War struggle with the Soviet Union.

In "Another Side of the Sit-Ins: Nonviolent Direct Action, the Courts, and the Constitution," John Kirk explores the convoluted response of state and federal courts to the charges of trespass brought against Little Rock student activists protesting lunch counter segregation because of jurisprudential tensions between civil rights and property rights. While clearly sympathetic to the aims of the sit-ins as a form of public protest, the U.S. Supreme Court proved consistently reluctant to rule in their favor over the private rights of property owners. It eventually overturned the convictions of the Arkansas students (and over three thousand other sit-in cases) on the basis of the outlawing of public segregation by the Civil Rights Act of 1964. However, its failure to clearly delineate the role of the state in adjudicating between individual liberties and private property rights had implications that remain unresolved a half-century later.

In "'Complicated Hospitality': The Impact of the Sit-Ins on the Ideology of Southern Segregationists," George Lewis moves the lens of analysis onto a vital but hitherto neglected aspect of student protest success—its impact on white segregationists. This essay shows how the sit-ins posed an array of fundamental challenges to the central tenets of Jim Crow ideology. As a consequence, they fundamentally undermined some basic assumptions of segregationist credo, notably its conviction that African Americans were content with the regional caste system, and thereby created divisions among southern resisters about how to combat them. As a result the sit-ins altered the fundamental balance of power in the freedom struggle, not only through their reinvigoration of nonviolent protest but also by wresting the tactical and intellectual initiative from those seeking to preserve segregation.

Clive Webb continues the exploration of the impact that the student sit-ins had on segregationists in "Breaching the Wall of Resistance: Southern White Reactions to the Sit-Ins." This essay acknowledges the importance of the protests in demonstrating to white defenders of Jim Crow the depth of black anger with this system and the consequent segregationist resort to defense of property rights rather than racist doctrine to legitimize their continued resistance to racial change. It also moves beyond monolithic interpretations of southern white reaction to show that this spanned the entire spectrum from confrontation to co-operation. It also considers some neglected influences on white response to the protests, notably international politics and Christian theology, and examines how segregationist politicians in the U.S. Congress incorporated a critique of the sit-ins into their opposition to enactment of federal civil rights legislation.

In "SNCCs: Not One Committee, but Several," Peter Ling takes issue with the imprecise nomenclature of the Student Nonviolent Coordinating Committee. Drawing on existing scholarship, this essay shows how the organization ceased to be a primarily student one after 1962, grew far removed from its philosophical commitment to nonviolence by 1966, and had always experienced tension between its coordination role and its cultural preference for the sovereignty of its local field offices. Adding a new dimension to this critique, Ling challenges the appropriateness in discussion of SNCC of employing the definite article: "the." Ling's examination of attendance lists at major SNCC meetings from 1960 through 1964 traces a shifting organizational membership to argue that there were several SNCCs rather than one. In his assessment, SNCC's evolution reflects a process not of individuals changing through experience of movement activism but of different individuals exerting influence at different times. As Ling argues, conventional understanding of the internal stresses resulting from the influx of student volunteers for the Freedom Summer project need to be reviewed in this context. Rather than dividing an organization that had forged a real unity, the newcomers only aggravated existing volatility and inchoateness.

Many commentators at the time recognized the dramas taking place as SNCC volunteers struggled in the dangerous circumstances of the rural Deep South to help impoverished African Americans in Mississippi and elsewhere achieve voting rights. Giving expression to this, some organizers and student volunteers looked to convey their experience in the form of literary fiction. In "SNCC's Stories at the Barricades," Sharon Monteith contends that the activist fiction writing is yet to receive the attention it deserves—either as personal narratives that are revealing of grassroots efforts to realize strategic goals in the face of massive resistance, or as imaginative and immediate responses to both the threat and the reality of racial terrorism. In focusing on James Forman's novel-length manuscript, "The Thin White Line," and Michael Thelwell's short story, "The Organizer," Monteith illustrates what a sample of these forgotten fictions tell us about the freedom struggle and about SNCC as an organization.

Joe Street's chapter, "From Beloved Community to Imagined Community: SNCC's Intellectual Transformation," traces the development of SNCC's concept of community, placing particular emphasis on the transition that occurred between the conclusion of the Mississippi Summer Project in 1964 and the expulsion of whites from the organization in 1967. The influx of new activists with fewer emotional and personal bonds to the original character of the organization made this arguably the most important period in its intellectual development. Street argues that the resultant transformation led SNCC away from the original biracial ideal of the "beloved community" toward a concept more in tune with Benedict Anderson's notion of an "imagined community" as its long-standing ambivalence about integration surfaced. His analysis particularly focuses on the ideas of those closely involved in the Atlanta Project until their expulsion for insubordination and the so-called Washington clique that took control of SNCC in 1966. Rejecting the traditional approach that interprets SNCC's development in terms of the decline of a redemptive organization, this suggests instead that its evolution was logical and understandable in relationship to its shifting notion of community.

Simon Hall examines another element of SNCC's intellectual transformation in "The Sit-Ins, SNCC, and Cold War Patriotism." While segregationists routinely denounced the outburst of student sit-in protest in 1960 as the work of Communists, civil rights activists were assiduous in linking their demonstrations to the international struggle between the free world and the forces of totalitarian ideology. Hall's analysis traces the use of Cold War patriotism by early student protestors and SNCC and its eventual replacement with a more critical internationalism that emphasized global solidarity among non-white peoples and condemned U.S. foreign policy as racist, expansionist, and imperialistic. While acknowledging that the change cannot be understood outside the broader context of SNCC's domestic disillusionment with white liberals and the rise of black nationalism, it argues that such a perspective had existed within the organization since its founding and had originally operated alongside Cold War patriotism. Ultimately, however, the abandonment of the latter with its combination of powerful moral suasion and steely pragmatism had a damaging effect on SNCC's capacity to attract wider public and political support.

Further developing consideration of the global aspects of the freedom struggle, Stephen Tuck argues in "From Greensboro to Notting Hill: The Sit-Ins in England" that the local and national struggles for racial equality in the United States and Britain can only be fully understood in their international context. The relationship between civil rights activists in the two countries was particularly close in the 1960s and triangulated with developments in Africa and the Caribbean—they followed each other's progress and setbacks, swapped ideas and tactics, and made transatlantic visits. For British blacks, the American civil rights movement provided models of protest and organization for adaptation at home. The sit-ins became a favored tactic of anti-racist activism, but because Jim Crow–style segregation was not deeply embedded in the United Kingdom, they never won the kind of headlines that the U.S. protests had attracted. Meanwhile, American campaigners for racial equality followed developments in Britain, which was more analogous than postcolonial Africa to their own situation. As such, transatlantic developments provided a cautionary tale of the socioeconomic discrimination, racial violence, and anti-immigration sentiment that a black minority experienced in a liberal democratic country. This was lesson that helped to inform SNCC's eventual call for Black Power as its official position.

Finally, Steven F. Lawson in "Still Running for Freedom: Barack Obama and the Legacy of the Civil Rights Movement" considers the relevance of the civil rights struggle of the 1960s for contemporary America. Despite the limited gains achieved through black suffrage and the evident income disparity between whites and other racial groups, he argues that progressive blacks and whites can take some comfort from the past as they look toward the future. The political emancipation of blacks, in which SNCC played a vital role, has made a critical difference. In combining protest with electoral politics, the civil rights movement transformed individuals and communities through collective struggle. Although Barack Obama lived afar from this development in time and space, he continues to carry on its legacy both by embracing its goals and transcending them. As Lawson shows, however, Obama has to operate in an environment in which conservatism has not lost its intellectual nerve as was the case in the 1930s and without the support of a grassroots social movement for progressive social change as existed in the 1960s.

A goodly number of people helped to bring this project to reality. James Ralph, Dean of Faculty and Rehnquist Professor of American History and Culture at Middlebury College, Vermont, was instrumental in the germination of our decision to hold a fiftieth-anniversary conference to mark the emergence of the sit-in movement and SNCC's formation. Thomas L. Blair, a conference attendee, provided insights from his personal experience in the struggle for racial equality in America. The editors, as ever, are indebted to the administrative staff of their respective institutions—Kate Bateman and Jean Petrovic of the Eccles Centre and Olga Jimenez of the Institute for the Study of the Americas—for their hard work and efficiency in making the original conference a successful event. They also thank Meredith Babb of the University Press of Florida for her immediate enthusiasm for the project and her advice on bringing it to completion.

Finally, every editor engaged in a collaborative undertaking such as this one is utterly dependent on the other contributors to deliver manuscripts that meet the demands of quality and timely submission. We are delighted to pay fulsome tribute to our colleagues' endeavors on this score. Along with Steven Lawson but from further afield, the co-editors were exposed to the broad influences of the civil rights movement in general and its student element in particular as they came to political consciousness in the 1960s. Coming from a younger generation, the other contributors have inherited a world that the 1960s freedom struggle helped to change for the better—even if that struggle remains unfinished. Their new and insightful research is testimony to the enduring interest of American history scholars in the United Kingdom in that momentous movement.

1

The New Movement

The Student Sit-Ins in 1960

IWAN MORGAN

On the afternoon of February 1, 1960, four African American students, all age seventeen or eighteen, from the all-black North Carolina Agricultural and Technical College (NCA&T) conducted a sit-in at the Woolworth store on Elm Street in downtown Greensboro to challenge its whites-only lunch-counter policy. Before the week was out, more than three hundred students would join them in sitting in at downtown lunch counters. The actions of Ezell Blair Jr., Franklin McCain, Joseph McNeil, and David Richmond generated a new wave of student protest by African Americans and their white sympathizers that would be of critical importance for the achievement of the civil rights revolution of the 1960s. The city that played unwilling host to this momentous episode had a relatively progressive reputation on racial issues and wanted to be seen as the prosperous gateway to the emerging Sunbelt South, but its place in history became irrevocably linked instead to the black freedom struggle. As journalist-scholar Taylor Branch commented, "Greensboro helped define the new decade." In like fashion, historian William Chafe observed, "Greensboro was the pivot that turned the history of America around."[1]

The wave of sit-ins that followed Greensboro and the failure of local white power structures to suppress them enhanced the self-confidence of student activists. Reflecting this, a meeting held on April 16–18, 1960, at Shaw University, an all-black college in Raleigh, North Carolina, agreed to form a new interracial organization to promote and support peaceful direct action against segregation. As historian Clayborne Carson observed, "SNCC's founding was an important step in the transformation of a limited student movement to desegregate lunch counters into a broad and sustained movement to achieve major social reforms."[2]

Initially, the new organization exercised little control over the protests that it was meant to coordinate, but it started to play a more assertive role as 1960 drew to a close. Its various changes of name reflected this evolution. Originally called the Temporary Coordinating Committee, it was renamed the Temporary Student Nonviolent Coordinating Committee in May 1960. At its Atlanta conference in October, the organization dropped "Temporary" from its title to become the Student Nonviolent Coordinating Committee (SNCC) in recognition that the struggle to overthrow racial inequalities would be long and difficult.[3]

The formation of SNCC, howsoever called, confirmed the emergence of a fresh element in the struggle for African American civil rights in the South. It was significant that after Greensboro, sit-in participants habitually spoke of being involved in a movement. In a report for the Southern Regional Council, an interracial group of civil rights moderates, Leslie Dunbar pinpointed this as a break from the past: "No-one ever speaks of the 'school desegregation movement.' One accomplishment of the sit-in, then, was to achieve, almost from the start, this recognition."[4]

The new movement would play a major role alongside more long-standing organizational actors in bringing about the civil rights revolution of the 1960s. Each of these contributed in its own way to the freedom struggle in the South. Nevertheless, the sit-ins and the formation of SNCC were crucial in galvanizing the other civil rights groups that had shown signs of losing momentum after the highs of the *Brown v. Topeka* judgments of 1954–55 and the Montgomery bus boycott in 1955–56. As historian Robert Cook observes, the student demonstrations "kick-started the civil rights movement into action by revealing the extent of grass-roots dissatisfaction with segregation and providing the existing protest with a mass constituency in the South."[5]

To set the context for the essays that follow, some explanation of the emergence and initial development of student civil rights activism in 1960 is necessary. It is important when looking back on the demonstrations of that seminal year from the vantage of more than a half-century later to understand that they were neither inevitable nor predictable. The outbreak of civil rights protest by African American students and their white supporters took the entire country no less than the segregationist South wholly by surprise.

Twenty-first-century familiarity with student protest as a political phenomenon derives from its frequent occurrence in many parts of the world since Greensboro. In the United States, student peace protest against the Vietnam War was an important factor in ultimately making

America's involvement in the southeast Asian conflict unsustainable. In France, the student demonstrations of May 1968 in support of university reform and broader socioeconomic change nearly drove President Charles de Gaulle from office. The Soweto student uprising of 1976 was an important challenge to South Africa's apartheid regime, which finally collapsed a decade and a half later. Hoping to emulate the Velvet Revolution against Communism in Eastern Europe, students in Beijing engaged in the Tiananmen Square democracy protests of 1989, which were brutally suppressed by the Chinese authorities.[6] As the Greensboro/SNCC fiftieth-anniversary year of 2010 drew to a close, Britain, France, Greece, Italy, and Spain experienced a new eruption of student protest against public-sector austerity measures pursued by their debt-ridden governments.[7]

In 1960, however, the ferment of student activism was unprecedented insofar as popular memory was concerned. Even more surprising to contemporaries, its instigators were young African Americans studying at the all-black colleges (and in some cases, high schools) of the South. Apart from relatively limited protest actions in the 1920s, black campuses had long been quiescent. In rising up, African American students had to break free from the shackles of time, place, and family. Cold War orthodoxy had broadly encouraged conformity and caution on the part of black college youth in the 1950s. According to an eminent African American sociologist, most were politically apathetic, shared white middle-class values, and were ambitious for material success. Scholar and activist Howard Zinn, who became an informal adviser to SNCC and wrote the first serious history of it, held the same opinion of the students he taught at Spelman College, an all-black women's school in Atlanta where he took a post in 1956. Shortly before the campus exploded into activism in 1960, students "were going about their duties trying to just move up in the ranks of society, and it seemed as if that was all that interested them."[8]

African Americans also had to confront the South's Jim Crow system of segregation, whose controls they had hitherto accepted. In the recollection of John Lewis, in 1960 a twenty-one-year-old student at the American Baptist Theological Seminary in Nashville, Tennessee, and one of the Nashville group that exerted leadership in the early SNCC, "All my life, I'd heard, seen and obeyed the rules. . . . I hated the rules but I'd always obeyed them."[9] Assessing the significance of the African American sit-in activists in shedding this mind-set, historian Wesley Hogan commented, "It understates their achievement to see this as an effort to alter the customs of white supremacy—even if the object was such a sweeping set of rules as the southern caste system. They succeeded where thousands of others had tried but failed: they innovated *concrete* ways to throw over an entire array of deferential behavior and ideas."[10]

Family expectations that a college education constituted the foundation for personal advancement reinforced the conformity of black youth. Many African American parents admonished their student offspring against doing anything that could harm career prospects and bring shame on the family name. As one white SNCC activist later remarked, "For most of those students who were sitting in . . . going to jail was about the worst possible thing that could happen and yet they were willing to put everything on the line; they were willing to sacrifice not only their future but their family's investment in them."[11]

Perhaps no one better exemplified the truth of this than John Lewis, the first in his family to go to college. His sense of exhilaration on being arrested for participation in the Nashville sit-ins in February did not expunge thoughts of parental reaction. "A lifetime of taboos from my parents," he recalled, "rushed through my mind as the officer gripped me by the bicep of my left arm. *Don't get in trouble. Stay away from Love Street. Only bad people go to jail.* I could see my mother's face now. I could hear her voice: *Shameful. Disgraceful.*" As he feared, his mother made no distinction between being jailed for drunkenness or for civil rights protest. "You went to school to get an education," she wrote him. "You should get out of this movement, just get out of that mess." As a result, Lewis "lost [his] family that spring of 1960."[12]

Other black families urged caution out of anxiety about the physical safety of their sons and daughters. As Nashville sit-in participant Bernard Lafayette recalled, "There was an ongoing debate between the students and their parents. They feared for our safety, because we were going up against a system that was not known to be very sympathetic or humane."[13] In turn, student protesters whose families lived near their colleges and high schools felt concern that parents, siblings, and other close relatives would be subjected to retaliatory victimization for their activities. Future SNCC leader Cleveland Sellers remembered how hard it was for him as a sixteen-year-old to tell his mother that he would be participating in the sit-ins against segregated lunch counters in Denmark, South Carolina, in mid-February 1960. Although she declared support for him, he "knew enough about the attitude of Denmark's whites to suspect that they would try to put pressure on the parents of those students involved in the demonstration."[14]

Almost at a stroke, mass engagement in the first spate of sit-ins liberated African American students from their habitual restraints. The four youthful protesters who started it all by requesting service at a segregated Woolworth lunch counter had no idea that they would be instrumental in launching a movement that would do much to bring about the most significant racial change in the South since Reconstruction. Sit-ins were hardly a novel form of protest. Groups linked to the main civil rights organizations had already experimented with this tactic.[15] The Congress of Racial Equality (CORE) had done so sporadically in the 1940s and 1950s. Some chapters of the National Association for the Advancement of Colored People (NAACP) Youth Council had followed suit. Rev. James Lawson, an ally of Martin Luther King Jr., had organized workshops for the Nashville Christian Leadership Conference that produced trial sit-ins in downtown stores in 1959.[16] Overall there had been sit-ins in at least sixteen southern cities during the late 1950s, but these had been isolated incidents that attracted little attention either from the press or the public and failed to arouse African American students and sympathetic white students into mass activism.

In contrast, news of the Greensboro protest immediately inspired similar demonstrations by students who emulated the original quartet in being peaceable, polite, and smartly attired. The sit-ins spread first to nearby Winston-Salem, Raleigh, and Durham and then to more distant North Carolina cities like Charlotte and Fayetteville. On February 11, Hampton, Virginia, became the first city outside the Tar Heel State to experience a sit-in. The next day, a sit-in took place in Rock Hill, South Carolina. By the end of the month the demonstrations had spread to seven states and affected over thirty communities. Within a short time, most of the major cities of the South had experienced sit-ins, including Richmond (February 20), Baltimore (February 22), Houston (March 4), New Orleans (March 8), and Atlanta (March 15). The most ambitious protest was in Atlanta, where student leaders from six colleges organized a campaign that demanded not only an end to public segregation but also equality in jobs, education, health care, and public services. Lacking the wholehearted support of local black leaders, including Martin Luther King Sr., however, it proceeded somewhat hesitantly until taking a more militant turn in late 1960.[17]

In total, demonstrations took place in seventy-eight towns and cities across the South and border states from February through June 1960. North Carolina led the way with eighteen, followed by Florida with twelve and Virginia with ten. According to one estimate, more than fifty thousand students participated in the protests during this period. With something like 90 percent of the students at NCA&T and three neighboring colleges taking part in the Greensboro demonstrations at some stage, one told a reporter that involvement was "like a fever. Everyone wanted to go."[18]

Those engaged in this new wave of activism were bound from the start by a common sense of participation in a regional freedom movement. The sporadic sit-ins of the past had never succeeded in transcending local concerns, but involvement in the post-Greensboro protests entailed much greater exposure to violence and legal retribution because of the broader threat they posed to the segregationist system and its values. Even participation in the Montgomery bus boycott had not carried the same level of risk because it fundamentally entailed passive rather than active resistance.

The sit-in movement gained significant and hard-fought victories in compelling the desegregation of lunch counters and other facilities over the course of 1960, but its main successes came in the Upper South and border states. The Jim Crow system remained largely intact in the Deep South as that *annus mirabilis* drew to a close. It took six months to achieve the desegregation of lunch counters in Greensboro (but a further three years of protest to integrate all restaurants, movie theaters, and other public spaces); Atlanta did not follow suit until September 27, 1961. Nevertheless, the victories of 1960 inspired optimism that the sit-in movement would eventually overthrow Jim Crow. As Morehouse College student and Atlanta protest leader Julian Bond predicted to fellow SNCC member Mary King, "I think SNCC's going to be gone in another five years. There isn't going to be a need for us and we're going to be moving on to other things."[19]

By the end of 1960 some three thousand students had gone to jail for taking part in the sit-ins, but incarceration inspired pride rather than shame. Paying tribute to the protestors in a rally at Durham, North Carolina, on February 16, Martin Luther King had urged them to continue their struggle and "show that we are willing and prepared to fill up the jails of the South." The Southern Christian Leadership Conference (SCLC) leader would himself be imprisoned some eight months later for taking part in an Atlanta sit-in on October 19, but the intercession of John F. Kennedy and other members of his presidential campaign team quickly secured his release. In the meantime, many students had already heeded his battle cry to fill the jails.

Eighty-two sit-in protestors arrested on charges of disorderly conduct in Nashville instituted the new phase of peaceful militancy by going to prison rather than pay fines. Twenty-two-year-old Fisk University student Diane Nash spoke for the group at the trial on February 29. "We feel," she declared, "that if we pay these fines we would be contributing to and supporting the injustice and immoral practices that have been performed in the arrest and conviction of the defendants." On March 2 another group of Nashville students targeted the city's main bus terminal, leading to sixty-three further arrests. Fearing that the jails could not hold everyone arrested if the sit-ins continued, and worried for his city's reputation in the glare of national media publicity, Mayor Ben West ordered the release of all the demonstrators on March 3. He also negotiated a suspension of the protests in return for the establishment of a biracial committee to examine how to deal with the segregation of downtown lunch counters.[20]

What could most accurately be described as the sit-in movement's first jail-in took place in the wake of the March 12 protests to desegregate a Woolworth lunch counter in Tallahassee, Florida. On March 18 eight students arrested in this demonstration refused to pay fines after being convicted of disturbing the peace by riotous conduct and unlawful assembly. In their case, national publicity and a supportive telegram from Martin Luther King did not produce release on mayoral order as in Nashville. They would serve their sixty-day sentences. One of them, Florida A&M student Patricia Stephens, whose sister Priscilla was also imprisoned, would have to wear dark glasses for the rest of her life because of damage to her eyes from being tear-gassed in the protest. Undeterred, she wrote a letter from Leon County jail that epitomized the spirit of the new movement and anticipated by three years King's more famous letter from a Birmingham jail. Smuggled out of the prison by a local minister, the letter was published by baseball star Jackie Robinson in his newspaper column. In it, Stephens declared, "This is something that has to be done over and over again, and we are willing to do it as often as necessary. We strongly believe that Martin Luther King was right when he said, 'We've got to fill the jails in order to win our equal rights.' When I get out, I plan to carry on this struggle. I feel I shall be ready to go to jail again if necessary."[21]

Within a short time, it was evident that the sit-ins had broken the mold of civil rights activism in a number of ways. The youthful dynamic of the movement was essential to its character and uniqueness. As

Martin Luther King acknowledged in the Durham rally where he urged sit-in protestors to fill up the jails, "What is fresh, what is new in your fight is the fact that it was initiated, led, and sustained by students. What is new is that American students have come of age. You now take your honored places in the world-wide struggle for freedom."[22]

The new movement's student-centered nature was critical to its determination to remain independent of established civil rights organizations like the NAACP and the SCLC, led by lawyers and ministers, respectively. College-based and community-focused activism generated a democratic spirit of togetherness that carried over into the formation of SNCC amid the demonstrations. In many respects the new group was born as an anti-hierarchical organization that upheld the sovereignty of local activists to determine their own agendas to challenge Jim Crow in their communities. Giving expression to this outlook, veteran civil rights campaigner Ella Baker, formerly with NAACP and presently with SCLC, perceived in SNCC an "inclination towards *group-centered* leadership, rather than toward a *leader-centered pattern of group organization*."[23]

Lacking families to support, jobs to lose, or community status to uphold, the youthful participants in the sit-ins felt they could be bolder than their elders. In the words of Franklin McCain, one of the original Greensboro four, "We wanted to go beyond what our parents had done." Like those who followed in their wake, these young demonstrators were suspicious of the restraining influence of anyone beyond their age group. Two of the four had links to the local NAACP youth chapter, but their decision to protest was a spontaneous one taken the night before at a "bull session" where they "gave our grandparents and parents hell for accepting unequal rights." A seventeen-year-old freshman in 1960, McCain recalled nearly forty years later that they did not tell any adult of their intentions because older African Americans "would have said, talk to the management and see if you can't sort this out around the conference table. But they didn't understand the urgency."[24]

It is, of course, possible to find plenty of seemingly contrary evidence attesting to the deep admiration that many young black activists felt for older role models who had instilled in them the self-esteem and personal confidence essential for their engagement in protest activity. Rodney Hurst, a sixteen-year-old participant in the Jacksonville sit-ins of August 27, 1960, the demonstration that probably encountered greatest violence in the first year of the protests and known in the movement as "Ax Handle Saturday," later testified to the influence of his high school history teacher in developing his sense of self-worth.[25]

A coterie of older advisers, including Ella Baker (1903–1986), James Forman (1928–2006), and James Lawson (b. 1928), influenced SNCC's early development, but it was their commitment to protest rather than their age that earned them respect within the sit-in movement. Critical of the NAACP's focus on fund-raising and court action, Lawson called the demonstrations "a judgment upon middle-class conventional, half-way efforts to deal with a radical social evil."[26] A native of Chicago, where he was a schoolteacher, Forman had come south in 1960 to support black tenants evicted from their farms in Fayette County, Tennessee, for attempting to vote. He had then been arrested for involvement in community protest for better employment opportunities and desegregation in Monroe, North Carolina, in August. A skilled administrator and publicist, he left his Chicago teaching post in August 1961 to become executive secretary of SNCC because he believed in its unique capacity to mobilize the peaceful activism of young blacks.[27] Though Baker was much older than the students, John Lewis considered her "in terms of ideas and philosophy and commitment . . . one of the youngest persons in the movement." As SNCC activist Mary King later remarked, Baker was "the person that you find repeatedly from the twenties through to the 1960s as the pivot, as the catalyst for many of the civil rights organizations. . . . [She] believed profoundly that there is leadership in everyone."[28]

Nevertheless, there was a prevailing suspicion in the new movement that the voice of age, particularly as represented by the black establishment, was the counsel of caution. This is what the Nashville group that was influential in the early SNCC had been taught at their Highlander training retreats in the late 1950s. Ella Baker also warned student activists against attachment to established civil rights organizations because "people and their ideas can be captured by those who have programs of their own." The architect of the Raleigh meeting where SNCC was founded, she saw its purpose as being to identify a cadre of student leaders to sustain the momentum of civil rights activism that the sit-ins had kick-started into life. Her letter of invitation to participants declared that the event would be "youth-centered" despite the presence of "Adult Freedom Fighters." Such admonitions did much to ensure that Martin Luther King's exhortation at the conference for the students to throw in their lot with the SCLC fell on deaf ears.[29]

James Forman later claimed that Baker "smashed" King's plans to dominate the student movement. Taylor Branch, among others, questioned whether the SCLC leader had any such intention.[30] What cannot be doubted is that King was an inspirational influence for many of the student activists. Many had read his account of the Montgomery bus boycott of 1955–56, *Stride towards Freedom*. A goodly number had heard in person, or heard of, King's sermons on the need to redeem the soul of America by ridding it of segregation. Others still had been inspired by his call to fill up the jails.[31]

For SNCC supporters, however, the heady appeal of running their own movement and being an organization of organizers made them resistant to becoming part of the King-led SCLC. "We had pioneered in nonviolent direct action," Julian Bond later commented, "Now we could show we understood the political implications of our movement." Testifying to SNCC's confidence in youth, some three-quarters of the first forty field workers it appointed (a number not reached until late 1962) were under twenty-two years of age. Going it alone meant that the new organization was perennially short of funds in its early stages, lacked skilled administrators, and was dependent on the SCLC for office space in its Atlanta headquarters, but this was deemed a worthwhile price for independence.[32]

The dangers of association with the African American establishment were already apparent to some student activists by the time of the Shaw University conference. To the disgust of Nashville protestors, who had suspended their sit-ins to await the deliberations of the mayoral-appointed civic committee that included two senior members of the black community, this body produced a report recommending only "partial" integration of lunch counters. For John Lewis this was "a betrayal of sorts . . . more evidence of the difference between the generations." In his view older blacks did not understand that what was at issue was "nothing less than being treated exactly the same as the white people with whom we shared citizenship in this country."[33]

The leadership of the NAACP, the largest and oldest civil rights organization, provided further evidence of the age gap in its approach to the protests. Visiting North Carolina after the Greensboro sit-in, National Youth Director Herbert Wright reported that the organization could galvanize a new campaign for racial justice in the South by taking the new movement under its wing, but he warned his superiors that failure to embrace young blacks right away would alienate them. Many NAACP local chapters in Greensboro and elsewhere supported and participated in community protests. Indeed, it was NAACP Youth Council members who carried out the Jacksonville sit-ins of "Ax Handle Saturday." Lawyers with NAACP connections often represented protesters brought to trial for their sit-in activities. Nevertheless, the national leadership was unwilling to commit to Wright's bold vision. NAACP chief Roy Wilkins was too cautious by temperament and doubted that the organization's primarily middle-class black members in the South would approve non-violent direct action.[34]

The NAACP was publicly supportive of the student protests but remained fundamentally committed to its traditional strategy of achieving racial change through the courts. In line with this, Thurgood Marshall, the great civil rights lawyer who had successfully pleaded the *Brown v. Topeka* school-desegregation cases before the U.S. Supreme Court, declared that sit-in protesters were mistaken in their policy of refusing bail to stay in jail. The NAACP luminary told students gathered at Fisk University on April 6, 1960, "Once you've been arrested, you've made your point. If someone offers to get you out, man, you get out." It became clear to John Lewis and other movement activists that this venerable civil rights champion, "along with so many of his generation, just did not understand the essence of what we, the younger blacks of America, were doing."[35]

Without doubt, recent events had brought home to young African Americans that their generation was on the front line of a reassertion of southern resistance to racial change. In the opinion of John Lewis, the year 1955 was "a watershed not just for me but for the movement as well."[36] Southern avowals of unyielding determination to resist the Supreme Court's "implementation ruling" on *Brown v. Topeka*, which ordered lower courts to require "a prompt and reasonable start to full compliance" with school desegregation, appeared to spark a new spate of racial violence against blacks. The worst incident was the horrific murder of fourteen-year-old Chicago native Emmett Till in Mississippi for allegedly sassing a white woman and the consequent acquittal of the two killers by an all-white jury despite clear testimony of their guilt from a black witness. The murdered youth "was three years older than me," Cleveland Sellers recalled, "and I identified with him."[37] Future Jackson sit-in activist Anne Moody, fifteen years old at the time of the killing, recalled wondering "what one had to do or not do as a Negro not to be killed" and looking at "Negro men as cowards" for letting whites murder fellow blacks.[38] Two years later, the white mob's abusive treatment of the nine African American students trying to enter Central High School in Little Rock confirmed to young blacks that school desegregation was more judicial theory than reality. One of the volunteers who participated in the attempted integration, which did not succeed until 1960, wrote in her diary, "It feels as though segregationists are attacking from all sides."[39]

The sit-ins gave young African Americans the means to strike back peacefully at the reaffirmation of the southern caste system. Reinforcing their determination to do so was the shame that many felt for their previous timidity in its face. Having criticized the older generation at their eve-of-protest bull session, the Greensboro four acknowledged their own apathy in resisting segregation. Young blacks, David Richmond admitted, knew all about the evils of this racist system, but "no one was doing anything about it." Accordingly, they challenged each other to take action. Franklin McCain recalled, "We were really hard on ourselves too. So we decided to do something."[40] The feeling of personal transformation they experienced on carrying out their first sit-in does much to explain why so many young African Americans saw participation in the movement as an opportunity for cathartic personal renewal. In essence, this act of protest for the common good gave them a sense of taking control of their own destiny.

McCain's views on this score arguably spoke for an entire generation of black students in 1960:

> If it's possible to have your soul cleansed—I felt pretty clean at that time. I probably felt better on that day than I've ever felt in my life. Seems like a lot of feelings of guilt or what-have-you suddenly left me, and I felt as though I had gained my manhood, so to speak, and not only gained it, but had developed quite a lot of respect for it. Not Franklin McCain only as an individual, but I felt as though the manhood of a number of other black persons had been restored and had gotten some respect from just that one day.[41]

African American female activists expressed similar sentiments. As Diane Nash observed, the black student engaged in civil rights protest became part of "a group of people suddenly proud to be called 'black'" and developed "a new awareness of himself as an individual."[42]

The transformational significance of taking a stand against Jim Crow was one reason why the sit-in movement placed more emphasis on action than on philosophy. It was unnecessary to engage in intellectual justification of a tactic that was sophisticated in its very simplicity as an instrument of mass direct action. As historian John Kirk observed, "In direct contrast to the Montgomery bus boycott, the 1960s sit-ins proved immediately exportable."[43] In addition to its ease of widespread adoption, this was a form of direct action that allowed for tactical escalation, as the jail-ins demonstrated. It was also difficult to suppress without resort to the kind of extreme violence that segregationists may have wanted to use but could not for fear of damaging their cause in the eyes of non-southerners and thereby provoking federal intervention. The mass participation nature of the sit-ins also challenged the fundamental belief of segregationists that African Americans accepted Jim Crow of their own volition, thereby undermining their habitual intellectual defense of the system.

The emphasis on action did not preclude any role for ideas in the new movement. Most of its African American participants found inspiration in the anti-colonial struggle in contemporary black Africa. As one journalist reported after visiting southern campuses in the spring of 1960, "Even the most unintellectual black students were envious of the African independence movement and vaguely moved by it."[44] Nevertheless, such sentiments had more to do with racial pride than with doctrinal theory.

For some activists, Christian idealism fused with belief in the nonviolent philosophy of Indian nationalist leader Mohandas Gandhi to provide intellectual legitimacy for protest. This was particularly true of the Nashville group's commitment to the concept of an interracial "beloved community." Guided by James Lawson, its members had schooled themselves in the doctrines and practice of nonviolent resistance. As Clayborne Carson commented, "Their rules of conduct for demonstrators became a model for protest movements elsewhere in the South." These included not striking back or cursing if abused, remaining courteous in the face of all provocation, and putting love and nonviolence uppermost. Testifying to the Nashville influence in the early SNCC, Lawson secured adoption at the Raleigh conference of the statement of purpose that he had drafted for the new organization. It avowed: "We affirm the philosophical or religious ideal of nonviolence as the foundation of our purpose, the presupposition of our faith, and the manner of our action."[45]

For the vast majority of African American students engaged in the 1960 sit-ins, however, nonviolence was a political weapon rather than a creed. At SNCC's founding meeting, Martin Luther King had called for principled rather than pragmatic adherence to it. "The tactics of nonviolence without the spirit of nonviolence," he declared, "may become a new kind of violence." Some of the Divinity students present could identify with this exhortation, but most of the other attendees probably had the same reaction as the Virginia student who commented, "I don't dig all this."[46]

Cleveland Sellers later explained the dominant mood of the early SNCC: "Theirs was the politics of direct action. They were not guided by grand political theories . . . only by their tenacious belief in the moral rightness of their cause." Even for Lawson protégée Diane Nash, it was participation in peaceful direct action that validated his philosophical concept rather than vice versa. Initially skeptical that the sit-in tactic would be effective, she took part because "it was the only thing that was going on in Nashville that was trying to do something to combat the problem. It was only in the process of using it that I finally became convinced." As one Charlotte student remarked, "The sit-ins were a means of expressing something that had been in our hearts for a very long time." This sentiment later found expression in SNCC's unofficial motto, drawn from the maxim of Robert Moses, who became its field representative in Mississippi in July 1960: "Go Where the Spirit Say Go and Do What the Spirit Say Do!"[47]

SNCC's focus on action rather than ideas in its early days meant that it could accept the support of leftist groups without ever embracing their views. Socialists had some influence at the Atlanta conference that marked the start of the organization's greater assertiveness in coordinating the movement, but most of the attendees had no interest in socialist ideas. Testifying to this, SNCC withdrew its invitation to Martin Luther King adviser Bayard Rustin to speak at this gathering after the Packinghouse Workers union threatened to withdraw vital financial support for the conference because of concerns over his radical reputation. Ironically, SNCC leaders would consider Rustin too moderate when the organization turned more radical in the mid-1960s. Robert Moses, later an iconic figure in SNCC's voter-registration project, initially encountered suspicion of his ideological leanings when he took up a post in its Atlanta headquarters in June 1960. Julian Bond recalled, "We thought he was a Communist because he was from New York and wore glasses and was smarter than we were."[48]

Black nationalist groups had an insignificant impact on the sit-in movement and the early SNCC. Cleveland Sellers, later an advocate of Black Power, recalled a Black Muslim minister making no impression on a group of activists with his "weak Marxist" analysis of the South and racial discrimination. As Bond observed, "It wasn't that there was no one to our left; there was. We just were not ready. We were into our own thing. We *knew* it was right. To our mind, lunch-counter segregation was the greatest evil facing black people in the country and if we could eliminate it, we would be like gods."[49]

In reality, the students who participated in the sit-ins of 1960 were mainly protesting against the pace at which racial change was taking place rather than its direction toward racial integration and assimilation. Encouraged by the *Brown v. Topeka* decision, many had hoped to go to an integrated high school with adequate facilities rather than the kind of training school that blacks usually ended up in—but in vain. Only 6 percent of schools in the South had started to desegregate by 1960. As such, segregated lunch counters were just a focus for their anger with the broader Jim Crow system that condemned them to second-class status. Giving expression to this, a placard carried by anti-segregation demonstrators in Chapel Hill, North Carolina, declared, "We do not picket because we want to eat. . . . [We do it] to protest the lack of dignity and respect shown us as human beings."[50]

The majority of southern black student protesters in 1960 wanted to share in the benefits of American society rather than to transform it. Attuned to the class-based politics of the old left, CORE organizer Debbie Louis perceived a materialistic logic in the early sit-ins. In her view, the students "were motivated by a determination to secure the means for their own economic and social mobility, which in the circumstances clearly necessitated a direct assault on the tradition and law which limited them absolutely." According to one social scientist, African American students attending high-quality schools—often private ones—in urban settings with a low proportion of black population were most likely to participate in the sit-ins, because higher awareness of the wider society instilled attitudes that led to protest activity. In similar vein, social psychologist Thomas E. Pettigrew declared, "The Negro American judges his living standards, his opportunities, indeed, even judges himself in the only cultural terms he knows—those of the United States and its 'people of plenty.'"[51]

Having come of political age a decade after Red Scare tactics had effectively silenced the likes of W.E.B. DuBois and Paul Robeson, the majority of the mainly middle-class and lower-middle-class southern black sit-in protestors of 1960 did not identify with the African American working-class struggles of the 1930s and 1940s. They also accepted the orthodoxy of America's Cold War against the Soviets as a struggle for global freedom. Indeed, many of the early SNCC activists made a direct connection between the freedom struggle in the South and the free world's struggle against communism. Testifying to this, representatives of the student movement appearing before the platform committee of the Democratic National Convention in Los Angeles in June 1960 declared that all

Americans must "enjoy the full promise of our democratic heritage" in order that America could fulfill "its responsibility to the free world."[52]

The sit-in movement signified its commitment to living out an idealized view of America through its willingness to accept the support of white sympathizers in the struggle to integrate the South. From the moment that three white women from the local University of North Carolina campus joined in the Greensboro protests on February 4, the demonstrations of 1960 had a biracial character. The same was true of SNCC. Mary Stembridge, a white Virginian studying at Union Theological Seminary in New York, became the first secretary of its Atlanta office. Other whites, such as Ralph Allen, Jack Chatfield, Mary King, and Bob Zellner, became long-term stalwarts of the organization, while many more supported its activities for short periods. Zellner, the grandson of a Klansman, became in mid-1961 the first white southerner to be appointed a SNCC field secretary. His whiteness made him a particular target for segregationist violence in the voter-registration march in McComb, Mississippi, in October 1961.[53] This continued a pattern already evident in sit-ins that had drawn a violent segregationist response in 1960, notably in Jacksonville's "Ax Handle Saturday."

White southern students became involved in the sit-ins in the main out of a sense that segregation was outmoded and morally wrong. Many responded to the inspirational courage of African American protestors in putting themselves in physical danger to make integrationist ideals a reality. Some became radicalized in revulsion against racial violence. As Bob Zellner remarked of the segregationist response to the Freedom Rides of 1961, "I couldn't believe the level of fury that was coming from my people and what was happening. I could not *not* get involved."[54]

Some white northerners also came south to join in the sit-ins or held parallel demonstrations against Woolworth stores in their own region. At SNCC's founding conference, James Lawson expressed concern that their participation in the new organization's leadership might dissipate the unity of what had started as an interracial southern movement. A compromise was finally agreed to set up a de facto all-southern planning committee, which northerners could eventually join by participating in nonviolent demonstrations against segregation in their own localities (but picketing non-segregated Woolworth stores did not count). Aware that racial inequality existed in different socioeconomic forms in their own region, the northerners initially had a broader view of the freedom struggle than did many southern blacks. After attending the

Shaw University meeting, Chicago University student Ted Dienstfrey expressed confidence that the sit-ins would overthrow Jim Crow with or without northern help. "All this will change," he continued, "but—and this is what no one at the Southern conference wanted to discuss—very much in American society will not change."[55]

Though African Americans welcomed white involvement in the sit-ins of 1960 and the early SNCC, there is no evidence that they systematically sought it. Noting the pride that black students took in their protest activities, political scientist Michael Walzer commented that he had "never heard a Negro ask, or even hint, that whites should join their picket lines" because they thought it better "if *they* came unasked." In particular, blacks were determined to preserve their leadership of the movement. Sympathetic to this outlook, Anne Braden of the Southern Conference Educational Fund, a biracial group committed to civil rights reform, observed that SNCC welcomed white support provided it did not replicate "the old pattern that has often prevailed even in liberal interracial organizations—that of white domination."[56]

Of course, SNCC would change dramatically over the coming decade. The signs of this were already evident by the end of 1960. For many of the organization's black activists, nonviolent direct action was the starting point for the emergence of a new political consciousness. In itself the integration of lunch counters and other public spaces like swimming pools, parks, libraries, and churches did not constitute the sum of their ambition. They increasingly regarded expansion of black suffrage as the key agency of socioeconomic change for impoverished blacks in rural communities. Gaining a bigger voice within SNCC, these more militant members expressed concern that sit-in activity had undergone a relative lull in the second half of the year, something they attributed to the organization's hitherto light-touch approach to its coordinating function. They now deemed it essential for SNCC supporters to engage in activism outside their own communities.

The election in October 1960 of Charles McDew, an Ohio black studying at South Carolina State College in Orangeburg, as SNCC chair in place of the Nashville group's Marion Barry, who returned to his postgraduate studies at Fisk, did much to advance this new agenda. Addressing the Antioch College Human Rights Conference shortly afterward, McDew avowed, "Our fight is not against persons, but persons involved in the promotion and perpetuation of the system we would revise. The sit-ins have inspired us to build a new image of ourselves in our own minds.

And, instead of sitting idly by, taking the leavings of a sick and decadent society, we have seized the initiative, and already the walls have begun to crumble."[57]

The Nashville group viewed any shift away from direct action as a betrayal of SNCC's mission. Tensions consequently increased within the organization over the course of 1961. In an effort to resolve these, the group approved Ella Baker's proposal at the Highlander meeting in August to create a direct-action wing headed by Diane Nash and a voter-registration wing led by Charles Jones, a student at Johnson C. Smith College in Charlotte, North Carolina. Nash and her allies remained suspicious that voter registration, which the new Kennedy administration promised to support with funds, was just a White House device "to get the niggers off the streets." In John Lewis's later assessment, there would be "no separation between [direct] action and voter registration" because they were an equal threat to and provoked the same violent response from diehard segregationists. At the time, however, the increasing focus on the latter marked a decline in influence of the Nashville group that was clearly signaled by SNCC's decision not to invite James Lawson to its second-anniversary conference in Atlanta in April 1962.[58]

SNCC would face other internal rifts in the years to come. Many of the black students who had participated in the sit-in phase of the freedom struggle ceased to be active in support of the group after voter registration became its principal concern from late 1962 onward. The newcomers who took their place increasingly brought a different outlook into the organization. They espoused more radical ideas of economic equality, questioned whether nonviolence was valid on the new front lines of the rural Deep South, doubted SNCC's future as an integrated organization, and increasingly regarded the United States as an imperialistic rather than democratic force in world politics. In addition they favored a more structured form of organizational leadership to drive through their new agenda.

All social movements change over time, and few come close to achieving all their goals. However, the often jaundiced eyes of the present should not lose a sense of wonder at the audacity and courage of African American students in launching their challenge to the southern caste system in 1960. One episode that took place at the outset of the sit-ins epitomized the change that was taking place. At the end of the first week of protests in Greensboro, a group of young, white working-class men, brandishing Confederate flags, heckled and jostled black demonstrators. Some strapping members of the NCA&T football team, American flags in hand, hurried to their defense. Accustomed to African American deference, the white youths asked in amazement, "Who do you think you are?" Back came the reply, "We the Union army."[59] This may not appear a wholly apt metaphor for an essentially peaceful movement, but in one way it perfectly linked the past and present. Just as the Confederacy ultimately had to concede defeat to a militarily superior foe, the segregationist South's failure to suppress the sit-in protests ultimately ensured its own defeat by a morally superior foe.

Notes

1. Taylor Branch, *Parting the Waters: America in the King Years 1954–1963* (New York: Touchstone, 1989), 272; Chafe quoted in "Protestors Recall Success of 1960 Sit-Ins: Museum Opens on Site of Segregated N.C. Lunch Counter Where 4 Young Men Changed History by Sitting in 'Whites Only' Section," February 1, 2010, http://www.cbsnews.com./stories/2010/02/01/national/main6162991.shtml. For race relations in pre-1960 Greensboro, see William H. Chafe, *Civilities and Civil Rights: Greensboro, North Carolina, and the Black Struggle for Freedom* (New York: Oxford University Press, 1980).

2. Clayborne Carson, *In Struggle: SNCC and the Black Awakening of the 1960s* (Cambridge: Harvard University Press, 1981), 19. See also Wesley Hogan, *Many Minds, One Heart: SNCC's Dream for a New America* (Chapel Hill: University of North Carolina Press, 2007).

3. Cleveland Sellers with Robert Terrell, *The River of No Return: The Autobiography of a Black Militant and the Life and Death of SNCC* (Jackson: University Press of Mississippi, 1990), 38–44.

4. The report was later published as Leslie Dunbar, "Reflections on the Latest Reform of the South," *Phylon* 22, no. 3 (1961): 249–57, quote on 249.

5. Robert Cook, *Sweet Land of Liberty? The African-American Struggle for Civil Rights in the Twentieth Century* (London: Longman, 1998), 114–15.

6. For a comparison of the famous episode of the Chinese student facing down a tank in Tiananmen Square and a lesser-known one in the SNCC-supported anti-segregation campaign in Cairo, Illinois, in 1962, see John Lewis with Michael D'Orso, *Walking with the Wind: A Memoir of the Movement* (San Diego: Harcourt Brace, 1998), 192.

7. For interesting commentary linking the 2010 student protests in Europe and the 1960 Greensboro sit-ins, see Gary Younge, "Students' Power Is Limited: But Their Anger and Revolt Can Prove Contagious," *The Guardian*, December 6, 2010, 29. The same author offers insightful analysis of racial issues and racial identity in late-twentieth-century Britain and America in *No Place Like Home: A Black Briton's Journey through the American South* (London: Picador, 1999).

8. E. Franklin Frazier, *Black Bourgeoisie* (New York: Collier, 1962), 76; Zinn quoted in *A Circle of Trust: Remembering SNCC*, ed. Cheryl Lynn Greenberg (New Brunswick,

N.J.: Rutgers University Press, 1998), 27. See too, Howard Zinn, *SNCC: The New Abolitionists* (Boston: Beacon Press, 1964).

9. J. Lewis, *Walking with the Wind*, 87.

10. Hogan, *Many Minds, One Heart*, 23.

11. Mary King remarks in Greenberg, *A Circle of Trust*, 23.

12. J. Lewis, *Walking with the Wind*, 44, 53, 100, 116. In many cases, the gathering momentum of the sit-ins did not dispel family disapproval of offspring going to jail for the cause. One of the protesters imprisoned for participation in the Rock Hill demonstrations of February 1, 1961, wrote his parents, "Try to understand that what I'm doing is right. It isn't like going to jail for a crime like stealing or killing, but we are going for the betterment of all Negroes." Quoted in James Peck, *Freedom Ride* (New York: Simon and Schuster, 1962), 78.

13. "Sit-ins Re-ignited the Civil Rights Movement 50 Years Ago," *USA Today*, February 1, 2010, www.usatoday.com/news/nation/2010-02-01-sit-ins-civilrights-Nhlz.

14. Sellers, *River of No Return*, 20–21. Segregationists often escalated pressure tactics into outright violence as the sit-ins spread. Members of Tugaloo College student Anne Moody's family were subjected to physical attack in retaliation for her involvement in the sit-in protests in Jackson, Mississippi, in May 1963. See Anne Moody, *Coming of Age in Mississippi* (New York: Doubleday, 1968), 240.

15. See Aldon D. Morris, *The Origins of the Civil Rights Movement: Black Communities Organizing for Change* (New York: Free Press, 1984).

16. For discussion of the Nashville group, see David Halberstam, *The Children* (New York: Fawcett Books, 1999).

17. See David J. Garrow, ed., *Atlanta, Georgia, 1960–1961: Sits-Ins and Student Activism* (Brooklyn: Carlson, 1989).

18. Michael Walzer, "A Cup of Coffee and a Seat," *Dissent*, Summer 1960, 114. On the spread of the sit-ins, see Harvard Sitkoff, *The Struggle for Black Equality, 1954–1992*, rev. ed. (New York: Hill & Wang, 1993), 61–87.

19. Mary King's remarks in Greenberg, *A Circle of Trust*, 25.

20. Branch, *Parting the Waters*, 277–79, quote on 278; J. Lewis, *Walking with the Wind*, 102–4.

21. For text of the letter (and other materials pertaining to this jail-in), see Marna R. Weston, "The Letter from the Leon County Jail: Patricia Stephens Due and the Tallahassee, Florida, Civil Rights Movement" (unpublished master's diss., Florida State University, 2005), 70–75, available at http://etd.lib.fsu.edu/theses/MarnaWestonthesis30June2005v9. See also Patricia Stephens Due and Tananarive Due, *Freedom in the Family: A Mother-Daughter Memoir of the Fight for Civil Rights* (New York: Ballantine Books, 2003); and Tananarive Due, "Passing the Torch, Assessing the Toll: The FAMU Jail-in 50 Years Later," *The Defenders*, March 1, 2010, http://www.thedefendersonline.com/2010/03/01.

22. Branch, *Parting the Waters*, 276.

23. Ella Baker, "Bigger Than a Hamburger," *Southern Patriot*, June 1960, 4, reprinted in *The Eyes on the Prize Civil Rights Reader: Documents, Speeches, and Firsthand Accounts from the Black Freedom Struggle, 1954–1990*, ed. Clayborne Carson et al. (New York: Penguin, 1991), 121.

24. Younge, *No Place Like Home*, 109. These remarks are taken from Younge's 1997 interview with McCain.

25. Rodney L. Hurst, *It Was Never about a Hamburger and a Coke! A Personal Account of the 1960 Sit-In Demonstrations in Jacksonville, Florida and Ax Handle Saturday* (Livermore, Calif.: Wingspan Press, 2008).

26. James Lawson, "From a Lunch-Counter Stool," reprinted in August Meier, Elliott Rudwick, and Franciso L. Broderick, eds., *Black Protest Thought in the Twentieth Century*, 2nd ed. (Indianapolis: Bobbs-Merrill, 1971), 308–15.

27. James Forman, *The Making of Black Revolutionaries* (Seattle: University of Washington Press, 1997). Julian Bond comments on the respect younger blacks had for Forman's activist experience, commitment, and skills in his preface to this reissued edition of this memoir, which was originally published in 1972.

28. Lewis quoted in Carson, *In Struggle*, 24; King quoted in Greenberg, *A Circle of Trust*, 24. See also Barbara Ransby, *Ella Baker and the Black Freedom Movement: A Radical Democratic Vision* (Chapel Hill: University of North Carolina Press, 2003).

29. J. Lewis, *Walking with the Wind*, 82; Baker, "Bigger Than a Hamburger," 4; Carson, *In Struggle*, 20.

30. Forman, *Making of Black Revolutionaries*, 282; Branch, *Parting the Waters*, 292.

31. Sitkoff, *Struggle for Black Equality*, 58–59, 74; J. Lewis, *Walking with the Wind*, 45–46, 50, 53, 63–64.

32. See, for example, Sellers, *River of No Return*, 35–37; and Julian Bond, "The Movement We Helped to Make," in Alexander Bloom, *Long Time Gone: Sixties America Then and Now* (New York: Oxford University Press, 2001), 15. See too Bond's remarks in Howell Raines, *My Soul Is Rested: Movement Days in the Deep South Remembered* (New York: Penguin, 1983), 101–2.

33. J. Lewis, *Walking with the Wind*, 106. It especially galled Lewis that one of them, Fisk University president James Wright (the other was Tennessee State University president W. S. Davis), had been the first black college president in the country to express support for the sit-ins just over a month earlier (102).

34. Chafe, *Civilities and Civil Rights*, 170; Cook, *Sweet Land of Liberty?* 116–18; Roy Wilkins with Tom Mathews, *Standing Fast: The Autobiography of Roy Wilkins* (New York: Viking, 1982), 237.

35. J. Lewis, *Walking with the Wind*, 107.

36. Ibid., 46.

37. Sellers, *River of No Return*, 14–15, 16. See also similar comments in J. Lewis, *Walking with the Wind*, 46–47, 66, and Hurst, *It Was Never about a Hamburger and a Coke!* 27.

38. Moody, *Coming of Age in Mississippi*, reprinted in Carson et al., *Civil Rights Reader*, 41–43.

39. Melba Pattillo Beals, *Warriors Don't Cry* (New York: Pocket Books, 1994), 85.

40. Carson, *In Struggle*, 15; Younge, *No Place Like Home*, 109.

41. Remarks in Raines, *My Soul Is Rested*, 78.

42. Diane Nash, "Inside the Sit-Ins and the Freedom Rides: Testimony of a Southern Student" in *The New Negro*, ed. Matthew H. Ahmann (New York: Biblo and Tannen, 1969), 49–50; Nash remarks in Greenberg, *A Circle of Trust*, 21–22.

43. John A. Kirk, *Martin Luther King Jr.* (Harlow: Pearson, 2005), 47.

44. Helen Fuller, "We Are All So Very Happy," *New Republic*, April 25, 1960, 13. For a similar observation, see Mary King's remarks in Greenberg, *Circle of Trust*, 23–24.

45. Carson, *In Struggle*, 21–24.

46. David L. Lewis, *King: A Biography*, 2nd ed. (Urbana: University of Illinois Press, 1978), 115–16; Carson, *In Struggle*, 19, 22–23; Sitkoff, *Struggle for Black Equality*, 84.

47. Sellers, *River of No Return*, 44; Nash oral history in Greenberg, *A Circle of Trust*, 19–22; Sitkoff, *Struggle for Black Equality*, 78; Eric R. Burner, *And Gently He Shall Lead Them: Robert Parris Moses and Civil Rights in Mississippi* (New York: New York University Press, 1994), 27.

48. Carson, *In Struggle*, 29; Sellers, *River of No Return*, 42–43; Burner, *And Gently He Shall Lead Them*, 24.

49. Sellers, *River of No Return*, 44–45.

50. Hurst, *It Was Never about a Hamburger and a Coke!*; J. Lewis, *Walking with the Wind*, 43–44; Sitkoff, *Struggle for Black Equality*, 77.

51. Debbie Louis, *And We Are Not Saved: A History of the Movement as People* (Garden City, N.Y.: Anchor, 1970), 51; John Orbell, "Protest Participation among Southern Negro College Students," *American Political Science Review* 61 (June 1967): 554–55; Thomas E. Pettigrew, *A Profile of the Negro American* (Princeton, N.J.: Van Nostrand, 1964), 191.

52. Carson, *In Struggle*, 10–11; Burner, *And Gently He Shall Lead Them*, 24–26.

53. See, in particular, Mary King, *Freedom Song: A Personal Story of the 1960s Civil Rights Movement* (New York: Morrow, 1987); Bob Zellner with Constance Curry, *The Wrong Side of Murder Creek: A White Southerner in the Freedom Struggle* (Montgomery: NewSouth Books, 2008); and Constance Curry et al., *Deep in Our Heart: Nine White Women in the Freedom Movement* (Athens: University of Georgia Press, 2000). White SNCC activists also contribute oral history remarks to Greenberg, *A Circle of Trust*.

54. Zellner quoted in Greenberg, *A Circle of Trust*, 108.

55. Ted Dienstfrey, "A Conference on the Sit-Ins," *Commentary*, June 1960, 527, reprinted in Carson et al., *Civil Rights Reader*, 122–24.

56. Walzer, "A Cup of Coffee and a Seat," 114; Anne Braden, "What Is White Person's Place in Current Struggle," *Southern Patriot*, September 1960, 4. For Braden see Catherine Fosl, *Subversive Southerner: Anne Braden and the Struggle for Racial Justice in the Cold War South* (New York: Palgrave Macmillan, 2003).

57. Carson, *In Struggle*, 27–30; Sellers, *River of No Return*, 44; Andrew B. Lewis, *The Shadows of Youth: The Remarkable Journey of the Civil Rights Generation* (New York: Hill and Wang, 2009), 81–82.

58. J. Lewis, *Walking with the Wind*, 179–80, 189–90.

59. Chafe, *Civilities and Civil Rights*, 119.

2

Another Side of the Sit-Ins

Nonviolent Direct Action, the Courts, and the Constitution

JOHN KIRK

On May 19, 2010, in the fiftieth-anniversary year of the southern student sit-in movement, Kentucky Republican senatorial candidate and prominent poster child of the Tea Party movement, Rand Paul, appeared to question the validity of the 1964 Civil Rights Act when interviewed on MSNBC's *The Rachel Maddow Show*. Paul conceded that he accepted at least nine of the ten titles in the legislation, but he balked at Title II, which, he claimed, infringed upon the rights of private business owners by dictating to them exactly whom they were obliged to serve. Host Rachel Maddow pressed him: "How about desegregating lunch counters? . . . Were you in favor of that?" Paul replied: "Well, what it gets into is, is that then if you decide that restaurants are publicly owned and not privately owned. . . . Does the owner of the restaurant own his restaurant? Or does the government own his restaurant?"[1]

Amid the ensuing storm of controversy, the Republican Party hierarchy quickly distanced itself from Paul's comments. The chastened candidate soon deemed it expedient to clarify that he did indeed support the 1964 Civil Rights Act and the desegregation of lunch counters. Unwittingly, Paul had stumbled into a long, ongoing debate that played an important role at the time of the sit-ins in 1960. The story of the sit-ins, the courts, and the Constitution has too often been overlooked by movement historians, who have tended to focus instead on the sit-ins in terms of their moral drama, local outcomes, and impact on movement politics. In contrast to the deceptively simple and straightforward act of sitting in, however, the legal and constitutional dimensions of the sit-ins raise profound and complex questions about civil rights in the

United States that, as the Rand Paul controversy demonstrated, were still relevant in the second decade of the twenty-first century.

This essay explores the legal and constitutional dimensions of the southern student sit-in movement. To do this it focuses on how a local sit-in and one specific lawsuit in Little Rock, Arkansas, precipitated the first landmark case before the U.S. Supreme Court after congressional enactment of the 1964 Civil Rights Act. The case poignantly winds through and illuminates the much larger story of the legal and constitutional dynamics of the southern student sit-in movement, providing a richer, more complex, and longer history of the sit-ins that is often absent from movement literature. At the same time, the essay highlights one of the neglected and untold stories of the civil rights struggle in Arkansas, a narrative conventionally dominated by the Little Rock school desegregation crisis of 1957.

The southern student sit-in movement that began in Greensboro on February 1, 1960, spread rapidly to other cities and states. Under pressure from the demonstrations and from the African American community's economic boycott of businesses that often accompanied them, a number of businesses—mainly in the Upper South and border states—either desegregated in accordance with locally negotiated settlements or did so voluntarily rather than face continued disruption during the course of 1960. In the Deep South, however, stronger segregationist resistance limited the early success of the new movement.[2]

In its response to the protests, Little Rock was more akin to the latter than the former. Until the school crisis, it had a reputation as a moderate Upper South city in a progressive Upper South state. The most active segregationists in the city and the state were not respected figures of great social standing as elsewhere in the South but people of lesser social, economic, and political standing. However, the school crisis, which took the city's moderate leadership by surprise, had given them the opportunity to transform their circumstances. The sit-in protests offered them hope of perpetuating their newfound influence through the agency of resistance.[3]

The sit-in protests began in Little Rock on the morning of March 10, 1960. Students from the city's African American Philander Smith College were well aware of what was happening elsewhere in the South. After discussing the matter on campus, they decided that the time had come to mount a demonstration of their own. Around fifty students marched from their college to the F. W. Woolworth store on Fourth and Main Streets to ask for service at its segregated lunch counter. Refusing to serve them, the store manager immediately alerted Little Rock police chief Eugene G. Smith about the protest. The assistant store manager called Woolworth's home office in St. Louis for instructions and then closed the lunch counter to the public. When Chief Smith arrived he asked the students to leave, with all but five agreeing to do so. Those remaining—Charles Parker, age twenty-two, Frank James, twenty-one, Vernon Mott, nineteen, Eldridge Davis, nineteen, and Chester Briggs, eighteen—were arrested for loitering.

The five students made bail of $100 each posted by the Little Rock National Association for the Advancement of Colored People branch. The protestors had forewarned the state NAACP president and co-owner of Little Rock's leading African American newspaper, the *Arkansas State Press*, Daisy Bates, of their intended sit-in. Her husband, L. C. Bates, arranged a bondsman, mobilized attorneys, and traveled to the jail himself to ensure the release of the protestors. Reporters on the scene asked him why the students had staged a sit-in. "Well, put it this way," Bates told them, "you can go anywhere in any store and buy anything but when you try to buy food you are trespassing and the kids can't understand it and neither can I."[4]

After the five arrestees left jail, Chief Smith's consultations with the Little Rock city prosecuting attorney and the Arkansas state attorney general resulted in two additional charges being brought against each of them under Arkansas's Act 17 of 1958 and Act 226 of 1959.[5] These two measures had been enacted amid a flurry of pro-segregation legislation approved by the Arkansas General Assembly of 1958 and the special session of the Arkansas General Assembly of 1959, with both legislative sessions taking place against the backdrop of the ongoing school desegregation struggle in Little Rock. Act 17 prohibited "any person from creating a disturbance or breach of the peace on any public school property, school cafeteria, or any public place of business." It carried a maximum fine of $500 and a maximum six-month prison sentence.[6] Act 226 prohibited "any person from creating a disturbance or breach of the peace in any public place of business." This measure carried a maximum fine of $500 and a maximum six-month prison sentence.[7]

Dr. M. Lafayette Harris, president of Philander Smith College, released a statement denying foreknowledge of the students' actions. "The college does not and has never subscribed to mass action in dealing with difficult problems," he declared. "A full scale investigation is already under way to determine the facts relevant to the incident."[8] Like many other presidents of African American colleges, Harris trod a fine line between supporting his students, maintaining good relations with the city's white community, and placating the college's board of trustees, who held varying opinions on the sit-ins.[9] Nevertheless, no student subsequently faced further action by the college.[10]

Support from others in the African American community outside of the NAACP was in short supply. The 1957 school crisis had not only disrupted existing lines of contact between African American leaders and the white community but also left a vacuum in African American community leadership that Daisy and L. C. Bates temporarily filled. As Regional National Urban League representative C. D. Coleman reported in 1959, "The one great problem facing Little Rock [is] the lack of unity, confidence and cooperation between Negro leaders and the lack of regular and orderly lines of communication between Negro organizations. . . . Disunity among Negro leaders [is of] greater concern than the school crisis."[11] In like vein, John Walker, the African American associate director of the Arkansas Council on Human Relations, the state affiliate of the Atlanta-based Southern Regional Council, observed in 1960, "Negro leadership is virtually nil." In his estimation, "the 'masses' of Negroes are anxious for more progressive leadership from new people."[12]

On March 17, the five students arrested in the sit-in appeared for trial at Little Rock's Municipal Court. Other Philander Smith students packed the courtroom in a show of solidarity. Judge Quinn Glover found the students guilty under Act 226 but dismissed the charges against them under state loitering statutes and Act 17 on grounds that this single measure sufficiently covered their offenses. Glover handed each of the accused a $250 fine and a thirty-day jail sentence. The students' lawyers, Little Rock attorney Harold B. Anderson and Pine Bluff, Arkansas, attorney George Howard Jr., indicated that the students' fines and sentences would be appealed.[13]

In a show of defiance, and to place further pressure on downtown merchants, some forty to fifty Philander Smith students immediately left the courtroom and headed downtown to stage further sit-ins. This time they targeted not only Woolworth's but also other major downtown stores. All the establishments closed their lunch counters to customers when sit-ins took place. The students later convened at the state capitol, where they sang "God Bless America" and "The Star-Spangled Banner" before dispersing.[14]

Efforts by the Little Rock NAACP to hold talks with the Little Rock Chamber of Commerce about desegregating lunch counters to halt the sit-ins drew a noncommittal response. An impromptu poll of white community leaders by the local *Arkansas Democrat* newspaper revealed that most rejected the sit-ins as an acceptable form of protest.[15] The reluctance of local whites to enter into a dialogue with African Americans mirrored the initial reactions to sit-ins in many other communities across the South. Meanwhile, public announcements by national chain stores, such as F. W. Woolworth, S. S. Kresge, S. H. Kress, and W. T. Grant, declared that the policy of segregation would continue.

In light of this, the NAACP's national office called for a boycott of stores to support the aims of the sit-in demonstrators. On March 31 the Little Rock NAACP adopted what it called a "Racial Self-Defense Policy" against discrimination by urging people not to patronize stores that practiced segregation. Local branch president Rev. J. C. Crenchaw sent a memorandum to every downtown store operating a segregated lunch counter to announce this policy. He also pleaded with "all religious institutions, fraternal organizations, fraternities, sororities, civic and political groups" in the African American community to withdraw patronage from targeted stores. The memorandum called for a rallying of the community in support of the sit-in activists. "HE NEEDS OUR HELP," it appealed, "we have the family purse and we have the ballot, and the NAACP is asking 'DO YOU HAVE THE WILL?'" The answer was seemingly no. Within just a week the boycott faded.[16]

As the NAACP mobilized economic boycotts to support the sit-ins in cities throughout the South, the NAACP Legal Defense Fund (LDF) deliberated on how best to help those arrested for taking part in the protests. On March 18, 1960, Thurgood Marshall called a conference of sixty-two LDF lawyers at Howard University in Washington, D.C., to develop a legal strategy for the sit-in cases. Four options came under review. First, sit-in participants could claim a violation of the Fourteenth Amendment's guarantee of due process if they were charged with a breach of the peace without any actual evidence of a disturbance having taking place. Second, they could claim that segregation laws violated the Fourteenth Amendment's equal protection clause, since whites were served at lunch counters when African Americans were not. Third, if sit-in participants were convicted of trespass in a place where segregation laws existed, this too would be a violation of the equal protection clause, since the trespass laws were not being equally applied to whites. Fourth, for any sit-in participants convicted on state-owned property, the Fourteenth Amendment's equal protection clause prohibited states from enforcing segregation statues.[17]

In the 1883 rulings collectively known as the *Civil Rights Cases*, however, the U.S. Supreme Court had made explicitly clear that the equal protection clause did not cover private individuals, organizations, or establishments. They were free to choose their own clientele even if that meant discriminating on the grounds of race.[18] What, then, would happen in a case where there was no connection between state action and the conviction of sit-in participants? Did owners of private establishments still have the right to discriminate, as the *Civil Rights Cases* suggested? LDF lawyers looked to the more recent case of *Shelley v. Kraemer* (1948) as a precedent for extending the Fourteenth Amendment's equal protection clause to private discrimination.[19] *Shelley* involved the use of restrictive covenants in property contracts to prevent the sale of homes to African Americans. The U.S. Supreme Court had ruled against the use of such covenants on the grounds that state action was required to enforce these private contracts. This allowed a very wide interpretation of what "state action" meant.[20] As LDF lawyer Jack Greenberg put it, "Since private decisions cannot be enforced without an ultimate, although sometimes only implicit, state sanction, is everything we do 'state action'? Do all personal decisions present constitutional questions? Where should the courts draw the line?"[21]

On April 11, the five Little Rock sit-in students arrested on March 10 appeared before Judge William J. Kirby in the city's Circuit Court to appeal their fines and sentences. In support of the NAACP's non-patronage campaign, all wore badges reading, "I am wearing 1959 clothes with 1960 dignity. I refuse to patronize segregated stores." Kirby set the trial date for April 27.[22] The following day, ten students entered the McLellan store at 10:15 A.M. and asked for service at the lunch counter. The manager promptly closed the counter. The same thing happened at the Woolworth, Blass, and Pfeifer establishments.[23]

On April 13, another group of students, Eugene D. Smith, age twenty-one, Melvin T. Jackson, twenty, McLoyd Buchanan, nineteen, William Rogers Jr., nineteen, Sammy J. Baker, eighteen, and Winston Jones, eighteen, held a sit-in at the Pfeifer department store. When the manager asked them to leave, all but Jackson agreed to go. As with the first group arrested on March 10, the police charged the six protestors under Act 226.

In a separate incident, two other students, Thomas B. Robinson, age twenty, and Frank James Lupper, nineteen, requested service at the Blass lunch counter. Informed by the store manager that he was not prepared to serve them, they refused his request to leave the premises. The assistant manager then called the police, who escorted the two protestors from the building. In addition to being charged under Act 226, Lupper and Robinson were indicted under Act 14 for their refusal to leave the store at the request of the manager. Enacted by the 1959 special session of the Arkansas General Assembly, this measure made it "unlawful for any person to refuse to leave the business premises of any person when so requested by the manager or owner thereof." The maximum fine and jail sentence allowed under its terms were $500 and thirty days.[24]

On April 15, students from local colleges and high schools, with the support of the local NAACP, sought to keep up pressure on downtown stores by picketing them. Around twenty students marched outside the Blass, Pfeifer, and McLellan stores holding placards that variously read: "We are not buying where we can't eat"; "Jailing our youth will not solve the problem"; and "Help us make democracy work. NAACP Youth Council." L. C. and Daisy Bates joined them at various points. The latter told reporters that "the picketing will continue indefinitely until the conscience of the community is made to realize that Negroes are being refused service in these places." She added, "The Negro is just not going to be satisfied with a situation where he can buy $1,000 worth of merchandise in one department of a store but he is considered trespassing and arrested if he attempts to spend one dime at the lunch counter." According to press reports, there were few incidents as a result of the picketing. Most shoppers ignored the protest, some gathered in groups to watch, and at one point a group of white teenagers sought to impede the pickets by standing in their way and blowing cigarette smoke in their faces. No arrests were made.[25]

On April 21, the trials of the second and third group of sit-in cases manifested the growing annoyance and irritation of the white judiciary with the latest turn in events. In the Municipal Court, Judge Glover imposed harsher penalties than in the first sit-in case in handing the group of six students charged under Act 226 a $250 fine and a sixty-day jail sentence each. The two students charged under Act 226 and Act 14 received even tougher sentences in the form of a $400 fine and ninety days in jail.[26]

The hearings of protestors challenging their convictions underscored the bench's intent to pursue a hard line against sit-ins. At the April 27 appeal of the five students arrested for the first Little Rock demonstration, Circuit Court Judge William J. Kirby handed each one a $500 fine and sixty days in jail, thereby doubling the sentences imposed by Glover in the Little Rock Municipal Court.[27] On May 31, hearing the second batch of sit-in appeals of the six students charged under Act 226, he again doubled the penalties for five of the defendants, imposing on them the maximum fine of $500 and sixty-day jail sentences. The remaining appellant, Melvin T. Jackson, who had refused to leave the lunch counter at the request of store officials, received not only a $500 fine but also a prison sentence of six months, the maximum allowed under the law.[28]

On June 17, Kirby presided at the appeal of Frank James Lupper and Thomas B. Robinson. Counseled by their attorneys, Harold Anderson and Arkansas NAACP Legal Redress Committee chairman Wiley Branton, the two students opted for a jury trial. The all-white jury took just fifteen minutes to find them guilty. Kirby handed both students a $1,000 fine and a seven-month prison sentence. In addition to the maximum fines and prison terms allowed under Act 226, this sentence imposed a further $500 fine and thirty-day jail sentence allowed under Act 14.[29] As in all the cases heard by Kirby in the Circuit Court, the students' lawyers indicated that they would appeal their cases to the Arkansas Supreme Court.[30]

The summer recess at Philander Smith ended the sit-ins, since many students left Little Rock to return to their homes elsewhere in Arkansas and other states.[31] However the protests revived in the fall semester under the banner of the newly formed Arkansas Student Nonviolent Coordinating Committee, popularly known as "Arsnick."[32] On November 8, 1960, the day of national and state elections, thirty students marched on the Little Rock courthouse waving banners of protest at continuing segregation in the city.[33] On November 29, thirteen students demanded service at the Woolworth lunch counter, but complied with the request of the new Little Rock police chief, R. E. Glasscock, to leave. Accordingly, no arrests were made.[34]

The next day, seven students who demanded service at the same lunch counter refused to leave and were arrested. Charles Parker, age twenty-two (who had participated in the first sit-in in March 1960 and whose conviction for this was already on appeal with the Arkansas Supreme Court), Lonnie McIntosh, twenty, Ted Hines, eighteen, Billy Bowles, eighteen, Edward Green, eighteen, Henry Daniels, eighteen, and Myrabel Callaway, eighteen, were all charged under Act 226.[35] On December 1, Little Rock Municipal Court Judge Quinn Glover deferred six of the seven new cases until after the Arkansas Supreme Court had heard the earlier sit-in cases.[36]

In the trickle of cases that came before the U.S. Supreme Court in its 1960 and 1961 terms, the nation's ultimate court of appeal consistently reversed the convictions of sit-in participants. However, it refused to extend the Fourteenth Amendment's equal protection clause to instances of private discrimination as NAACP lawyers wanted. Doing so, the Court believed, would be tantamount to ordering private businesses to desegregate. Instead, the majority of justices sidestepped the equal protection clause in devising other ways to reverse sit-in convictions. In the case of *Boynton v. Virginia* (1960), for example, the Court used the Interstate Commerce Act to reverse the conviction of Bruce Boynton, an African American Howard University law student arrested for refusing to leave the white section of a bus terminal restaurant in Richmond, Virginia, in December 1958. In the case of *Garner v. Louisiana* (1961), the convictions of sit-in protestors in Baton Rouge were reversed on the grounds that there was insufficient evidence that their actions had caused a breach of the peace under state trespass laws.[37]

On January 16, 1961, the Arkansas Supreme Court heard its first sit-in cases, with Branton and Anderson again representing the appellants. The former raised several points along the lines that LDF lawyers had previously discussed. First, he argued that the students' Fourteenth Amendment right to equal protection was being violated. He conceded that businesses had the right to choose their own clientele, but he characterized the use of criminal laws against African Americans who asked for service as amounting to "state support [for] private prejudice," since whites asking for similar service were not treated in the same way. Second, Branton insisted that Act 226 and Act 17 should both be declared unconstitutional, since they handed powers to the state that were far too vague and sweeping. In contrast to an existing state law that defined disturbance of the peace as the commitment of a "willful and malicious act," he pointed out that the new measures made no such distinction. Third, even if the Court found the state acts constitutional, Branton claimed that there was too little evidence upon which to find the students guilty. Fourth, he charged that the fines and the sentences handed down by the lower courts "were unusually harsh because the students had espoused an unpopular cause." Branton believed that the sentences were specifically aimed to halt the protests and "break the spirit of other Negroes working for racial equality" rather than to ensure justice. He contended that if the court did uphold the students' sentences, at the very least the fines and jail terms should be reduced.[38]

For the state, Russell G. Morton, an administrative aide to Arkansas attorney general J. Frank Holt, contended that the students had not been arrested for requesting service but for refusing to leave the premises when asked to do so and because their refusal to leave meant that there was a threat of disruption and violence. The charges against them, Morton insisted, had nothing to do with their color, while their fines and sentences did not exceed what was provided for under the law.[39]

The Arkansas Supreme Court took the cases under submission but waited almost two and a half years to hand down a ruling. This delay in adjudging the constitutional issues under consideration held up the consideration of cases still going through the lower courts.[40] The state supreme court excused its inaction by pointing to a lack of direction from the U.S. Supreme Court, which remained seemingly reluctant to tackle the central Fourteenth Amendment constitutional question in the sit-in cases.

In its 1962 term, the flow of sit-in cases that reached the U.S. Supreme Court increased in volume. In deciding the first group of these under *Peterson v. City of Greenville*, the justices overturned the convictions of sit-in participants on the basis that local ordinances required segregation in restaurants, thereby demonstrating a clear link between state action and racial discrimination. In the second group, decided under *Lombard v. Louisiana*, sit-in convictions were overturned because city officials had made it clear prior to the sit-ins that participants would be prosecuted. This, the Court ruled, gave explicit state sanction to uphold segregation. In *Griffin v. Maryland*, the majority of justices looked to stretch the idea of state action even further. Those supporting a liberal interpretation of this concept overturned the convictions on grounds that the protestors had been asked to leave by a deputized county sheriff who worked as a security guard for the company where the sit-ins had taken place. The case proved so divisive that the Supreme Court decided to hear rearguments in its 1963 term before handing down a ruling.[41]

The 1962 term came to an end with the justices still dismissing convictions without tackling the thorny constitutional question of extending the provisions of the equal protection clause. Unwilling to wait further, the Arkansas Supreme Court handed down its ruling in the local Little Rock sit-in cases on May 13, 1963. Chief Justice James D. Johnson (a former president of the Associated Citizens' Councils of Arkansas, which was dedicated to resisting school desegregation) ordered the convictions of all students arrested under the breach of the peace provisions of Act 226 to be overturned. The state court accepted Wiley Branton's argument that there was insufficient evidence to support the convictions. Echoing the reasoning of the U.S. Supreme Court in its sit-in cases, it pointed out that the students had been asked to leave the stores by local police who lacked the authority to make such a request. In any case, there was no actual evidence of a breach of the peace in any of the incidents.[42]

The Arkansas Supreme Court adopted a very different perspective in hearing the cases of Frank James Lupper and Thomas B. Robinson, both charged under the anti-trespass provisions of Act 14. Since they had refused to leave the premises at the direct request of a store official, it held that they were guilty of trespass. Insisting that this decision did not violate the appellants' Fourteenth Amendment rights, the state court ruled, "By its terms and on its face, the statute applies to all who refuse to leave and it is not restricted to Negroes. There is nothing uncertain, indefinite or vague about Act 14. It prohibits trespass." The court also held that the students had no inherent right to service at lunch counters and that store owners could legitimately choose to serve or not to serve customers at their discretion. In short, this was exactly the sort of ambiguous case that the NAACP feared would be vulnerable to unfavorable state review if the U.S. Supreme Court did not extend the meaning of the equal protection clause. In the hope of resolving the constitutional principle at stake, it took the case on appeal to the nation's highest court once the state court refused a rehearing.[43]

In its 1963 term the U.S. Supreme Court found it increasingly difficult to fall back on its preferred approach of extending the parameters of what state action meant. In the case of *Bell v. Maryland* and the two South Carolina cases of *Barr v. City of Columbia* and *Bouie v. City of Columbia*, none of the previous caveats for state action appeared to apply. Amid much internal debate and dissent, in June 1964 the majority of justices agreed to dismiss all of the convictions. In *Bell* the Court remanded the case back to the Maryland state courts for reassessment in the light of recently passed city and state laws that forbade discrimination in places of public accommodation. In *Barr* and *Bouie* it overturned sit-in convictions on the basis that South Carolina's supreme court had misconstrued the state trespass statute to mean not just unauthorized entry into an establishment but also an unauthorized refusal to leave the property.[44]

Just when the U.S. Supreme Court appeared to have stretched to the limits its capacity for judicial support of the sit-ins without reinterpretation of the equal protection clause, the U.S. Congress came to its rescue. On July 2 the legislature approved the Civil Rights Act of 1964, one of whose provisions outlawed segregation in public facilities and accommodations. Much like the Supreme Court, however, Congress was ambiguous about the question of state action. Title II of the legislation, Section

201 (a), stated, "All persons shall be entitled to the full and equal enjoyment of the goods, services, facilities, and privileges, advantages, and accommodations of any place of public accommodation, as defined in this section, without discrimination or segregation on the ground of race, color, religion, or national origin." It went on in Section 201 (b) to list a number of places covered by the act, and it defined "public accommodation within the meaning of this title if its operations affect commerce, or if discrimination or segregation by it is supported by State action."

But what exactly constituted state action? Section 201 (d) of the act said that it meant, "if such discrimination or segregation (1) is carried on under color of any law, statute, ordinance, or regulation; or (2) is carried on under color of any custom or usage required or enforced by officials of the State or political subdivision thereof; or (3) is required by action of the State or political subdivision thereof." Following the Supreme Court's lead, this constituted a liberal reading of what state action meant.

In Section 201 (e) the act addressed private property rights in stating, "The provisions of this title shall not apply to a private club or other establishment not in fact open to the public, except to the extent that the facilities of such an establishment are made available to the customers or patrons of an establishment within the scope of subsection (b)." In essence, the only establishments that were not covered by the act were those that did not require state action to enforce discrimination or segregation and those that did not rely on interstate commerce. In practice, therefore, the number of exemptions from the terms of the legislation was likely to be very small.[45]

The Little Rock case of Lupper and Robinson, consolidated with the South Carolina case of *Hamm v. City of Rock Hill*, were the first to be heard by the U.S. Supreme Court after the passage of the 1964 Civil Rights Act. By that time, Little Rock had already desegregated its downtown facilities. Another wave of sit-ins had occurred in late 1962, spurred by white SNCC activist Bill Hansen, who had come to the city to help revive the protests at the request of the Arkansas Council on Human Relations. The new demonstrations finally convinced the Little Rock business community that it was more cost-effective to desegregate than to face further disruption. In the first six months of 1963, a phased plan of desegregation of downtown facilities was carried out with little fuss or disruption. All sit-in cases, save those of Lupper and Robinson, were subsequently dismissed by the local and state courts.[46]

The pending sit-in cases from Arkansas and South Carolina together with the new civil rights legislation from Congress introduced another pressing constitutional question for the U.S. Supreme Court. Could the provisions of the 1964 Civil Rights Act be applied retrospectively and thereby used to quash all the convictions of those charged with defying the segregation laws that Congress had now made illegal? The Court employed the legal doctrine of abatement to rule that it could. This allowed for the setting aside of pending judgments due to a change in the law that rendered invalid the laws under which the original charges were brought. Although the doctrine had never before been used to annul state criminal convictions because of a change in federal statutes, it expeditiously achieved what the Court had leaned toward throughout the sit-in cases: the reversal of all convictions. As a consequence of its ruling more than three thousand sit-in cases pending before the courts were summarily dismissed.[47]

In two landmark rulings shortly after enactment of the 1964 Civil Rights Act, the Supreme Court upheld congressional power to pass desegregation law that applied to accommodations involved in interstate commerce, rather than relying on the provisions of the Fourteenth Amendment's equal protection clause. This new direction had received the support and encouragement of the Kennedy and Johnson administrations. *Heart of Atlanta Motel, Inc. v. United States* (1964) ruled that the motel was obliged to accommodate African American patrons, since a failure to do so would interfere with interstate commerce. *Katzenberg v. McClung* (1964) similarly adjudged that Ollie's Barbecue in Birmingham, Alabama, could not refuse to serve African American customers, since the food cooked in the restaurant originated out of state.[48]

Legal scholars have lamented the failure of the liberal-inclined Supreme Court headed by Chief Justice Earl Warren to address the extent of the equal protection clause when it had the opportunity, and very likely the will, to do so. This omission allowed its more conservative successors, particularly under the chief justiceship of William Rehnquist, to narrow the scope of both the commerce clause and state action considerably. In *United States v. Morrison* (2000), the Supreme Court invalidated a section of the Violence against Women Act of 1994 that gave victims of gender-motivated violence the right to sue their attackers in federal court. This judgment relied on an earlier ruling, *United States v. Lopez* (1995), which limited the commerce clause to activities that had direct economic consequences. The Rehnquist court also revisited the 1883 *Civil Rights Cases* to limit the definition of state action in favor of private individuals, moving in precisely the opposite direction of the Warren Court in the sit-in cases. Thus, while the immediate issues of segregation and discrimination that the sit-ins addressed in the early 1960s have been consigned to the past, the fundamental questions of law they raised remain as contested and unresolved fifty years later as they were then.[49]

This brings us back to Rand Paul. It is important to note that his comments in May 2010 were not necessarily out of step with the sentiments of the Republican Party in their intent, even if they were so in terms of their framing of the argument. However, the notion that the 1964 Civil Rights Act infringed the rights of private business was misplaced. The Supreme Court in the 1960s precisely avoided tackling that question, and contemporary political circumstances in 2010 did not warrant a revisiting of that complicated constitutional issue. The libertarian Paul's argument was ideologically coherent, but it was not politically expedient. The way to roll back the 1964 Civil Rights Act, conservatives appear to have concluded, is to narrow the extent and scope of state action and the commerce clause rather than widen them, as the Supreme Court did in the 1960s. Instead of claiming that private businesses should have the right to refuse African Americans service, the argument against government interference is foregrounded because it is more palatable, more on message, and on its face at least, less color-blind, even though it is ultimately capable of achieving the very same outcomes that Rand Paul falteringly tried to advance.

Small wonder, then, that the Republican hierarchy moved so swiftly to distance themselves from Paul's comments and to tell him in no uncertain terms to shut up. Less concerned at his faux pas, Kentucky voters still elected Paul as their senator in the November 2010 midterm elections, placing him in an ever-more-conservative Congress alongside a conservative Court. In the fiftieth-anniversary year of the sit-ins, though there was little danger of segregated lunch counters being reinstated, the fundamental legal and constitutional questions the demonstrations against them had raised were as vulnerable to being undermined as they had ever been. Being more abstract and less immediately visible than desegregated lunch counters, the legal and constitutional dimensions of the sit-ins are easy to overlook, but their importance should by no means be underestimated. After all, the sit-ins belong to what is quite rightly termed the civil *rights* movement, rather than simply to a civil *appearances* movement.

Notes

1. See the transcript at http://voices.washingtonpost.com/right-now/2010/05/rand_paul_telling_the_truth.html.

2. Overviews of the sit-ins include Clayborne Carson, *In Struggle: SNCC and the Black Awakening of the 1960s* (Cambridge: Harvard University Press, 1981), 9–18; Wesley C. Hogan, *Many Minds, One Heart: SNCC's Dream of a New America* (Chapel Hill: University of North Carolina Press, 2007), 13–14; James H. Laue, *Direct Action and Desegregation, 1960–1962: Toward a Theory of the Rationalization of Protest* (Brooklyn: Carlson, 1989), 75–95; Aldon D. Morris, "Black Southern Student Sit-in Movement: An Analysis of Internal Organization," *American Sociological Review* 46, no. 6 (1981): 744–67; Martin Oppenheimer, *The Sit-in Movement of 1960* (Brooklyn: Carlson, 1989); and Howard Zinn, *SNCC: The New Abolitionists* (Boston: Beacon Press, 1965), 16–39.

3. See, in particular, Elizabeth Jacoway, "Taken by Surprise: Little Rock Business Leaders and Desegregation," in *Southern Businessmen and Desegregation*, ed. Elizabeth Jacoway and David R. Colborn (Baton Rouge: Louisiana State University Press, 1982), 12–41; David L. Chappell, "Diversity within a Racial Group: White People in Little Rock, 1957–1959," *Arkansas Historical Quarterly* 54 (Winter 1995): 444–56; C. Fred Williams, "Class: The Central Issue in the Little Rock School Crisis," *Arkansas Historical Quarterly* 56 (Autumn 1997): 341–44; Pete Daniel, *Lost Revolutions: The South in the 1950s* (Chapel Hill: University of North Carolina Press, 2000), 251–83; John Kirk, "The 1957 Little Rock Crisis: A Fiftieth Anniversary Perspective," in Kirk, *Beyond Little Rock: The Origins and Legacies of the Central High Crisis* (Fayetteville: University of Arkansas Press, 2007), 1–14.

4. Frank James, "'Up Against the Obstacles,' Little Rock, Arkansas," item 17, reel 4, frame 0980, Student Nonviolent Coordinating Committee Papers, Microfilm, Roosevelt Study Center, Middleburg, the Netherlands [hereafter SNCC Papers–RSC Microfilm]; Daisy Bates to Roy Wilkins, February 23, 1960, group III, series A, container 20, folder "Bates, Daisy, 1957–1960," National Association for the Advancement of Colored People Papers, Manuscript Division, Library of Congress, Washington, D.C.; "Arkansas Council on Human Relations, Narrative Quarterly Report, January-March, 1960," series 1, box 27, folder 228, Arkansas Council on Human Relations Papers, 1954–68, Special Collections Division, University of Arkansas Libraries, Fayetteville [hereafter ACHR Papers]; *Arkansas Democrat* (Little Rock), March 10 and 17, 1960; *Arkansas Gazette* (Little Rock), March 11, 1960.

5. *Arkansas Gazette*, March 11, 1960.

6. Act 17 of the 1958 Session of the Arkansas General Assembly.

7. Act 226 of the 1959 Special Session of the Arkansas General Assembly.

8. "An Appeal to the Negroes of Little Rock," series 1, box 33, folder 335, ACHR Papers; *Arkansas Democrat*, March 13, 1960.

9. For a discussion of these issues see Hurley Doddy, "Editorial Comment: The 'Sit-In' Demonstrations and the Dilemma of the Negro College President," *Journal of Negro Education* 30 (Winter 1961): 1–3.

10. *Arkansas Democrat*, March 15 and 16, 1960.

11. C. D. Coleman to M. T. Puryear, memorandum, October 5, 1959, group II, series D, container 26, folder "Affiliates File, Little Rock, Arkansas," National Urban League Papers, Manuscript Division, Library of Congress, Washington, D.C.

12. John Walker to Paul Rilling, November 17, 1959, reel 141, frame 0234–0235, Southern Regional Council Papers, Microfilm, Manuscript Division, Library of Congress, Washington, D.C.

13. "Arkansas Council on Human Relations, Narrative Quarterly Report, January–March, 1960," series 1, box 27, folder 228, ACHR Papers; "Monthly Report of Clarence A. Laws, Field Secretary, SWR, February 26–March 31, 1960," box 4, folder 10, Daisy Bates Papers, State Historical Society of Wisconsin, Madison; *Arkansas Democrat*, March 17, 1960; *Arkansas Gazette*, March 18, 1960.

14. *Arkansas Democrat*, March 17, 1960; *Arkansas Gazette*, March 17, 1960.

15. *Arkansas Democrat*, March 11, 1960.

16. Rev. J. C. Crenchaw to all religious groups, fraternal organizations, fraternities, sororities, civic and political groups, memorandum, March 30, 1960, series 1, box 31, folder 322, ACHR Papers; "Monthly Report of Clarence Laws, Field Secretary, SWR, February 26–March 31, 1960," and "1960 Annual Report of L. C. Bates, Field Secretary, Arkansas, December 3, 1960," box 4, folder 10, Bates Papers; *Arkansas Democrat*, April 1, 1960; *Arkansas Gazette*, April 1, 1960; Gilbert Jonas, *Freedom's Sword: The NAACP and the Struggle against Racism in America, 1909–1969* (New York: Routledge, 2005), 174–77.

17. Jack Greenberg, *Crusaders in the Courts: How a Dedicated Band of Lawyers Fought for the Civil Rights Revolution* (New York: Basic Books, 1994), 275–76. For discussion of the equal protection clause see Michael Klarman, "An Interpretive History of Modern Equal Protection," *Michigan Law Review* 90 (November 1991): 213–18.

18. *Civil Rights Cases*, 109 U.S. 3 (1883).

19. *Shelley v. Kraemer*, 334 U.S. 1 (1948).

20. For a discussion of housing, race, and the law, see Stephen Grant Meyer, *As Long as They Don't Move Next Door: Segregation and Racial Conflict in American Neighborhoods* (Lanham, Md.: Rowman and Littlefield, 2000).

21. Greenberg, *Crusaders in the Courts*, 276.

22. *Arkansas Democrat*, April 11, 1960.

23. *Arkansas Democrat*, April 12, 1960.

24. Act 14 of the 1959 Special Session of the Arkansas General Assembly.

25. *Arkansas Gazette*, April 16, 1960.

26. "1960 Annual Report of L. C. Bates, Field Secretary, Arkansas, December 3, 1960," box 4, folder 10, Bates Papers; *Arkansas Democrat*, April 13 and 21, 1960.

27. *Arkansas Democrat*, April 27, 1960; *Arkansas Gazette*, April 28, 1960.

28. *Arkansas Gazette*, May 31, June 1, 1960.

29. "1960 Annual Report of L. C. Bates, Field Secretary, Arkansas, December 3, 1960," box 4, folder 10, Bates Papers; *Arkansas Democrat*, April 27, June 17 and 18, August 17, 1960; *Arkansas Gazette*, April 27, June 1, 1960. On Branton see Judith Kilpatrick, *There When We Needed Him: Wiley Austin Branton, Civil Rights Warrior* (Fayetteville: University of Arkansas Press, 2007).

30. *Arkansas Democrat*, May 11, June 29, August 17, 1960.

31. *Arkansas Democrat*, June 4, October 4, 1960.

32. "Arkansas Council on Human Relations, Narrative Quarterly Report, October-November, 1960," series 1, box 27, folder 228, ACHR Papers; *Arkansas Democrat*, September 6, November 29, 1960.

33. Worth Long Jr. to Edward B. King Jr., n.d., item 88, reel 19, frame 0189, SNCC Papers–RSC Microfilm.

34. *Arkansas Democrat*, November 29, 1960.

35. *Arkansas Democrat*, November 30, 1960; *Arkansas Gazette*, December 1, 1960.

36. *Arkansas Democrat*, December 1, 1960. In the case of Charles Parker, who had already been arrested and sentenced for his role in the March 1960 sit-in, Glover handed down a $500 fine and a six-month prison sentence.

37. *Boynton v. Virginia*, 364 U.S. 454 (1960); *Garner v. Louisiana*, 368 U.S. 157 (1961). On the Supreme Court's 1960 and 1961 terms and the sit-ins, see Derek Bell, *Race, Racism, and American Law*, 5th ed. (New York: Aspen Publishers, 2004), 544–547; Brad Ervin, "Notes: Result or Reason: The Supreme Court and the Sit-In Cases," *Virginia Law Review* 93 (May 2007): esp. 188–200; Greenberg, *Crusaders in the Courts*, 306–8; Thomas Lewis, "The Sit-in Cases: Great Expectations," *Supreme Court Review* 136 (1963): 101–51; Bernard Schwartz, *Super Chief: Earl Warren and His Supreme Court: A Judicial Biography* (New York: New York University Press, 1983), 402–4; McKenzie Webster, "Note: The Warren Court's Struggle with the Sit-In Cases and the Constitutionality of Segregation in Places of Public Accommodations," *Journal of Law and Politics* 17 (Spring 2001): esp. 376–79.

38. *Arkansas Gazette*, January 1 and 17, 1961.

39. *Arkansas Gazette*, January 17, 1961.

40. *Arkansas Democrat*, December 1, 1960; January 16, 1961; *Arkansas Gazette*, April 20 and 28, 1961, March 18, July 11, October 17, November 1, 1962, May 14, 1963.

41. *Peterson v. City of Greenville*, 373 U.S. 244; *Lombard v. Louisiana*, 373 U.S. 267; *Griffin v. Maryland*, 378 U.S. 130. On the Supreme Court's 1962 term and the sit-ins see Bell, *Race, Racism, and American Law*, 547–48; Ervin, "Notes: Result or Reason," 200–212; Greenberg, *Crusaders in the Courts*, 306–8; Schwartz, *Super Chief*, 479–86.

42. *Briggs v. State*, 236 Ark. 596, 367 S.W. 2d 750. On Johnson's career see Elizabeth Jacoway, "Jim Johnson of Arkansas: Segregationist Prototype," in *The Role of Ideas in the Civil Rights Movement*, ed. Ted Ownby (Jackson: University Press of Mississippi), 137–55.

43. *Briggs v. State*, 236 Ark. 596, 367 S.W. 2d 750; *Arkansas Gazette*, May 15, June 4, 1963.

44. *Bell v. Maryland*, 378 U.S. 226; *Barr v. City of Columbia*, 378 U.S. 146; *Bouie v. City of Columbia*, 378 U.S. 347. On the Supreme Court's 1963 and 1964 terms and the sit-ins, see Bell, *Race, Racism, and American Law*, 548; Ervin, "Notes: Result or Reason," 212–21; Greenberg, *Crusaders in the Courts*, 311–15; Monrad G. Paulsen, "The Sit-In Cases of 1964: 'But Answer Came There None,'" *Supreme Court Review* 137 (1964): 137–70; Lucas A. Powe, *The Warren Court and American Politics* (Cambridge, Mass.: Belknap Press, 2000); Schwartz, *Super Chief*, 508–25; Webster, "Note: The Warren Court's Struggle," 379–83, 388–405.

45. Civil Rights Act of 1964 (Pub.L. 88–352, 78 Stat. 241, July 2, 1964). On the act

see Hugh D. Graham, *The Civil Rights Era: Origins and Development of National Policy, 1960–1972* (New York: Oxford University Press, 1990); Robert D. Loevy, *To End All Segregation: The Politics of the Passage of the Civil Rights Act of 1964* (Lanham, Md.: University Press of America, 1990); Robert D. Loevy, ed., *The Civil Rights Act of 1964: The Passage of the Law That Ended Racial Segregation* (Albany: State University of New York Press, 1997); Clifford M. Lytle, "The History of the Civil Rights Bill of 1964," *Journal of Negro History* 51 (October 1966): 275–96; Robert Mann, *When Freedom Would Triumph: The Civil Rights Struggle in Congress, 1954–1968* (Baton Rouge: Louisiana State University Press, 2007); Denton L. Watson, *Lion in the Lobby: Clarence Mitchell, Jr.'s Struggle for the Passage of Civil Rights Laws* (New York: William Morrow, 1990); Charles W. Whalen and Barbara Whalen, *The Longest Debate: A Legislative History of the 1964 Civil Rights Act* (Cabin John, Md.: Seven Locks Press, 1985); Rebecca Zietlow, *Enforcing Equality: Congress, the Constitution, and the Protection of Individual Rights* (New York: New York University Press, 2006), 97–127.

46. John A. Kirk, *Redefining the Color Line: Black Activism in Little Rock, Arkansas, 1940–1970* (Gainesville: University Press of Florida, 2002), 154–58.

47. *Hamm v. Rock Hill*, 379 U.S. 306 (1964); *Lupper v. Arkansas*, 379 U.S. 306 (1964); *Arkansas Gazette*, October 11 and 13, 1964; "Note: Constitutional Law: Supreme Court Avoids Question of State Action in Sit-In Cases by Extending the Doctrine of Abatement," *Duke Law Journal* 3 (1965): 640–48; Schwartz, *Super Chief*, 552–55. According to one source, the sit-in appeals had a 93.4 percent success rate before the Supreme Court; Joel B. Grossman, "A Model for Judicial Policy Analysis: The Supreme Court and the Sit-In Cases," in *Frontiers of Judicial Research*, ed. Joel B. Grossman and Joseph Tannehaus (New York: John Wiley, 1969), 438.

48. *Heart of Atlanta Motel, Inc. v. United States*, 379 U.S. 241 (1964); *Katzenbach v. McClung*, 379 U.S. 294 (1964). On the two cases see Richard C. Cortner, *Civil Rights and Public Accommodations: The Heart of Atlanta and McClung Cases* (Lawrence: University Press of Kansas, 2001).

49. *United States v. Lopez*, 514 U.S. 549 (1995); *United States v. Morrison*, 529 U.S. 598 (2000). On Morrison, the Rehnquist Court, and Equal Protection, see Robert C. Post and Reva B. Siegal, "Equal Protection by Law: Federal Anti-Discrimination Legislation after Morrison and Kimmel," *Yale Law Journal* 110 (December 2000): 441–526.

3

"Complicated Hospitality"

The Impact of the Sit-Ins on the Ideology of Southern Segregationists

GEORGE LEWIS

On the first Sunday of March 1960, Kelly Miller Smith Sr. rose to address the congregation of his First Baptist Church in Capitol Hill, Nashville. He was well aware that his audience included many of the eighty-five students who had recently been arrested in the Nashville sit-ins. Under the guidance of direct-action advocate James Lawson, he had helped to train them in the civil disobedience workshops that had been running in his church basement since 1958. "Father, forgive them, for they know not what they do," Smith began, in pointed reference to the city's segregationists. He continued:

> The students sat at the lunch counters alone to eat, and when re-fused service, to wait and pray. And as they sat there on that South-ern Mount of Olives, the Roman soldiers, garbed in the uniforms of the Nashville policemen and wielding night sticks, came and led praying children away. As they walked down the streets, through a red light, and toward Golgotha, the segregationist mob shouted jeers, pushed and shoved them, and spat in their faces, but the suffering students never said a mumbling word. Once the martyr mounts the Cross, wears the crown of thorns, and feels the pierce of the sword in his side there is no turning back.[1]

Historians of the sit-ins have neither replicated the lyricism of Smith's extended metaphor nor substantively challenged its content. The domi-nant analytical view continues to be that much of the sit-ins' success was predicated upon the ability of protestors to juxtapose outward displays of their own morality and higher purpose with the base racism and im-patient, febrile violence of their segregationist foes. Assessment of the

41

historical significance of the protests also remains little altered. Their primary importance is still understood to lie in their ability to sharpen the senses of an inchoate civil rights movement and, in particular, to bring a physical theater to the metaphysical judicial battles over the question of segregated public spaces, the legal pedantry and complexity of which had limited appeal to white liberals.[2] Such views are, however, the product of a long-standing critical imbalance. For, while historians have continued to bring depth to their analyses of the sit-ins, they have done so while retaining too narrow a focus, concentrating on only one side of what was clearly a two-sided battle. Movement activists have been viewed in increasingly rich textures, but their segregationist foes continue to be neglected and remain in monochrome.

The historical narrative conventionally depicts segregationists as a homogeneous group that reacted with little agency within broadly drawn thematic pathways. They are seen as attempting to curtail the sit-in movement through reactive extralegal violence and parallel resorts to the law, notably through enactment of restrictive ordinances and statutes.[3] If the nuanced focus long afforded to their activist foes is brought to bear on segregationists, however, it immediately becomes evident that the historiographical orthodoxy is flawed. First, it is clear that segregationists were simply too diverse and multifarious to conform to the simplistic, static patterns that have routinely defined them. In this sense, restoring Jim Crow's defenders as three-dimensional historical actors reinforces the scale of the challenge facing the civil rights protesters in their campaign to overthrow it. More importantly, only when that correction of focus is made can a key facet of the sit-ins' lasting historical impact be fully understood. These protests undermined not only the physical barriers of Jim Crow, as historians have long recognized, but also many of the ideological tenets that were fundamental to the sustainability of the system of southern segregation.

The benefits of taking a more holistic historical approach are most easily exemplified through reexamination of the violence that was a near ubiquitous response to the protests. Historians have tended to reflect the Student Nonviolent Coordinating Committee's (SNCC's) strategic perspective in focusing exclusively on the tactical uses of nonviolence.[4] It is abundantly clear from the contemporary evidence, however, that there was an equally strategic deployment of violence by segregationists in their counter-campaigns. When sit-in protests began in Jacksonville, Florida, in August 1960, for example, a crowd of whites estimated at two hundred congregated in Hemmingway Park to oppose them. As one eyewitness reported, "There were signs saying 'Get Your Free Baseball Bats here.' They, also, had clubs and axe handles. Some were parading around the store with baseball bats over their shoulders and small confederate flags on the tops of the ax handles." Simply noting the brutality of that environment, however, belies the long-term processes that lay behind its creation. The apparently careless introduction of weaponry was far from the simple, short-term, and reactive development that it first appears, and it was certainly not the first step of a deterministic march toward inevitable bloodshed. Rather, it reflected a growing realization among some segregationists that demonstrable acts of violence were not always necessary by 1960. For civil rights protestors, the social memory of previous episodes of racial intimidation that had escalated into brutal violence remained crystalline. Accordingly, the segregationist deployment of intimidatory tactics was often as terrifying as actual physical attacks on them.[5]

The more closely the evidence is examined, the clearer it becomes that segregationist tactics rarely remained static and often evolved at a similar pace to those of the protesters. In part this reflected a recognition that, while there were continuities between past and present black protest, the motivations that drove African American sit-in activists and their white allies had undergone significant change. As Richard H. King has argued, many proponents of nonviolent direct action acted with a selflessness that challenged the prevailing orthodoxy of the post–World War II United States, in which "the primacy of self-interest" was taken to govern political engagement.[6] Many segregationists astutely recognized that their adversaries had begun to prioritize their own perception of the public good over personal safety. As a consequence, they developed alternative means of intimidation, as twenty-year-old civil rights activist Anne Moody found to her cost. Though maltreated, she herself came to no great physical harm during the Jackson, Mississippi, sit-in of May 28, 1963. In the aftermath of the protest, however, she grew increasingly fearful for her family's safety. Moody recalled waiting "to hear in the news that someone in Centreville [her hometown] had been murdered. If so I knew it would be a member of my family."[7]

When intimidation did translate into true violence at the scene of the sit-ins, this was neither as all-encompassing nor as haphazard as often portrayed. Nonviolence workshops such as those in Smith's church basement were designed to ensure that each protestor was prepared for the outbreak of visceral, race-based violence. When it did occur, however, segregationists did not simply attack protestors randomly, but proved particularly keen on targeting those white demonstrators whose presence made many sit-ins interracial affairs. In his personal chronicle of the campaign to desegregate Knoxville, Tennessee, in July and August 1960, Presbyterian clergyman Merrill Proudfoot noted that "most of the hostility is vented against whites."[8] Anne Moody similarly recalled that, when "some old man in the crowd ordered the students to take us off the stools," and a "big husky boy" asked "Which one should I get first?" the reply was, "That white nigger."[9] A white student from Florida State University, Richard Frank Parker, was arrested along with black protestors on vagrancy charges for their part in the Jacksonville sit-ins. He alone received a savage beating that resulted in a broken jaw and concussion. After hospital treatment, the NAACP's Ruby Hurley reported that Parker was taken back to the jail and further charged with fighting.[10] An earlier incident of racial targeting in Birmingham, Alabama, had involved a twenty-one-year-old white civil rights supporter, a part-time preacher and student at Birmingham-Southern College whom police charged with "intimidating a witness." According to one reporter, however, he was "slight . . . weighing about 137 pounds," stood only five foot, eight inches tall, wore thick glasses, and "suffers from asthma and is noticeably shy and diffident."[11]

The details of those legal charges—"vagrancy," "fighting," "intimidating a witness"—are also important in highlighting the shortcomings inherent in presenting a homogenized view of a single segregationist response to the sit-ins. Such a foreshortened view has neglected the important point that, besides those who willfully engaged in violence, the forces of massive resistance were well populated with trained lawyers who remained above the physical fray but still had a marked effect on the segregationist response to the sit-ins. Indeed, a number of Jim Crow apologists were sufficiently attuned to the potential effectiveness of this new style of protest to realize that it would be counterproductive to have test cases involving local segregation laws reaching federal courts on appeal. Accordingly, they developed a series of ploys that allowed for racially motivated arrests on purportedly non-racial grounds.

Ross Barnett used the political capital earned in his successful gubernatorial election—he took his oath of office in Mississippi just thirteen days before the Greensboro sit-ins began—to pressure the state legislature into enacting a slew of anti-protest measures. None had a specifically racial focus, but each was developed with racially motivated intent, even when dealing ostensibly with obstruction of public highways, redefinitions of the laws of trespass, and expanding what could be designated disorderly conduct.[12] Thus, when the "Tugaloo nine" were arrested for their part in a "read-in" at Jackson Municipal Library, Municipal Judge James Spencer found them guilty of breach of the peace.[13] It proved a popular tactic that was widely copied by other states. A Georgia law enacted in 1960 decreed it illegal to refuse to leave any business if requested to do so by the owner or manager.[14] In February of that year, the sit-ins in Rock Hill, South Carolina, had encountered considerable segregationist violence, but the only arrests were those of forty-three demonstrators, each of whom was charged with trespassing.[15]

As the campaigns against sit-ins continued, segregationists proved that their choice of language on the arrest docket was not the only place in which they were applying legal sanctions with an increasingly astute strategic vision. In Jackson, for example, arrested demonstrators who refused to walk to waiting paddy wagons were denied the positive publicity that would have been generated by press images of white policemen forcing them into vehicles by the decision to entrust such arrests not to white police officers but to African American trustees from the city jail. To counter their "jail not bail" tactic, Mayor Allen Thompson had also organized extra prison space. In the immediate aftermath of eighty-eight arrests, for example, he announced to waiting reporters, "We can handle 100,000 agitators." Even the itinerant segregationist mob that regularly confronted Mississippi's sit-in protestors displayed a new level of sophistication after being initially outwitted by feints and false leads. In Anne Moody's words, "They no longer looked for us, or for the demonstration. They just followed the newsmen and photographers. They were much smarter than the cops, who hadn't caught on yet."[16]

A more nuanced understanding of the segregationist response to the sit-ins necessitates recognition of its strategic dimension, but this still glosses over the real historical impact of the protests. Historian Clayborne Carson has noted that the central role of southern black colleges as the early incubators of the sit-ins "surprised many observers who were aware of the[ir] restrictive rules and conformist atmosphere."[17] Any element of surprise was greater still among those whites who had an intellectual stake in the Jim Crow system, for the sit-ins posed such fundamental questions as to render continued segregation ideologically untenable. It is in this context that their primary importance must be recognized and measured. As Wesley C. Hogan observes, "Scholars and journalists paid a good deal of attention to the sit-ins, but almost none of their accounts penetrated deeply into the movement or were able to explain the source of its power." In pinpointing the source of that power as the collective will of a close group to maintain protests that challenged Jim Crow physically, Hogan neglects the effect that the sit-ins had on segregationists intellectually.[18]

The full extent of that impact can only be realized by refocusing the lens through which historians have traditionally viewed the sit-in protests to consider the segregationist perspective, and thus to add a new dimension to the history of the freedom struggle. It is clear from the memoirs and oral histories of sit-in activists, for example, that the initial reaction of those segregationists who were personally confronted by protesters was often indecisive. Joseph McNeil explained to a student reporter that the immediate response to the Greensboro Four was mostly incomprehension. They were "completely ignored" by a waitress who "said nothing." The lunch counter manager and the store manager also refused to talk to them. When the police arrived, they just "stared at us and walked up and down the aisle, but said nothing to us."[19]

Protestors believed that this reaction was an effort at intimidation or a sign of imminent violence. A wider view incorporating not only segregationists who were prone to violence but also those who strove to maintain an intellectual defense of Jim Crow suggests a more plausible alternative. Put simply, those sitting in were ignored because lunch counter staff and store managers preferred not to be confronted by their presence, not least because segregationists were increasingly bereft of solutions to the multiple problems that the protests posed. It was a predicament symptomatic of the broader dilemma they faced.

By the close of the 1950s, Jim Crow was still postulated upon many of the intellectual rationales and founding assumptions that had underpinned and then sustained white supremacy in the region since its articulation in early-nineteenth-century apologias for slavery. As South Carolina writer, educator, and segregationist Louis D. Rubin Jr. noted in 1957, white southerners shared a predilection for looking backward rather than forward, often with "paralyzing effects." The "foremost" contemporary example of this was the "Negro issue." In his assessment, the racial arguments advanced by southerners had remained unchanged "for the past 150 years." The steep decline in the published output of segregationists appears to validate Rubin's contention. Broadsheets, handbills, and magazines may have continued to spew forth from the Citizens' Councils, but there was a marked diminution of publications attempting to intellectualize the South's position for a more general audience. The vast majority of such resistance-era tracts dated from the 1950s, prior to the activist phase of the civil rights movement, and failed entirely to engage with the questions that the sit-ins posed.[20]

In spite of his frustration with the southern tendency to look backward, Rubin's own thinking was rooted in the past. Acknowledging that what "was adequate in 1870" to deal with blacks was not so by 1960, he warned fellow segregationists of "the manifest fact that the African slaves brought over from the jungles in the eighteenth century have been changing, learning, growing." Such thinking ironically presented future historians with clear examples of the sort of racial paternalism that had traditionally undergirded the white South.[21]

Rubin's continued adherence to such an outmoded position caused rifts among the writers and editors of *The Lasting South*, published in 1957. The book clearly reflected the difficulties that the self-styled intellectuals of southern segregation increasingly found in articulating a vision for the region. Implicitly critical of Rubin, who was one of the coeditors, the preface noted that contributors "do not agree about all the ways by which the South should act to retain its individuality." While united in arguing for the maintenance of the region's "traditions," there was "no unanimity of opinion among the essayists, or, for that matter, among the editors themselves," on the "segregation issue."[22]

Race-based paternalism still reigned supreme in the white South that was confronted by the sit-ins. North Carolina attorney general Malcolm B. Seawell typically asserted that the student protests were causing "irreparable harm"—not to the financial position of the chain stores affected by sit-ins but to relations between black and white. In 1960, Mayor William Enloe of Raleigh adjudged it "regrettable that some of our young Negro students would risk endangering . . . race relations by seeking to change a long-standing custom in a manner that is all but destined to fail."[23]

This paternalism, of course, spawned a number of interlocking assumptions, each of which has particular relevance for historical analysis of the sit-ins. First, southern blacks were thought to be content with the racial situation as it existed. In segregationist eyes, their innate inferiority made them grateful for whites' social support. Testifying to this outlook, Montgomery, Alabama, Chamber of Commerce official Carl H. Bear asserted in May 1960 that the majority of local blacks "realize that equality is a status in society which must be earned and cannot be accomplished by force, nor can it be conferred by judicial decree or legislative enactment. They know that this earned equality will require much more education, extending over a period of many years."[24]

The second segregationist assumption was that "contentment" among the southern black population would never lead any of its members to "agitate" for greater rights. To Jim Crow supporters, only northerners and other outsiders believed anything to the contrary, and none of them could hope to comprehend the true state of southern race relations. Thus, South Carolina essayist and academic Ellington White was able to write at the end of the 1950s, "If the Southerner has been at fault in simplifying the Negro . . . then we can also say that the North has been equally at fault in simplifying the relation between the Negro and the Southern white." More pointedly still, "the outsider has repeatedly assumed an authority in this matter beyond his knowledge."[25] As Richmond novelist and independent scholar Clifford Dowdey succinctly put it, "the habit of explaining the sins of The South has become something like a game played for its own sake by amateurs. The game, as played in New York, bears no relation to the business of life, as lived in the South."[26]

Given the stagnant state of southern segregationist ideology, the impact of the sit-ins reached far beyond those public spaces that the protestors had targeted for immediate desegregation. They demonstrated categorically that southern blacks—and, indeed, a number of southern whites—were not, after all, content with the racial status quo and the maintenance of segregation. In reality, it was southern segregationists who misunderstood the relative contentment of the southern African American population, not northern commentators; southern blacks were not at a heritable intellectual disadvantage to southern whites—after all, they were winning significant victories over Jim Crow supporters with a campaign of civil disobedience that was highly sophisticated in its very simplicity.

It is in regard to such miscalculation that the more detailed examination of segregationist violence becomes analytically important. The disproportionate level of attacks on white sit-in protestors and the way in which segregationists honed in on their involvement in interracial protests was no mere coincidence. Jim Crow supporters took particular offense at the presence of whites born and bred in the South at the epicenter of protest, as this belied the argument that segregation was only understood by those who grew up within its complex and peculiar customs. The actions of these southern heretics went "against the grain," to borrow a phrase from historian Anthony P. Dunbar. Indeed, their involvement in the sit-ins showed that it was Ellington White, and not "the Northerner," who was guilty of oversimplification in arguing that there was a single relationship between the blacks and whites of the South.[27]

In this context, it becomes clear that the sit-in movement was in the process of winning victories in two parallel categories: concrete success over the customs and ordinances of segregation, and psychological and intellectual triumphs over the ideology of the segregationist South more broadly. It is a reflection of Jim Crow's ideational atrophy, as well as shifting national and international attitudes to white supremacy more generally, that non-southern media outlets offered such a paucity of opportunities for segregationists to articulate their ideological opposition to the sit-ins. As one of the region's most thoughtful spokesmen, James Jackson Kilpatrick, had noted even before the close of the 1950s, "When the literate Southern conservative—and there are some literate Southern conservatives—seeks access to the major media of national communication, he finds the borders closed to him as though he carried typhoid."[28]

Kilpatrick himself had a rare opportunity to enunciate the regional conservative viewpoint when NBC executives selected him to present the segregationist case in a live TV debate against Martin Luther King Jr. in November 1960 on the question, "Are the Sit-In Strikes Justifiable?"[29] In the later stages of their exchanges, Kilpatrick was remarkably assured in questioning King on an individual's right to defy a law that was subjectively deemed to be "unjust," but he was poorly served by the decision of program executives to reduce the show's usual hour-long running time to thirty minutes.[30] In contrast, he was unimpressive at the start of the program, when moderator John McCaffery sought to keep the debate focused on the sit-ins and away from wider issues of segregation.

Faced with the specific question of whether the sit-ins were justifiable, Kilpatrick was uncharacteristically evasive. Accusing both sides of exaggerating the crisis, he claimed that the right to eat was surely less important than the right to vote, to own property, or, he claimed, to serve on juries. He then embarked on the "relative civilizations" argument that, alongside paternalism, had been a mainstay of southern white supremacist ideology since the days of slavery. "We believe," Kilpatrick avowed, "that it is an affirmatively good thing to preserve the predominant racial characteristics that have contributed to Western civilization over the past two thousand years." This was why segregationists continued to "believe in public policies that promote separation of the races in those few essential social areas where intimate personal association, long continued, would foster a break-down, especially among young people, of those ethnic lines that seem to us important." In his view, the sit-ins needed contextualization, not only in terms of "the total problem of race relations that has occupied the South not merely since 1954 but for a very long period in our history" but also in terms of what King was demanding. Willfully misconstruing his opponent's position, Kilpatrick claimed that King sought "the obliteration of race altogether" by means of a "Waring blender process on our society."[31]

As the following passage indicates, however, Kilpatrick interspersed his traditional defense of segregation with some startling deviations from orthodoxy:

> Now, to the extent that integrated lunch counters and tea rooms in our department stores would contribute toward that breakdown, I would regard them as unwise. But I would say that as a practical matter I am inclined to believe this extent is relatively small. The business of eating lunch in a big city dime store, so far as I can see, is a largely impersonal exercise in indigestion. It involves no long-continued intimacy, and I would suppose that in the course of time most of the South's larger cities could adjust to this change as they have adjusted to an end of segregation on public transportation lines and in their parks. Indeed, my impression is that more than a hundred public eating facilities in private stores in the South already have taken this step.

Such rhetoric underlined the fundamental problem facing Kilpatrick and the segregated South. The sit-ins operated in a different context and under different imperatives from earlier assaults on Jim Crow, owing to their speed, their dynamism, their personnel, and their ubiquity. The *Brown* decision had wound its way through the appeal court systems for over three years before the U.S. Supreme Court finally offered its verdict. Within six months of the first sit-in of 1960, by contrast, Florida alone had seen victories against segregated lunch counters in fifteen establishments across five cities.[32]

The carefully inserted caveat in the position Kilpatrick described— that close personal contact was only problematic if "long continued"— was a pragmatic rearguard concession to sustain the segregationist position, given that some desegregation had already taken place without provoking a societal implosion. More importantly still, the ease with which sit-in tactics could be applied to a variety of different venues increased the difficulty of suppressing them. Events had forced Kilpatrick to claim publicly that eating sandwiches in an interracial setting was not a devastating blow against Jim Crow. As a National Council of the Protestant Episcopal Church report had recognized in the spring of 1960, however, part of the genius of the sit-in movement lay in its flexibility. The protests, it declared, "have not been confined to restaurants alone," but had already spread to municipally supported libraries and art galleries, as well as "eating places operated in conjunction with inter-state commerce facilities."[33]

In one of the starkest indications that the sit-in protesters had eroded the pillars of contemporary segregationist ideology, there is significant evidence to suggest that, three months before he went on national television to defend its rationale, Kilpatrick had already come to the conclusion that the South's position was untenable. Both privately, and, indeed, publically, he had acknowledged the protests' wider impact. In terms of the latter, one of his *Richmond News Leader* editorials in August 1960, titled "Reflections on the Sit-Ins," read like an audible sigh of defeat. "There is undoubtedly some sort of 'moral right' that vests in a Negro customer who is encouraged to buy a suit of clothes but is denied the privilege of buying a sandwich," he wrote, still—just—clinging to the segregationist distinction between rights and privileges. "We have said a hundred times that the South is not static, as its detractors insist. The South changes; it changes socially, economically, culturally, politically, as it should and must change. Today, in Richmond, we have a change to accept." Privately, Kilpatrick later admitted to the *Richmond Times-Dispatch*'s Earle Dunford, he knew the fight was lost when the flagship department store of the former Confederate capital yielded to the protests. "My turning point came with the desegregation of Thalhimers lunch counter," he confided. "That was kind of the watershed point, I guess—the turning of the tide."[34]

Few divined that watershed as accurately or as swiftly as Kilpatrick. As the sit-in protestors continued to prove on an almost daily basis that so many of the founding assumptions of Jim Crow were deeply flawed, segregationists of every stripe searched for solutions with increasing desperation. Even the Citizens' Councils, which at times had worked as the engine room for massive resistance, were left flailing in despair. Indeed, *The Citizens' Council* went so far as to eschew that shibboleth of the southern segregationist position, the primacy of states' rights, in its call for an end to the protests. In what was, for a segregationist publication, a shrewd satire of the movement's strategy of triggering federal intervention to protect African American civil rights in southern states, the newspaper argued that the sit-ins were directed not by disaffected southerners but by "various . . . Northern-led groups." Accordingly, it reasoned, the orders to stir up the South's contented African Americans were being transmitted across state lines. "If this is not a clear cut violation of Federal Law," an editorial wanted to know, "what is? If this situation does not cry out for a full-scale FBI investigation and Justice Department prosecution of the guilty parties, what does?" Answering its own question, it concluded: "Here is an excellent opportunity for the Federal government—and most particularly, the Justice Department—to prove that it is sincere in its desire to protect the rights of *all* citizens. For obviously these 'sit-down' lunch counter demonstrations are violating the basic civil rights of a majority of the people of the South."[35]

For segregationists seeking a more sophisticated and substantive riposte to the sit-ins, the legal sphere continued to hold the greatest hope. Lawyer, part architect of Virginia's resistance strategies, and close confidant of Kilpatrick, David J. Mays retained a confidence that the courts would provide redress against the protests, which he considered a tactical error on the part of the civil rights movement. "This effort of the Negroes is self-defeating," he declared, "since they have now turned from the federal courts to extra- and illegal actions." In a similar vein, he was scornful of King's defense of lawbreaking in the televised debate with Kilpatrick.[36]

Not everyone was as sanguine about judicial support for the segregationist position. A faction of the faculty at Vanderbilt University sensed the changing atmosphere and issued a statement urging the need to "distinguish both morally and legally between perpetrators of actual violence who defy the peaceful traditions of this community by reviling, beating, and otherwise persecuting their fellow men, and citizens who peacefully and lawfully assert their rights."[37] This was increasingly the outlook of the judicial system. As early as February 1960, Claude Sitton noted in the *New York Times* that the courts were no longer willing to endorse the uneven reading of the Constitution that had long brought legal sustenance to Jim Crow. "Some newspapers noted the embarrassing position in which the variety chains found themselves," he reported. "The *News and Observer* of Raleigh remarked editorially that in these stores the Negro was a guest, who was 'cordially invited to the house but definitely not to the table. And to say the least, this was complicated hospitality.'"[38] The Supreme Court's judgment in *Garner v. Louisiana* (1961),

which struck down the convictions of a cohort of Louisianan sit-in protestors arrested for "disturbing the peace," signaled its rejection of the
segregationist reading of the Fourteenth Amendment. In essence, the
ruling established two principles: eating at a lunch counter was not a
privilege, but a right; equal protection was not to be suspended in the
public spaces of privately owned businesses.[39]

The "complicated hospitality" of allowing blacks to shop in stores that
denied them a seat at the lunch counter required segregationist ideology
to perform multiple contortions in its efforts to resist the deceptively
simple tactics of the sit-ins. For those segregationists who rarely looked
up beyond the boundaries of their own locality, and who shared in the
southern fondness for looking backward rather than toward the future,
the full impact of the protests was not immediately recognizable. Their
complacent belief that the participants could be intimidated, arrested,
or made subject to new legal restraints provided nothing more than the
briefest of solutions. Other segregationists understood not only that
such parochial views of resistance would inevitably lead to defeat but
also that the sit-ins, even if curbed in the short-term, threatened irreparable long-term damage to the white South's way of life.[40]

For those segregationists able to take a fully contextualized view of
their position, it was clear that the sit-ins represented the final dispel-
ling of the paternalism myth. As a result, any analysis of the collective
impact of these protests must resist the lure of scrutinizing little beyond
their effect on the freedom movement, of which they were such a signal
part. It must also register the full significance of their bearing on massive resistance. The sit-ins, in short, rendered many of the segregationist
South's most cherished defenses anachronistic, implausible, and untenable. In so doing, they wrested the momentum of the freedom struggle
away from the defenders of Jim Crow and threw it decisively behind the
proponents and strategists of nonviolent direct action.

As the Southern Regional Council's Harold Fleming told one reporter,
Brown may have been the legal turning point, but "the sit-ins are the
psychological turning point in race relations in the South. This is the first
step to real change—when the whites realize that the Negroes just aren't
having it any more."[41] As was so often the case, it was Kilpatrick, an
adopted southerner from Oklahoma, who was able to articulate the true
nature of the segregationist position before the majority of his peers had
begun to comprehend it. "Life is short, honest to God it is, and life is too
short to waste it in vain and abortive causes that offer no conceivable

hope of advantage anywhere," he wrote on the first anniversary of the sit-ins. "I don't mind taking up lost causes—it is the fate of every South-erner—but I want to be a little selective in the lost causes I take up."[42]

Notes

1. Smith quoted in Louis E. Lomax, *The Negro Revolt* (New York: Harper & Broth-ers, 1962), 126; Wesley C. Hogan, *Many Minds, One Heart: SNCC's Dream for a New America* (Chapel Hill: University of North Carolina Press, 2007), esp. 16–26. Smith supplemented his church-based leadership role with the chairmanship of the local chapter of the NAACP and was the founding president of the Nashville Christian Leadership Conference.

2. See, for example, David R. Goldfield, *Black, White, and Southern: Race Relations and Southern Culture 1940 to the Present* (Baton Rouge: Louisiana State University Press, 1990), 120–21 (given the paucity of recent scholarly attention for the sit-ins, his bibliographical essay also remains instructive, especially 294–97); and Hogan, *Many Minds, One Heart*, 23.

3. In terms of the historiography of massive resistance, Numan Bartley, *The Rise of Massive Resistance: Race and Politics in the South during the 1950's* (Baton Rouge: Louisiana State University Press, 1969), concentrates firmly on the 1950s; Francis M. Wilhoit, *The Politics of Massive Resistance* (New York: George Braziller, 1973), ignores the sit-ins in its analysis of resistance's "critical confrontations"; and the essays in Clive Webb, ed., *Massive Resistance: Southern Opposition to the Second Reconstruction* (New York: Oxford University Press, 2005), have too much work to do in other impor-tant areas in their collective corrective of an outdated historiography.

4. See, for example, Hogan, *Many Minds, One Heart*, 34–38.

5. "Report on Situation in Jacksonville by Robert Saunders, Field Secretary and Mrs. Ruby Hurley, Regional Secretary," August 29, 1960, National Association for the Advancement of Colored Peoples White Reprisals and Resistance Papers [hereafter NAACP-WRRP], reel 6, frame 0915 (consulted at David Wilson Library, University of Leicester).

6. Richard H. King, *Civil Rights and the Idea of Freedom* (New York: Oxford Univer-sity Press, 1992), esp. chapter 3 (quote on 62).

7. Anne Moody, *Coming of Age in Mississippi* (London: Peter Owen, 1968), 240. In retaliation for her protest activity, Moody's younger brother, "Junior," barely escaped from a mob that cornered him at home; her uncle was subject to a severe beating; and her younger sister, Adline, and mother, Toosweet Davis, were hounded by night riders.

8. Merrill Proudfoot, *Diary of a Sit-In* (Chapel Hill: University of North Carolina Press, 1962), 106.

9. Moody, *Coming of Age in Mississippi*, 237–38.

10. "Jackson Situation by Mrs. Ruby Hurley," August 30, 1960, NAACP-WRRP, reel 6, frame 920.

11. Harrison E. Salisbury, "Fear and Hatred Grip Birmingham," *New York Times*, April 12, 1960. A southern reader immediately challenged this article for using "empurpled language" and ignoring the moderate "middle ground" in favor of reporting on extremism. Joseph F. Johnston Jr., letter to the editor, *New York Times*, April 12, 1960.

12. Erle E. Johnston Jr., *Mississippi's Defiant Years, 1953–1973: An Interpretive Documentary with Personal Experiences* (Forest, Miss.: Lake Harbor Publishers, 1990), 99–100.

13. Ibid., 99–100, 129.

14. "Negroes in South Hail Sit-in Ruling," *New York Times*, December 12, 1961.

15. Claude Sitton, "Negro Sitdowns Stir Fear of Wider Unrest in South," *New York Times*, February 15, 1960.

16. Moody, *Coming of Age in Mississippi*, 242–43.

17. Clayborne Carson, *In Struggle: SNCC and the Black Awakening of the 1960s* (Cambridge: Harvard University Press, 1981), 12.

18. Hogan, *Many Minds, One Heart*, 42–43.

19. Albert L. Rozier Jr., "Students Hit Woolworth's for Lunch Service," *The Register* (North Carolina A&T), February 5, 1960, in *Reporting Civil Rights: Part One: American Journalism, 1941–1963*, ed. Clayborne Carson et al. (New York: The Library of America, 2003), 431–32. Anne Moody further attests to that sense of bewilderment in her memoir of the Jackson campaign: the waitresses she encountered ran to the back of the store, pausing only to turn off the lights before deserting the counter, including the white customers who were sat there. Moody, *Coming of Age in Mississippi*, 236.

20. See, in particular, Herman Talmadge, *You and Segregation* (Birmingham: Vulcan Press, 1955); Tom Brady, *Black Monday* (Winona, Miss.: Association of Citizens' Councils of Mississippi, 1955); Wesley Critz George, "Human Progress and the Race Problem" (N.p., 1957), based on his "Dartmouth Address," October 12, 1955; *The Congressional Committee Report on What Happened When Schools Were Integrated in Washington, D.C.* (Washington, D.C.: Government Printing Office, 1956); and Charles J. Bloch, *States' Rights: The Law of the Land* (Atlanta: Harrison Co., 1958). The *Congressional Committee Report*, released on December 28, 1956, was widely reprinted by various Citizens' Council organizations. See, for example, *Congressional Committee Report on What Happened When Schools Were Integrated in Washington, D.C.* (Greenwood, Miss.: Educational Fund of the Citizens' Councils, n.d.), copy in NAACP-WRRP, reel 13, frames 0494–0504. Despite appearances, James Jackson Kilpatrick, *The Southern Case for School Segregation* (New York: Crowell-Collier Press, 1962), does not fit the same segregationist mold of the above tracts. In a private letter to one of his former publishers, Henry Regnery, in 1961, Kilpatrick declared, "I am not at all anxious to do the book. Between you and me, I am so sick of this whole subject I wish I never had to write another line about it." He was more enticed by the publisher's promise to produce "a large printing and no restriction on what I write" and by the security of financial reward. As his close associate David Mays noted in August 1962, "Jack makes only $10,000 per year as editor of the News Leader and is always alert to ways of making an extra dollar for his family's needs." See Kilpatrick to Regnery, October

19, 1961, box 5, "1959–63 Personal Correspondence 'Q-R' (1 of 2)," James J. Kilpatrick Papers, University of Virginia Special Collections, Charlottesville; and Mays Diaries, August 11, 1962, Virginia Historical Society, Richmond.

21. Louis D. Rubin Jr., "An Image of the South," in *The Lasting South: Fourteen Southerners Look at Their Home*, ed. Louis D. Rubin Jr. and James Jackson Kilpatrick (Chicago: Henry Regnery, 1957), 10–11.

22. Louis D. Rubin and James Jackson Kilpatrick, preface to Rubin and Kilpatrick, *The Lasting South*, ix–x.

23. Other Tar Heels simply found it "incomprehensible" that any such demonstration would be necessary in their state. See Sitton, "Negro Sitdowns Stir Fear of Wider Unrest," and the same author's "A Chronology of the New Civil Rights Protest, 1960–1963," in *Freedom Now! The Civil Rights Struggle in America*, ed. Alan F. Westin (New York: Basic Books, 1964), 80.

24. Bear quoted in Dan Wakefield, "Eye of the Storm," *The Nation*, May 7, 1960, article reproduced in Carson et al., *Reporting Civil Rights*, 473.

25. Ellington White, "The View from the Window," in Rubin and Kilpatrick, *The Lasting South*, 166.

26. Clifford Dowdey, "The Case for the Confederacy," in Rubin and Kilpatrick, *The Lasting South*, 33.

27. Anthony P. Dunbar, *Against the Grain: Southern Radicals and Prophets, 1929–1959* (Charlottesville: University Press of Virginia, 1981); White, "The View from the Window," 166.

28. Kilpatrick, "Conservatism and the South," in Rubin and Kilpatrick, *The Lasting South*, 195.

29. George Lewis, *Massive Resistance: The White Response to the Civil Rights Movement* (London: Hodder, 2006), 111.

30. For a discussion of those format changes, see John P. Shanley, "The Nation's Future," *New York Times*, November 28, 1960.

31. "Transcript of NBC's 'The Nation's Future,'" November 26, 1960, in "Kilpatrick, James J.," Virginia Commission on Constitutional Government Papers, Record Group 70, State Government Records Collection, Library of Virginia, Richmond.

32. "Memorandum, Florida State Conference of Branches," August 18, 1960, NAACP-WRRP, reel 6, frame 0914.

33. Division of Racial Minorities, Division of Christian Citizenship, to the Members of the Protestant Episcopal Church, "Protestant Episcopal Church: The National Council. Background Paper on the Student 'Sit-In' Protest Movement in the Light of the Church's Authoritative Statements," April 1, 1960, NAACP-WRRP, reel 8, frame 0470.

34. *News Leader* editorial, August 31, 1960, and Kilpatrick quoted in Earle Dunford, *Richmond Times-Dispatch: The Story of a Newspaper* (Richmond: Cadmus, 1995), 397, 407.

35. "Seditious Sit-Downs—An Editorial," *The Citizens' Council*, March 1960, 3.

36. Mays was astounded by King's assertion that "observance of law is a matter of individual conscience, in other words every man is a law unto himself." Mays Diaries, April 8, November 26, 1960.

37. The statement continued: "We think the law must be equitably enforced as well as equally observed. It follows that when members of one group and their supporters are arrested on narrow legal grounds while, at the same time, individuals who commit acts of violence against them are suffered to act freely, the law itself is being used unjustly." Reproduced in "Protestant Episcopal Church: The National Council," reels 8–9.

38. Sitton, "Negro Sitdowns Stir Fear of Wider Unrest."

39. *Garner v. Louisiana*, 368 U.S. 157 (1961). For a commentary see Kenneth L. Karst and Wiliam W. Van Alstyne, "Comment: Sit-Ins and State Action—Mr Justice Douglas, Concurring," *Stanford Law Review* 14, no. 4 (1962): 762.

40. The objectivity needed to understand such a view was most often found in the reports of the national press: Claude Sitton, for example, noted, "The demonstrations were dismissed at first as another college fad of the 'panty-raid' variety," but that view "lost adherents . . . as the movement spread. . . . Some whites wrote off the episodes as the work of 'outside agitators.' But even they conceded that the seeds of dissent had fallen in fertile soil." See "Negro Sitdowns Stir Fear of Wider Unrest."

41. Fleming quoted in Wakefield, "Eye of the Storm," in Carson et al., *Reporting Civil Rights*, 473.

42. Kilpatrick's reply to letter of "Mr Flax," February 21, 1961, "1960–62 Personal Correspondence F," box 2, Kilpatrick Papers.

4

Breaching the Wall of Resistance

White Southern Reactions to the Sit-Ins

CLIVE WEBB

Opinion polls could not have been clearer. White southerners were almost unanimous in their condemnation of the sit-ins. According to one 1961 survey, 84 percent opposed not only the tactics but also the aims of the protesters.[1] Another poll showed that even whites who sought rapprochement with civil rights activists or were openly sympathetic with their cause disputed the legitimacy of the demonstrations. While it was predictable that only 17 percent of self-described racial moderates approved of the protests, even among integrationists the figure was a meager 34 percent.[2]

What southern whites were much less sure of, however, was how to stop black activism. It was in fact this indecision and disarray that facilitated the demonstrations in the first place. Despite the resolute defiance of the Deep South, the high tide of massive resistance had started to recede by 1960. Segregationists had inflicted unintentional self-harm when they refused to comply with federal court orders to admit black students to public schools. The consequences of this strategy—a breakdown of law and order, school closures, public-relations damage, retraction of northern and federal investment—convinced increasing numbers of white southerners that uncompromising resistance served little purpose.

Although the defenses of white supremacy had begun to falter, in the sit-ins they faced an assault of hitherto unseen scale and force. There is an increasing trend among historians to elide the civil rights protests of the 1950s and 1960s into a century-long struggle for racial equality. This tendency to stress historical continuity over discontinuity minimizes the distinctiveness of black protest in the decades that immediately followed

World War II. Although the sit-ins drew on historical antecedents, they represented an unprecedented challenge to southern white supremacy. White southerners understood this as their traditional tactical response to black insurgency proved increasingly ineffective. Their recognition that sheer force was insufficient to withstand the tide of reform, their resort to increasingly narrow legal defenses of segregation, and their inability to find in their religion support for their racial beliefs all demonstrate an awareness of the historical rupture precipitated by the sit-ins. The defensiveness and disunity with which they reacted demonstrated, as Harold Fleming of the Southern Regional Council argued, that the sit-ins were "the psychological turning point in race relations in the South."[3]

Ironically, their own racism undermined the ability of segregationists to defend Jim Crow against the sit-in demonstrators. Deluded by their own propaganda about the mutual trust and understanding between black and white southerners, they could not initially comprehend the indigenous nature of the student revolt. Their inability to believe that black youth possessed either the motivation or ability to organize an insurgency against segregation left them confused as to who their enemies were and what tactics to use against them. Some accused communists. According to Governor LeRoy Collins of Florida, "if the leaders in the Kremlin had worked up a plan to weaken us throughout the world, I can think of none which would be more effective than the script we are now following."[4] Others blamed northern civil rights organizations including the Congress of Racial Equality and, especially, the National Association for the Advancement of Colored People.[5] Even segregationists who conceded that the students were not puppets whose strings were being pulled by outside forces underestimated their sense of purpose and their organizational prowess. According to the 1961 poll cited earlier, 50 percent of segregationists attributed the sit-ins to "youthful exuberance" or "ignorance." Only 12 percent conceded that a desire for racial equality motivated the demonstrators.[6] Not until the protests spread across the region did segregationists really grasp who or what they were really up against.

"We call upon all proper authorities," declared the Citizens' Council, the most powerful of the political organizations sworn to uphold segregation, "to take the necessary action to prosecute leaders of the sit-down movement to the fullest extent."[7] Local and state officials certainly drew on all the power at their disposal in an effort to repress the protests. State legislatures enforced old trespass statutes or enacted new laws that empowered the police to make more than three thousand arrests and the courts to impose tough sentences over the course of 1960, none more so than the four-month sentence received by Martin Luther King Jr. for his involvement in an Atlanta sit-ins on October 19.[8] State authorities also retaliated against the colleges that served as the recruiting grounds for the movement, forcing the dismissal of 58 professors and the expulsion of 141 students.[9] In some states they also attempted to outmaneuver the protests through the use of paid informants who infiltrated the movement and passed on details about its members, resources, and tactics.[10]

Some scholars maintain that white southern newspapers tried to contain the threat posed by the sit-ins by minimizing or entirely omitting coverage in their pages. This was to an extent true of the Deep South, but press outlets in other parts of the region provided extensive reportage.[11] More generally, Paul Wehr points out, white newspapers editorialized against the demonstrations, but their detailed reporting of those events unwittingly provided not only inspiration but also tactical instruction to African Americans in other communities.[12]

Meanwhile, the rise of radical black protest revitalized grassroots segregationist organization. Within three days of the launch of the Rock Hill, South Carolina, sit-ins in February 1960, for example, 350 local whites founded a Citizens' Council that threatened to boycott any store that served black demonstrators.[13] The sit-ins also precipitated a sharp rise in membership of the Ku Klux Klan and the consolidation of the previously splintered Invisible Empire into a more united political force. Klansmen dramatized their renewed strength on the night of Saturday, March 26, 1960, when they burned more than one thousand crosses throughout the South. The Klan also inflicted some of the bloodiest violence against black demonstrators. In Houston, three masked men beat a protester with a chain, carved "KKK" into his chest, and hanged him by his knees on a tree. In Jacksonville, Florida, Klansmen led a mob of three thousand whites that assaulted NAACP Youth Council activists in Hemming Park with axe handles, baseball bats, and barbed wire.[14]

Incidents such as these exposed the complicity of law enforcement officers and the judiciary in suppressing black political dissent. Jacksonville police were passive spectators of the violence in Hemming Park, intervening only when the situation started to spill out of control and even then arresting more African Americans than whites. Municipal Court Judge John Santora also imposed fines or jail terms on fifty-seven blacks and only twenty-six whites, but he made an example of white sit-in leader Richard Parker, who, despite having suffered a broken jaw, received a ninety-day prison sentence for inciting a riot.[15] In Orangeburg, South

Carolina, police arrested nearly four hundred demonstrators, herded them into a crowded stockade, and drenched them with fire hoses.[16]

Such incidents were far from the norm, however. The authorities in many communities exercised considerable restraint, and there were relatively few serious outbreaks of violence.[17] When violence did occur, the customary segregationist tactic of intimidation proved counterproductive. It tended to strengthen the public voice of pragmatic white southerners who calculated that the cost of uncompromising resistance to racial reform was too much to pay. Racial disorder tarnished the reputations of southern communities and deterred northern capital investment. A *Tampa Tribune* editorial on the turmoil in Jacksonville concluded that the "constitutional right to peaceable assembly does not include sanction for guns, knives, baseball bats or axe handles" and denounced the mayor and police for not averting an incident that "gave their city and all Florida a black eye."[18] The progressive white political leadership in cities such as Nashville, Tennessee, was especially anxious not to suffer a repeat of the violence that had already shaken their communities in reaction to school desegregation. When a bomb demolished the home of black leader Z. Alexander Looby in April 1960, a three-word headline in the *Nashville Tennessean* captured the urgent response of city hall: "INTEGRATE COUNTERS—MAYOR."[19] As the sit-ins spread, city leaders across the South warned local citizens not to repeat the political and economic damage that whites in cities such as Jacksonville and Nashville had done to their own communities. Voicing such concern, the *Petersburg Progress-Index* warned the residents of this Virginia city that the proper authorities should handle the protests. "Everybody else," it declared, "would be wise to get as far away from them as possible."[20]

Racial violence also compromised a segregationist leadership desperate to convince a skeptical northern public that it was motivated less by racial prejudice than a desire to uphold the sacred constitutional principle of federalism. The southern press often blamed black activists whose criminal behavior had supposedly provoked whites. The *Chattanooga News–Free Press*, for instance, attributed the riot that erupted on the downtown streets of the Tennessee city to "trouble-making Negro demonstrators."[21] Yet the more astute massive resisters understood that the white mobs that brutally assaulted peaceful black demonstrators had irrevocably surrendered the moral high ground. In the words of moderate Atlanta newspaperman Ralph McGill, mob violence "left them naked to civilization."[22] Segregationist ideologue James Kilpatrick ruefully contrasted "the colored students, in coats, white shirts, ties" with white hoodlums "come to heckle, a ragtail rabble, slack-jawed, black-jacketed, grinning fit to kill."[23] The sit-ins exposed the paradoxical dilemma at the heart of massive resistance. Segregationist leaders were forced to dissociate themselves from the white rank and file because their resort to racial demagoguery and violence made it impossible to persuade the rest of the nation of the political legitimacy of their cause. Without the support of the white lower classes, however, the segregationist leaders had no movement to command.

Segregationist politicians tried but failed to turn the violence to their advantage. Within weeks of the first demonstrations, the U.S. Senate opened debate on a new federal civil rights bill. The proposed law provided for federal inspection of local voter-registration polls, introduced penalties against any interference with an individual who tried to register or cast a vote, and made it a crime to use threats or force to obstruct a federal court order. Southern Democrats attempted to obstruct the bill by organizing what became the longest filibuster in Senate history, stretching over forty-three hours from February 29 to March 2, 1960.

Seizing on the protests to justify their action, filibuster supporters accused civil rights activists of collusion with the liberal northern news media to mount the sit-ins in the hope of stirring public sympathy for the measure's enactment. According to Congressman Robert Ashmore (D–South Carolina), the demonstrations were "a planned and concerted effort to agitate, and create dissension to the point of violence. And evidently, those directing the demonstrations thought it wise to stage their publicity stunts while Congress is considering civil rights legislation."[24]

In like vein, the leader of the southern senatorial bloc, Richard Russell (D-Georgia), asserted that black activists had conspired to "start a race riot of terrible proportions" in the South "to force Senate passage of a civil rights bill." He also accused the northern press of deliberately misrepresenting the demonstrations in order to strengthen popular support for federal intervention in southern race relations. According to Russell, when black students illegally trespassed on private property the liberal media portrayed them as exercising a legitimate right to protest, but when southern whites demonstrated against school desegregation they were accused of riot and sedition. It was a double standard to criticize segregationists for repressing the legal rights of African Americans but condone the criminal behavior of black demonstrators who threatened to ruin white businesses.[25]

Senate hard-liners received the support of the southern press. Even racially moderate newspapers claimed that the lawlessness of the protesters undermined the moral argument for a federal civil rights law. As the *Kingsport News* of Tennessee put it, "this business is simply handicapping those who are fighting for Civil Rights legislation in the Congress."[26] When some of the demonstrations descended into violence, segregationist politicians saw it as grist for their mill. Southern Democrats seized on an incident in Columbia, South Carolina, where black demonstrators had reportedly smashed the windows of a drive-in restaurant, to insist it was whites whose rights were most in need of protection. Congressman John Bell Williams (D-Mississippi) denounced what he also saw as the double standard of the media. "In their usual manner of reporting such incidents, national news mediums referred to this as a 'demonstration,'" he complained, "while the same thing done by white hoodlums would have been called 'mob' action."[27]

As further disorders erupted on the streets of southern cities, it nonetheless became obvious, even to many elements of the white southern press, that black activists were not the belligerents. Historians see the sit-ins, with smartly attired and courteously behaved black students confronting brutal white racists, as a potent enactment of politics as street theater. Segregationist politicians were powerless to prevent southern whites from performing the roles scripted and directed by black protesters that cast them as the villains in the drama. As the demonstrations continued, the rhetoric of southern senators became more strained and defensive. The dignity with which demonstrators faced hostile white thugs undermined whatever legal or moral force southern politicians' arguments possessed.

While southern newspapers continued to accuse demonstrators of criminal behavior, they recognized that whites could not resist the sit-ins by themselves stepping outside the law. In Tennessee, for example, the *Kingsport News* declared: "The mobs that seek to break up the sit-downs and the protest parades are outside the law . . . law enforcement authorities should stop that and so demonstrate that the state does demand respect for law from everyone. . . . This sort of thing weakens the hands of those Southerners who are struggling to prevent undue Federal action."[28] Southern senators appear to have conceded the point, since they stopped using the sit-ins as a means to frame their resistance to the civil rights bill.

The defensiveness of segregationists is further evident from their avoidance of white-supremacist arguments to support their opposition to the sit-ins. Instead, their principal argument was that privately owned businesses had the right to serve who they wanted. "No customer has a right to demonstrate inside a store," asserted one South Carolina newspaper. "The moment he does so, he can be ejected and arrested for disorderly conduct."[29] Segregationists cited both a statement by Harry Truman in support of private property rights and the U.S. Supreme Court decision in *National Labor Relations Board v. Fansteel Metallurgical Corp* (1939) outlawing sit-down strikes as evidence that their position was rooted less in provincial prejudice than broad legal and constitutional principle. The omission of race nonetheless represented a tacit admission that white southerners were attempting to defend the indefensible.

The sit-ins not only disconcerted segregationists but also shattered the complacency of white southern moderates. In cities such as Atlanta, Durham, and Nashville, business-oriented administrations collaborated with accommodationist black community leaders to ameliorate the harsher aspects of segregation. The gradualist reformism of these moderates was at odds, however, with student demonstrators impatient for immediate change.[30] Unable to satisfy the protesters with limited concessions, they reacted with resentful criticism that betrayed a paternalistic presumption that slow and deliberate policies would accomplish change better than the impulsiveness of young blacks. According to one South Carolina newspaper, reform "will come from neither white nor Negro agitators, but from those, white and black, who keep their feet solid on the ground and their heads cool and objective."[31]

In many instances these arguments about the unilateral action of the students undermining what had been achieved through mutual endeavor was a smoke screen for a complete failure to address black discontent. This is evident from a Virginia newspaper editorial claiming the sit-ins threatened the "sympathetic . . . racial co-existence" that had endured since the local community drove out northern carpetbaggers and "convinced the colored people that they had been the tools of unscrupulous self-seekers, just as they are today."[32] An editorial by Mississippi racial moderate Hodding Carter also betrayed an attitude of complacency if not insincerity toward black demonstrators. Although he appeared to understand the mounting frustration of African Americans with the courts' failure to fulfill the expectations created by the *Brown* decision, he contended that the provocative tactics used by student demonstrators would only prove counterproductive. As he asserted, the sit-ins "may seem to shorten the way to eventual equality, but in truth they make the road ahead more rocky." Encouraging black protesters to revert to a litigation strategy that he acknowledged brought change at an agonizingly slow pace was indicative of Carter's failure to grasp the moral urgency of civil rights reform. Having advised African Americans to pursue their cause through the legal system, he nonetheless anticipated that their efforts to integrate lunch counters would end in failure, since "no court ever ruled that anyone engaged in private enterprise need serve any customers if he does not wish to do so. We do not believe any court ever will, or should." Those last two words exposed the preceding counsel to black activists as disingenuous.[33]

Sit-in demonstrations struck not only at the tactics used to defend segregation but also at its intellectual foundations. The Supreme Court's decision in *Brown v. Board of Education* had troubled the consciences of some white southern Christians, who privately and sometimes publicly wondered whether their religion legitimated racial segregation. The sit-ins further sharpened the focus of this theological debate. Black student demonstrators proclaimed that their actions were imbued with divine purpose. "With God on our side," exclaimed Ezell Blair of the Greensboro Four, "who can be against us?" This implicit equation of support for segregation with sin represented a bold challenge to white southern Christians. The Atlanta Committee on Appeal for Human Rights more confrontationally accused those who resisted racial equality of denigrating the core principles of the Christian faith. "We want to state clearly," read their declaration in the *Atlanta Constitution*, "that we cannot tolerate, in a nation professing democracy and among people professing Christianity, the discriminatory conditions under which the Negro is living today."[34]

How white southerners responded to these charges is difficult to assess without resort to generalization. According to one estimate, there were at the time of the sit-ins around 55,000 mainstream denomination churches in the South and countless other religious fringe groups.[35] Despite their common faith, white southern Christians did not speak with one voice on the sit-ins. On the contrary, the protests exposed and exacerbated inter- and intra-denominational cleavages over the race issue. They divided minister from minister, clergymen from congregations, and metropolitan areas from small towns and the countryside.

Local, state, and national ministerial associations offered fervent support for the student demonstrators. The religious organizations that issued statements in support of the protesters' right to disobey discriminatory and immoral laws are too many to list in their entirety, but the included the General Assembly of the United Presbyterian Church, the National Council of the Episcopal Church, the Methodist Church Board of Social and Economic Relations, the Home Missions of the

Congregational and Christian Churches, the American Friends Service Committee, and the National Council of Churches.[36] Princeton divinity professor Paul Ramsey even produced a book-length study on the Christian obligation to support the demonstrations.[37]

As Will D. Campbell, a white southern liberal who worked as a field officer for the National Council of Churches, observed, the sit-ins emboldened many national religious bodies to take a more radical stand on civil rights. The Supreme Court's decision in *Brown v. Board of Education* induced declarations from church leaders that it was a Christian duty to obey the law. In supporting the sit-ins, however, their position altered to advocating disobedience of any law that was unjust and immoral.[38] The General Assembly of the United Presbyterian Church, for instance, moved in line with the new militancy of black activists by passing a resolution endorsing civil disobedience. Commissioners declared that the church governing body "commends and encourages those persons who are seeking by non violent means to bring about equality for all."[39] In seeking biblical sanction for the demonstrators who act on higher moral law in defying man-made statutes, the leaders of this and other denominations cited the Old Testament story of Shadrach, Meshach, and Abednego, who were rescued from the fiery furnace for their defiance of King Nebuchadnezzar.[40]

Black activists drew inspiration and support from their own churches, but the intervention of white religious leaders imbued the demonstrations with greater moral authority and respectability than they would have otherwise commanded in the broader community. Dr. Ernest Trice Thompson, the highest elected officer of the Southern Presbyterian Church, asserted that the sit-ins forced white Christians to confront "discriminations which should be forgotten and which will pass. All discriminations will, and must, disappear."[41]

Yet church leaders' support for black student activism also aroused considerable ministerial dissent, especially in the Deep South. The white southern clergyman who commanded more power and influence than any other, the revivalist Billy Graham, gave succor to Christian segregationists by seeming to oppose the sit-ins. Graham had aroused the ire of many southern whites by asserting that there was no biblical basis to the separation of the races.[42] The confrontational tactics of sit-in demonstrators nonetheless ran counter to his gradualist approach to race relations. Interviewed by a reporter, the evangelist asserted, "No matter what the law may be—it may be an unjust law—I believe we have a Christian responsibility to obey it." Pressed to clarify whether he disapproved of the demonstrations, he further obscured his meaning by replying, "I did not say that. I do not know the legal ramifications of this particular situation."[43]

Graham may have attempted to appease both sides in the civil rights struggle, but his statement only empowered segregationists. African Americans denounced his apparent inability to understand the moral imperative of their protests. One black clergyman postulated that Graham knew black demonstrators had right on their side but had allowed his conscience to be overpowered by "the prospect of southern revival money."[44] Although the evangelist appeared to be in dispute with black activists over means rather than ends, segregationists interpreted his line of reasoning as being consistent with their own theological defense of Jim Crow. They construed his comments as an implicit reference to Romans 13:1–7, in which St. Paul instructs Christians to submit themselves to law and established authority because "the powers that be are ordained of God."[45]

Few southern clergymen claimed divine sanction for segregation as forcefully as Baptist minister George Dorsett, chaplain of the North Carolina Ku Klux Klan, who helped coordinate the counterprotests in Greensboro.[46] There were nonetheless prominent ministers who condemned the sit-ins as atheistic assaults on the social order and decried the resolutions made in support of the demonstrations by national religious organizations. The Episcopalian bishop of Alabama, Charles Carpenter, denounced civil disobedience as "just another name for lawlessness" and encouraged the members of his diocese to ignore the declaration of support for the sit-ins by the national council of the church.[47] Fellow Episcopalian Jeffrey Alfriend, pastor of the St. John's Church in Tallahassee, expressed his opposition to the protests in more explicitly racist terms that emphasized white southern fears of miscegenation. "I am very tired of hearing it said, 'This is a matter of Christian conscience,'" he declared indignantly. "With me, it certainly is not. It is a matter of biological expediency and ordinary common sense."[48]

Ministers from other denominations also made angry retorts to resolutions advocating civil disobedience made by national religious bodies. A Presbyterian minister in Athens, Georgia, complained of a resolution by his church's general assembly commending the sit-ins, "It will make our task more difficult in dealing with the problem."[49] A similar statement in support of the demonstrations from the Lutheran Human

Relations Association of America drew the fire of a Savannah, Georgia, minister who accused its members of issuing edicts from "theological ivory towers."[50]

These criticisms alluded to the difficulties faced by white southern ministers who supported racial equality in principle but were in practice constrained by the prejudices of their congregations. Harvard social psychologist Thomas Pettigrew estimated that four out of every five white southern ministers supported racial integration but that pressure from their parishioners inhibited their practical involvement in civil rights activism. While it is difficult to determine the accuracy of this calculation, there is no doubt that racially moderate clergymen had reason to fear reprisal.[51]

One of the most potent instruments of grassroots segregationist resistance within southern white churches was the Methodist Laymen's Union. Founded in reaction to the *Brown* decision, the body declared that its sole purpose was to "prevent either the sudden or the gradual integration of Negroes and whites." Members condemned as an "approval of lawlessness" a resolution of the General Conference of the Methodist Church commending the dignified conduct of sit-in demonstrators. Having failed to insert a clause stressing the sanctity of individual property rights, they threatened to withhold the donations made by local churches to the governing body. The union also orchestrated a campaign of intimidation against ministers who supported or participated in sit-ins.[52]

The protests precipitated similar conflict between moderate clergymen and reactionary congregants across the South. Three Methodist ministers who wrote a letter in support of local demonstrations to the *Rock Hill Herald* were fired from their pulpits.[53] A similar fate befell twenty-eight Methodist clergymen in Mississippi who signed a statement encouraging freedom of expression on the race issue. Fear for their safety forced them one by one to flee the state.[54] Unitarian minister Charles White McGehee withstood pressure following his declaration of support for local sit-ins from a Jacksonville newspaper that encouraged its readers to purge the Florida city of "race-mixing preachers," but he still had to be guarded around the clock by members of his congregation.[55]

Newspapers in other southern cities launched smear campaigns against liberal clergymen. Merrill Proudfoot, a Presbyterian clergyman and theology professor active in the Knoxville sit-ins, despaired that there was not another white minister in the city "who has sufficient conviction about the justice of our cause to risk offending some members of his congregation." The fate of those clergymen who eventually overcame their fears, however, only appeared to excuse their earlier caution. When several ministers issued a public statement in support of the protests, segregationists retaliated by distributing handbills throughout the city, accusing the signatories of being communists whose desecration of "the laws of God" rendered them "unfit to stand in the pulpit." Acting on this instruction, the board of one Baptist church summarily fired their minister.[56]

In criticizing the timidity of white ministers, we should recognize that many black clergymen whose power bases relied on the maintenance of segregation also opposed the protests. The segregationist press gave widespread coverage to Dr. J. H. Jackson Jr., the influential president of the National Baptist Convention, who condemned what he saw as the reckless irresponsibility of the demonstrators. From the opposite political side, Knoxville activist Merrill Proudfoot lamented that "as disappointed as I am about the white ministers, it is the absence of the Negro ministers which weighs heaviest on me."[57]

The sit-ins at lunch counters troubled the consciences of many white southern Christians, but it was the kneel-ins at churches that really awakened them to the impossibility of reconciling support for segregation with their religious faith. It was a commonplace expression of the time that the most segregated time of the week was Sunday morning, when blacks and whites attended separate religious services. The Southern Baptist Convention and the Presbyterian Church in the United States had both declared at the time of the *Brown* decision that segregation was antithetical to Christian doctrine. Scholars such as David Chappell have used these resolutions to argue that white southern church leaders offered little cultural or intellectual reinforcement to the defense of Jim Crow. As David Reimers has pointed out, however, "the problem lay in implementation."[58]

The first kneel-ins occurred on Sunday, August 7, 1960, when twenty-five students attempted to gain admittance to services at six white churches in Atlanta. Calling attention to the maintenance of the color line in houses of worship represented a more immediate challenge to the consciences of white southerners. Since the rights of private property ownership used to oppose the lunch counter protests did not apply to churches, it was more difficult to deny that the exclusion of African Americans reflected racial prejudice.

Many white churches nonetheless closed their doors to black demonstrators. Atlanta journalist Ralph McGill denounced ushers at white churches across Georgia who, when confronted by kneel-in demonstrators, acted "like doorkeepers at a secret lodge."[59] His criticism did little to stir shame or remorse among Christian segregationists. State authorities filed a suit against Martin Luther King enjoining him from "advising or counseling the invasion of private premises and the interruption of white church services."[60] Two years after McGill appealed to the Christian consciences of white Georgians, police arrested black activists who attempted to participate in services at a church in Albany.[61]

African American activists suffered similar exclusion when they attempted to integrate services at white churches in other southern states, including Alabama and Tennessee.[62] When black demonstrators tried to attend services at the Southside Baptist Church in Miami, Rev. Ben Peacock led his congregation out of the building.[63] In Mississippi, demonstrators endured arrest and incarceration when they attempted to kneel-in at churches near the state capitol building in downtown Jackson.[64]

The obdurate resistance of many churches to black worshippers arguably reveals much about the mind-set of southern whites on the race issue. The "movement disruption costs" associated with integration of churches was much greater than providing lunch-counter service to African Americans. Although the integration of lunch counters was an affront to many southern whites, they could tolerate it provided there was minimum disruption to their own consumer experience. Religious faith and worship was more fundamental to the self-identification of white southerners than the right to eat a hamburger at a racially exclusive lunch counter. For many whites in the Bible Belt it was the core of their being. Their opposition to the kneel-ins demonstrates that while they could make a calculated concession on the race issue by accepting the integration of public spaces, their acceptance of African Americans did not extend to the inner spaces of their hearts and souls.

The resistance of religious institutions to racial integration nonetheless provoked much soul-searching on the part of some individual congregants. There are a number of white racial conversion narratives that stem from the uneasy confrontations between these churchgoers and black demonstrators. In Augusta, Georgia, a woman who had opposed accepting black students from Paine College into her church later confided to Ralph McGill, "I knew it would disturb our church if they were admitted. But what I didn't know was that it would disturb it more deeply and fundamentally to keep them out. . . . Even the more angry and determined members protest too much. They reveal by their very anger and protestation their own sense of guilt and the uncomfortable fact that a Christian church can do what we have done."[65]

The resistance of southern white churches to racial integration created conflict not only with national but also international religious organizations. Although segregationists insisted that the maintenance of the color line was a matter of individual state sovereignty, the kneel-ins forced them to confront the broader international consequences of resisting racial reform.

In August 1960, representatives from fifty countries attended a meeting of the World Council of Churches in St. Andrews, Scotland. Their deliberations focused on the need to forge greater global unity among Christians. Delegates discussed numerous issues, including how in a time of Cold War to enhance relations between Christians in the East and West. The admission of delegates from five newly decolonized African nations also influenced their formal declaration that segregation based on race was contrary to biblical doctrine. This pronouncement swayed Ralph McGill to warn his fellow white southerners that their refusal to admit African Americans to places of worship had repercussions far beyond the confines of their community, state, or region. With the United States and Soviet Union in fierce competition to secure alliance with the new independent republics of Asia and Africa, failure to uphold the principles of democracy and freedom could alienate potential Cold War partners and tip the delicate geopolitical balance irrecoverably toward communism. Referring to the resistance encountered by kneel-in demonstrators, McGill declared, "there is no blinking the fact that the Christian church is being hurt in the testing time to which it is being subjected. . . . All these incidents are grist in the mills of Communist and Moslem propaganda."[66]

It was doubtful that a white moderate like McGill would persuade hard-line segregationists to submit to racial integration in the interest of promoting the strategic global interests of the United States. "The agitators are always referring to what other countries will think of the United States," declared a defiant Dean Fleming, secretary of the Alabama Baptist Laymen. "We are not a bit interested in what they think of us."[67]

Southern white supremacists might not care about the rest of the world, but the rest of the world was sharpening its critical focus on them. In particular, members of the international community drew uncomfortable comparisons between segregation in the American South and apartheid in South Africa. On March 21, 1960, police in the South African township of Sharpeville shot dead sixty-nine black people protesting the restrictive pass laws. The simultaneous timing of the sit-ins and the

Sharpeville massacre formed clear parallels between racism in the American South and South Africa in the minds of many political analysts. According to one commentator, the southern states had, with the exception of the Little Rock school crisis, evaded the levels of international criticism directed toward the apartheid regime in South Africa. Media coverage of the sit-ins, however, meant that this situation was changing: "America's continuing inability to resolve her interracial problem with dispatch is beginning to weigh more heavily in the international field than her failure to match the Russians in rocketry."[68] A resolution by the United Nations General Assembly condemning the Nationalist government in South Africa had, for instance, prompted calls for similar censure of southern segregationists.[69] The connection became still more obvious in late 1960 when black demonstrators modeling their tactics on African American activists staged sit-ins at restaurants in Cape Town.[70]

The comparison drawn by other nations between South Africa and the American South further was a political embarrassment to the United States. Northern political and spiritual leaders attempted to reassert the moral authority of their nation by rallying to the cause of the sit-ins. The chief executive of the United Presbyterian Church, Dr. Eugene Carson Blake, asserted that American clerical authorities could not in conscience condemn South African apartheid "as long as they did not support the lunch-counter sit-ins in the South."[71] Similarly, while the U.S. government saw South Africa as an important trading partner and Cold War ally, it could not remain silent on the Sharpeville massacre without compromising its authority as leader of the free world. In protesting the violence, however, State Department officials exposed themselves to accusations of hypocrisy because of the persistence of racial discrimination in their own country.

The more astute segregationists understood that the only way for Washington to resolve this problem was to intervene more decisively in southern race relations. Although they denied comparisons in terms of how they treated their black populations, segregationists defended South Africa from State Department criticism because of what they perceived as the disturbing parallel between this encroachment on national sovereignty and the threat of federal intervention in southern state affairs. One Mississippi newspaper declared that while the Sharpeville massacre was an affront to "all civilized people," the State Department had acted incautiously in criticizing the South African government. "For a fair approximation of how most white South Africans must feel now, we might imagine our reaction if, immediately following the jailing of Negro 'sit-ins' by local police, the Soviet Union were to issue an immediate official protest. Whether we were right or wrong, we'd be correct in thinking it was none of their business."[72]

The morally equivocal tone of the last sentence exposed an increasing lack of conviction about the innateness of southern race relations. It would have been difficult only a few years earlier to find a Mississippi newspaper editorial arguing so tenuously that the need for the South and thereby the entire country to protect against communist propaganda outweighed consideration of whether segregation was morally right or desirable. Defensiveness rather than defiance had started to characterize white southern rhetoric.

Segregationists tried to cast southern race relations in a more favorable light through comparison with other parts of Africa, particularly the bloody turmoil in the Congo, which, they argued, served as a prophetic warning of what could happen if they did not resist the new black militancy and retain control of their region. When the sit-ins sparked violence in some southern cities, the segregationist press compared the situation with events in the new African republic. "From Congo to Jacksonville, the story was the same," affirmed one South Carolina newspaper, "a clash between whites and blacks."[73] Press reports revealing that whites rather than blacks were the perpetrators of the violence nonetheless stripped the paternalistic veneer from southern race relations and exposed a reality closer to South Africa's. A Kentucky newspaper published an editorial cartoon that conceded the comparison. It depicted two figures standing side by side as a group of young black people approach them, one of them a shotgun-brandishing hooded skeleton that represents apartheid, the other a southern Klansman wielding a bullwhip. Some white southerners had begun to see themselves through the eyes of the rest of the world and were disturbed by what it revealed.[74]

The cartoon demonstrated how the sit-ins stimulated a new level of introspection on the part of white southerners about their treatment of African Americans. Among the writings of segregationists, however, few self-reflective sources provide explicit insight into the psychological impact of the sit-ins. Segregationists seldom commented directly on how their racial convictions were affected by black protesters who, rather than being intimidated by imprisonment, wore it as a badge of honor or proclaimed their moral superiority in protest songs satirizing white adversaries who "love segregation like a hound dog loves a bone."[75]

The lesson in those communities where downtown businesses desegregated their facilities was that reform could be accomplished without complete disruption to the pattern of everyday life. As a report by the Southern Regional Council concluded, this owed much to the absence of boastful celebration by black demonstrators.[76] In the Deep South, however, the sit-ins had been unable to breach the "wall of resistance" defended by whites implacably opposed to integration.[77] It was nonetheless evident even to segregationists in these states that they had underestimated not only the depth of African Americans' disaffection but also their ability to mobilize and maintain collective action for reform.

As numerous commentators observed, the success of the sit-ins elsewhere in the region escalated the sense of isolation and alarm among Deep South segregationists. In late 1960, Mayor Allen Thompson of Jackson, Mississippi, accepted an invitation to appear on a nationally televised debate about the sit-ins. Pressure from the segregationist Citizens' Council, however, led to his withdrawal. According to one newspaper, this intervention exposed segregationists' increasing lack of conviction that they could win the intellectual and moral argument on race relations. After all, "if the Deep South's position is correct on sit-ins, what better way to present it than on national television?" In coercing Thompson to pull out of the program, the council revealed "its rabid fear of opposition and its almost pathological insecurity."[78] Violence and intimidation succeeded for now in suppressing civil rights protest, but these tactics also betrayed the desperation of segregationists, who in reaction to the sit-ins sensed they could only postpone, not prevent, civil rights reform.

The support of both national political parties for the sit-ins certainly warned white southerners to expect tougher federal enforcement of civil rights. Democratic presidential candidate John F. Kennedy asserted that the sit-ins honored a tradition of political protest enshrined in the origins of the United States, exclaiming that "the American spirit is coming alive again."[79] The Democratic Party's adoption of a strong civil rights platform prompted speculation that white southerners would abandon their traditional partisan loyalties to support Republican presidential candidate Richard Nixon. Far from presenting himself as a viable alternative to disaffected southern Democrats, however, Nixon avowed support for what he identified as the "essentially moral" cause of the sit-ins. This contrasted with his so-called southern strategy to capitalize on the backlash against civil rights reform in the 1968 race for the White House.[80]

Without the ability to foresee the future, segregationists had to contemplate alternative strategies intended to retain their influence in Washington. James Kilpatrick encouraged southern whites to cast their ballots for unpledged electors who in a closely contested race could demand concessions in return for their electoral votes. Another southern editorialist urged southern Democrats and conservative Republicans to form a congressional bloc. Numerous newspaper leaders promoted a third-party challenge, albeit with little optimism that it could succeed where the earlier Dixiecrat revolt of 1948 had failed. The tone of many of these press columns was indeed desperate. Regardless of the outcome of the election, the alignment of both political parties with the aims and tactics of the sit-ins instilled even the most optimistic of these editorials with a sober perspective on segregationists' waning political clout in Washington.[81]

Sensing that great changes were afoot, white moderate journalist Harry Ashmore had published *An Epitaph for Dixie* in 1958.[82] At that juncture, however, it seemed premature to write the inscription on Jim Crow's headstone before he was actually dead and buried. The corpse of southern white supremacy still had life left in it by the end of 1960, but the sit-ins had ensured that its end was nigh. The unprecedented insurgency of southern blacks exposed and exacerbated the disunity and defensiveness of whites in the region.

Doubtless reinforced by generational affinity, a sense that white supremacy was morally indefensible had inspired many white students to join with their black counterparts in challenging the color line.[83] Nevertheless, the sit-ins also had a profound impact on the racial beliefs of older whites that were elemental for the preservation of Jim Crow. In dramatizing the depths of black disaffection with segregation, the protests exposed the traditional white fallacy that African Americans were satisfied with their lot within the caste system. "We know what our Negroes want" had long been the complacent refrain of the white South. During the Nashville protests, the vice-president of a downtown department store reflected on the reassertion of this mantra by no-surrender segregationists: "I think the best way to determine what the Negroes want would be to put yourself in their position and figure out what you would want."[84] While conceding that he could not entirely comprehend what it meant to be a black person in the Jim Crow South, this effort at empathetic understanding demonstrated a transformation in the mindset of many whites. By encouraging whites to see the world through their eyes, black activists had indelibly altered the region not only in physical terms but also on a deeper philosophical level. Jim Crow segregation could not long survive this change.

Notes

1. Sharon A. Bramlett, "Southern vs. Northern Newspaper Coverage of a Race Crisis—The Lunch Counter Sit-In Movement, 1960–1964: An Assessment of Press Social Responsibility" (Ph.D. diss., Indiana University, 1987), 7.

2. Donald R. Matthews and James W. Prothro, *Negroes and the New Southern Politics* (New York: Harcourt, Brace and World, 1966), 435.

3. Numan V. Bartley, *The New South, 1945–1980* (Baton Rouge: Louisiana State University Press, 1995), 299–300. The most important articulation of the "long civil rights movement" thesis is Jacquelyn Dowd Hall, "The Long Civil Rights Movement and the Political Uses of the Past," *Journal of American History* 91 (March 2005): 1233–63.

4. *Florence Morning News*, March 19, 1960. Editorial opinion in Florida and the rest of the South endorsed that of Governor Collins. See, for example, the assertion that neither southern blacks nor whites benefited from the sit-ins, "the only people they make happy are the leaders in Moscow," in the *Sarasota Journal*, October 7, 1960.

5. *Florence Morning News*, March 19, 1960; Hugh Davis Graham, *Crisis in Print: Desegregation and the Press in Tennessee* (Nashville: Vanderbilt University Press, 1967), 196.

6. Matthews and Prothro, *Negroes and the New Southern Politics*, 437.

7. "Seditious Sit-Downs," *The Citizens' Council*, March 1960, 1–2, South Carolina Library, University of South Carolina, Columbia.

8. Bartley, *The New South*, 302; *Memphis Commercial Appeal*, March 23, 1960; *Mississippi Clarion Ledger*, March 24, 1960; *Aiken Standard and Review*, April 1, 1960.

9. Matthews and Prothro, *Negroes and the New Southern Politics*, 408–9.

10. Zack J. Van Landingham, "Sit Down Protest Strikes Jackson, Mississippi," report, March 23, 1960, Sovereignty Commission Online, Mississippi Department of Archives and History Digital Collections, http://mdah.state.ms.us/arrec/digital_archives/sovcom/result.php?image=/data/sov_commission/images/png/cd06/041685.png&otherstuff=2|133|0|1|1|1|1|41067|.

11. For examples of press restrictions, see Merrill Proudfoot, *Diary of a Sit-In* (Chapel Hill: University of North Carolina Press, 1962), 70, and Laurie B. Green, *Battling the Plantation Mentality: Memphis and the Black Freedom Struggle* (Chapel Hill: University of North Carolina Press, 2007), 254.

12. Bramlett, "Southern vs. Northern Newspaper Coverage," 26. See also Lisa L. Zagumny, "Sit-Ins in Knoxville, Tennessee: A Case Study of Public Rhetoric," *Journal of Negro History* 86 (Winter 2001): 47; and Kenneth T. Andrews and Michael Biggs, "The Dynamics of Protest Diffusion: Movement Organizations, Social Networks, and News Media in the 1960 Sit-Ins," *American Sociological Review* 71 (October 2006): 765–66, 769.

13. *Rock Hill Evening Herald*, February 15, 1960; Miles Wolff, *Lunch at the Five and Ten: The Greensboro Sit-Ins: A Contemporary History* (New York: Stein and Day, 1970), 63.

14. *New York Times*, March 27, 1960; Arnold Forster and Benjamin R. Epstein, *Report on the Ku Klux Klan* (New York: Anti-Defamation League, 1965), 20–21; Matthews and Prothro, *Negroes and the New Southern Politics*, 409; Thomas F. Parker, ed., *Violence in the U.S.* (New York: Facts on File, 1974), 16–18.

15. Rodney L. Hurst Sr., *It Was Never about a Hot Dog and a Coke! A Personal Account of the 1960 Sit-In Demonstrations in Jacksonville, Florida and Ax Handle Saturday* (Livermore, Calif.: WingSpan Press, 2008), 70–83; James Max Fendrich, *Ideal Citizens: The Legacy of the Civil Rights Movement* (Albany: State University of New York Press, 1993), 17; 1961 U.S. Commission on Civil Rights, *Report, Volume 5: Justice* (Washington, D.C.: Government Printing Office, 1961), 37–38; Parker, *Violence in the U.S.*, 18; *The Student Voice*, October 1960, 15.

16. Jack Bass and W. Scott Poole, *Palmetto State: The Making of Modern South Carolina* (Columbia: University of South Carolina Press, 2009), 98.

17. Michal R. Belknap, *Federal Law and Southern Order: Racial Violence and Constitutional Conflict in the Post-Brown South* (Athens: University of Georgia Press, 1995), 77–78.

18. 1961 U.S. Commission on Civil Rights, *Report, Volume 5: Justice*, 39.

19. David Halberstam, *The Children* (New York: Random House, 1998), 234.

20. *Petersburg (Va.) Progress-Index*, August 3, 1960.

21. Graham, *Crisis in Print*, 196.

22. Ralph McGill, *The South and the Southerner* (Athens: University of Georgia Press, 1992), 282.

23. Bartley, *The New South*, 301–2.

24. *Congressional Record*, 86th Cong., 2nd sess., vol. 106: part 4, 5446.

25. Dewey W. Grantham, *The South in Modern America: A Region at Odds* (New York: HarperCollins, 1994), 198.

26. *Kingsport (Tenn.) News*, March 22, 1960.

27. *Congressional Record*, 86th Cong., 2nd sess., vol. 106: part 4, 5061.

28. *Kingsport News*, March 17, 1960.

29. *Florence (S.C.) Morning News*, March 23, 1960. For a similar editorial accusing "black brigands" of violating private property rights, see the aforementioned "Seditious Sit-Downs" editorial published in *The Citizens' Council*.

30. Kevin M. Kruse, *White Flight: Atlanta and the Making of Modern Conservatism* (Princeton, N.J.: Princeton University Press, 2005), 181–83.

31. *Florence Morning News*, August 31, 1960. For similar editorial opinions, see *Petersburg Progress-Index*, April 10, 1960, and *Kingsport News*, February 10, 1960.

32. *Danville (Va.) Bee*, April 4, 1960.

33. *Delta Democrat Times*, April 13, 1960.

34. Proudfoot, *Diary of a Sit-In*, 156; Jack L. Walker, "Sit-Ins in Atlanta: A Study in the Negro Revolt," in *Atlanta, Georgia, 1960–1961: Sit-Ins and Student Activism*, ed. David J. Garrow (Brooklyn: Carlson, 1989), 66. See also the letter sent by the Greensboro Student Executive Committee to the national office of Woolworth's in Wolff, *Lunch at the Five and Ten*, 37.

35. McGill, *The South and the Southerner*, 275.

36. For a more extensive inventory of national church bodies that supported the

demonstrations, see Martin Oppenheimer, *The Sit-In Movement of 1960* (Brooklyn: Carlson, 1989), 80–82.

37. Paul Ramsey, *Christian Ethics and the Sit-In* (New York: Association Press, 1961).

38. Will D. Campbell, *Race and the Renewal of the Church* (Philadelphia: Westminster Press, 1962), 28–29.

39. *Chicago Tribune*, May 26, 1960.

40. Michael B. Friedland, *Lift Up Your Voice Like a Trumpet: White Clergy and the Civil Rights and Antiwar Movements, 1954–1973* (Chapel Hill: University of North Carolina Press, 1998), 50.

41. Daniel H. Pollitt, "Dime Store Demonstrations: Events and Legal Problems of First Sixty Days," *Duke Law Journal* 9 (1960): 320–21.

42. David L. Chappell, *A Stone of Hope: Prophetic Religion and the Death of Jim Crow* (Chapel Hill: University of North Carolina Press, 2004), 140.

43. *Miami News*, November 27, 1960. Graham continued to occupy an uneasy middle ground on the race issue during the direct-action campaigns of the 1960s, for instance encouraging Martin Luther King during the Southern Christian Leadership Conference campaign in Birmingham to "Put the brakes on a little bit." *New York Times*, April 18, 1963.

44. *Washington Afro-American*, December 13, 1960.

45. For more on this biblical defense of segregation, see Peter C. Murray, *Methodists and the Crucible of Race, 1930–1975* (Columbia: University of Missouri Press, 2004), 108–9.

46. Proudfoot *Diary of a Sit-In*, 46; Wolff, *Lunch at the Five and Ten*, 130–35.

47. Gardiner H. Shattuck Jr., *Episcopalians and Race: Civil War to Civil Rights* (Lexington: University Press of Kentucky, 2000), 103. The Episcopal Society for Cultural and Racial Unity described Carpenter's intervention as "unfortunate," but there does not appear to have been any attempt to censure him. *New York Times*, April 11, 1960.

48. *Delta Democrat Times*, May 5, 1960.

49. *Modesto Bee*, May 25, 1961.

50. Kathryn M. Galchutt, *The Career of Andrew Schulze: Lutherans and Race in the Civil Rights Era, 1924–1968* (Macon, Ga.: Mercer University Press, 2005), 172.

51. *New York Times*, June 28, 1960.

52. Donald E. Collins, *When the Church Bell Rang Racist: The Methodist Church and the Civil Rights Movement in Alabama* (Macon, Ga.: Mercer University Press, 1998), 20, 58, 63–68; Murray, *Methodists and the Crucible of Race*, 105; "Clergy Praises Negroes," *The Citizens' Council*, May 1960, 1.

53. Pete Daniel, *Lost Revolutions: The South in the 1950s* (Chapel Hill: University of North Carolina Press, 2000), 285.

54. John R. Salter, *Jackson, Mississippi: An American Chronicle of Struggle and Schism* (Malabar, Fla.; Robert E. Krieger, 1987), 73.

55. Hurst, *It Was Never about a Hot Dog and a Coke!* 121–23, 143–44.

56. Proudfoot, *Diary of a Sit-In*, 62–63, 88–91, 101, 161–62.

57. *Middlesboro Daily News*, December 3, 1960; Proudfoot, *Diary of a Sit-In*, 63.

58. David L. Chappell, "Disunity and Religious Institutions in the White South," in *Massive Resistance: Southern Opposition to the Second Reconstruction*, ed. Clive Webb (New York: Oxford University Press, 2005), 137; David M. Reimers, *White Protestantism and the Negro* (New York: Oxford University Press, 1965), 185.

59. *Miami News*, August 29, 1960. Concurring with this assessment, one historian commented, "Georgia's white churches nearly unanimously turned a deaf ear to the just grievances of blacks." See Donald L. Grant, *The Way It Was in the South: The Black Experience in Georgia* (Athens: University of Georgia Press, 2001), 398.

60. *Baltimore Afro-American*, September 20, 1960. A Superior Court judge dismissed the suit, but the determination of state authorities to resist church integration was clear.

61. *Los Angeles Times*, August 20, 1962.

62. *Milwaukee Journal*, April 22, 1963; Collins, *When the Church Bell Rang Racist*, 64–66.

63. *Lakeland Ledger*, September 4, 1960; *Rock Hill Herald*, September 5, 1960.

64. *New York Times*, December 16, 1963; *Sarasota Herald-Tribune*, February 14, 1964; *Washington Afro-American*, April 28, 1964.

65. McGill, *The South and the Southerner*, 223.

66. Ralph McGill, "World Christianity Is on Trial," *Miami News*, August 29, 1960. For more information on the meeting of the World Council of Churches, see *Glasgow Herald*, August 8, 25, 1960.

67. *Delta Democrat Times*, May 5, 1960.

68. *Montreal Gazette*, February 27, 1960.

69. *Sarasota Herald-Tribune*, March 27, 1960.

70. *Chicago Tribune*, November 27, 1960; *Christian Science Monitor*, January 23, 1961; *New York Times*, January 29, 1961.

71. *Melbourne Age*, April 20, 1960.

72. *Delta Democrat Times*, March 24, 1960. The paper editorialized to the same effect in its edition of April 13, 1960.

73. *Florence Morning News*, August 31, 1960. See also Daniel, *Lost Revolutions*, 286–87.

74. *Middlesboro (Ky.) Daily News*, April 4, 1960.

75. James Bevel, Bernard Lafayette, Joseph Carter, and Samuel Collier, "You Better Leave Segregation Alone," *Sing for Freedom: The Story of the Civil Rights Movement through Its Songs* (Smithsonian Folkways—SFW40032).

76. *New York Times*, June 6, 1960.

77. Howard Zinn, *SNCC: The New Abolitionists* (Boston: Beacon Press, 1964), 17.

78. *Delta Democrat Times*, October 13, 1960.

79. *New York Times*, June 25, 1960.

80. *New York Times*, May 17, 1960; *Blytheville Courier News*, August 18, 1960; *Florence Morning News*, August 31, 1960.

81. *Florence Morning News*, August 21, 1960; *Kingsport News*, March 19, 1960; *Delta Democrat Times*, July 13, 1960.

82. Harry Ashmore, *An Epitaph for Dixie* (New York: Norton, 1958).

83. See, for example, Christina Greene, *Our Separate Ways: Women and the Black Freedom Movement in Durham, North Carolina* (Chapel Hill: University of North Carolina Press, 2005), 79–82.

84. Edwin Randall, *The Sit-In Story: The Story of the Lunch Room Sit-Ins* (Smithsonian Folkways Recordings, 1961).

5

SNCCs

Not One Committee, but Several

PETER LING

Of all the civil rights organizations of the 1960s, none is more revered than the Student Nonviolent Coordinating Committee (SNCC). As scholars have moved away from the Montgomery-to-Memphis master narrative that attached the rise and fall of civil rights activism to the life and work of Rev. Martin Luther King Jr., SNCC has emerged as the touchstone of the authentic movement experience.[1] Despite this centrality to the history of the civil rights movement, the precise character of SNCC's membership remains undefined. Even the basic task of drawing up a roster of members has not been done. In part this is because the lack of a subscription requirement for membership meant that definitive listings of who belonged to the organization and at what stage were never kept.

Recent scholarship has particularly valued SNCC's work as representative of the larger civil rights movement because it was group-centered and directed primarily toward organizing at a local level.[2] These were the SNCC characteristics that group spokespersons had themselves extolled. Accordingly, there was a large pantheon of individuals rather than one dominant leader at the center of its history. This included older mentors such as Ella Baker, Rev. James Lawson, and Howard Zinn, and a larger, more variegated group of younger activists such as Marion Barry, Julian Bond, H. Rap Brown, Stokely Carmichael, James Forman, Lawrence Guyot, Prathia Hall, Casey Hayden, Joyce and Dorie Ladner, Bernard Lafayette, John Lewis, Bob Moses, Diane Nash, Bernice Johnson Reagon, Ruby Doris Smith Robinson, Cleveland Sellers, Charles Sherrod, Marian Wright Edelman, and Bob Zellner.[3]

Ironically, this collective profile has allowed SNCC to retain its heroic status, whereas revisionist assessments of Martin Luther King diminished the standing of his organization, the Southern Christian Leadership Conference (SCLC). The accusation made in contemporary movement circles that the SCLC was a "hit-and-run" organization, which entered communities like Albany, Georgia, in 1961–62, Birmingham, Alabama, in 1963, St. Augustine, Florida, in 1964, and Selma, Alabama, in 1965, used them to capture national headlines, and then abandoned them to deal with the aftermath of intense racial confrontations, has been amplified by the new scholarship's extensive treatment of SNCC's organizing efforts at the grass roots, notably in Mississippi. As a result, one facet of SNCC's exalted reputation is a sense that its staff showed perseverance and dedication in the most difficult circumstances. The individuals named above certainly furnish ample evidence for this claim. However, it is necessary to ascertain to what extent they were truly representative of SNCC before the organization in its entirety can also be characterized in this way.

Of course, this list of just twenty-four names is incomplete, and comprises only those few main figures who have attracted scholarly attention. Arguably, it is most flawed in its failure to include local figures such as Fannie Lou Hamer, who worked so closely with SNCC in Mississippi as to be part of its deliberations. Admittedly the same is true of other civil rights organizations. There were local people who participated in SCLC campaigns with an intensity that made them important within that organization for a brief period. At the same time, there were individuals in both organizations whose involvement was fleeting and brief, and it is important to understand that this transiency is a characteristic feature of social movements. Nevertheless, the general perception of SNCC is of an organization collectively composed of exceptionally dedicated activists who stayed with the organization from its inception in 1960 through to its decline in the late 1960s and effective dissolution early in the following decade. Commenting on SNCC's development in its first eighteen months of existence, historian Andrew Lewis observes: "The tentative sense of group identity evident in Raleigh had blossomed into a tight-knit community of young activists. They were a 'circle of trust' and a 'band of brothers,' they pledged."[4]

Challenging such orthodoxy, this essay contends that SNCC was a protean, volatile entity composed of a fluctuating membership. It was most united when operating as a loose confederation of people whose focus was emphatically local. The less coherently defined SNCC was, the happier its members were with it. This claim is best corroborated by the swiftness of SNCC's disintegration after Stokely Carmichael's election as chair in place of John Lewis in 1966 supposedly signaled a move to a more tightly structured organization along the lines recommended by James Forman at the previous year's Waveland meeting.[5] In fact, the true SNCC that still enthralls its chroniclers was a constellation of "SNCCs" with each local group working principally with and addressing the needs of its immediate community.

The formation of a temporary Student Nonviolent Coordinating Committee at the Raleigh conference on April 15, 1960, was an important event in the development of the broader civil rights movement. However, SNCC changed significantly over time, arguably more than any other organization within the civil rights movement. By the summer of 1964 its full-time staff could not properly be described as students, nor had they been since voter registration superseded nonviolent direct action as SNCC's primary focus in 1962. Certainly, the student volunteers who came into Mississippi for the 1964 Freedom Summer encountered an organization whose commitment to nonviolence and the ideal of the beloved community, as embodied in its original statement of purpose, was by no means a group norm. SNCC's founding declaration reflected the temporary ascendancy of its Nashville contingent, mentored by Rev. James Lawson. At its peak during the Freedom Rides of 1961, the influence of this group had steadily abated as the voter registration work in Mississippi, southwest Georgia, and other rural areas of the Deep South became SNCC's main focus over the course of 1962.

Emily Stoper, in her 1968 Harvard dissertation, observed that "the rather vague nature of SNCC membership makes it difficult to get accurate figures at any given time on the size of SNCC or the percentage of any group within it." She also noted that it would be inaccurate to limit membership to those "on staff" (in other words, receiving payment), since so many of SNCC's activities were performed by volunteers, who frequently attended staff conferences prior to 1964.[6] This essay is guided by these observations and is intended to amplify our understanding that SNCC was a continuously evolving organization by stressing its significant turnover of personnel.

Historical scholarship has conventionally attributed the fundamental changes within SNCC to a process of radicalization through which its members revised their positions as a result of shared experiences. This argument that SNCC abandoned its early faith in interracial liberalism and principled nonviolence owing to the failure of white liberal leaders to keep their promises to the organization and to the brutality and moral intransigence of their white supremacist opponents can be documented in the case of some of its leading figures. John Lewis's controversial speech at the March on Washington in 1963 was subject to censorship by organizers of this event partly because it articulated strongly SNCC's mistrust of the Kennedy administration. Robert Moses's impassioned rejection of the proposed compromise that would have seated two representatives of the Mississippi Freedom Democratic Party as delegates at large at the 1964 Democratic National Convention was another sign of the growing alienation of SNCC leaders from the liberal establishment. "We are not here to bring politics into our morality," Moses told Martin Luther King, "but to bring morality into our politics."[7] However, Lewis, who attended SNCC's founding conference at Raleigh in April 1960, and Moses, who came to work at its Atlanta headquarters in July of that year, were remarkable figures and, by virtue of that fact, unrepresentative.

Lewis was among the few from the Nashville group who stayed with SNCC until his ouster as chairman in the summer of 1966. By then his faith in nonviolence and his belief that the existing political order could be reformed placed him at odds with figures like Stokely Carmichael. A child of Caribbean immigrants, Carmichael grew up in the Bronx and entered the movement via Howard University's Non-violent Action Group (NAG), which had not sent representatives to the Raleigh conference. NAG had staged sit-ins and other demonstrations against segregation in Washington, D.C., and had provided some of the student volunteers whom another Nashville group leader, Diane Nash, had summoned to continue the Freedom Rides in 1961. However, the campaign that was the fulcrum of its experience took place in Cambridge, a small city of some twelve thousand inhabitants on Maryland's eastern shore. This began in early 1962 and escalated to a crisis that resulted in martial law being declared in June 1963. Crucially, the NAG cadre saw nonviolence as a tactical choice, whereas the Nashville movement had been guided by James Lawson to accept it as a way of life. It was this distinction between pragmatic and principled nonviolence that inclined Lewis to see his removal as SNCC chair as the final culmination of a division between northern and southern students that had been a source of tension within the organization from its outset.

From its inception, SNCC had benefited in terms of its image promotion from the interest of social scientists and the efforts of its own publicists. Accordingly, its early historiography mainly featured doctoral dissertations and insider accounts, notably Howard Zinn's *The New Abolitionists*. The eruption of student activism intrigued social scientists because it marked such a sharp break from the conformity and consensus that were conventionally regarded as the hallmarks of American culture in the 1950s.[8] The SNCC publicists, including the organization members who toured college campuses promoting the cause and raising funds, were always likely to record incidents that stressed the exceptional bravery of individuals in the face of southern white repression.[9] Neither group paid heed to those whose fleeting involvement in the cause sent them easily into oblivion. The ordinary people who touch the outer edge of genuine activism may be more typical of their generation, but they do not command the interest of history. Scholars tend to insert a passing reference to them in the story of the past, but only after this has been set by narratives about its leading figures.

The path blazed by Clayborne Carson in his study *In Struggle* (1981) has largely determined the course of SNCC historiography. The moments of controversy he identified, beginning with the decision at Raleigh to found an independent student group rather than acquiesce in schemes to put students under SCLC leadership and ending with the tensions between the more separatist-orientated Atlanta project workers and a liberal integrationist faction over the expulsion of whites in late 1966, have continued to shape scholarly accounts. Perhaps surprisingly, those whom Carson dubbed "hard-liners" in the debates over a tighter organizational structure in 1965 were the first to publish their memoirs. Both James Forman in *The Making of Black Revolutionaries* (1972) and Cleveland Sellers in *The River of No Return: The Autobiography of a Black Militant and the Life and Death of SNCC* (1973) indicated how a paradoxical narrative of raised consciousness and organizational declension made SNCC into the crucible for Black Power. In the early 1970s, the disenchantment with integrationism and the preeminence of a cultural identity that celebrated African American distinctiveness meant that even a more moderate SNCC figure like Julian Bond could be identified in what was essentially a campaign biography as *Julian Bond, Black Rebel*.[10]

Over the same period, the women's movement probed its own development through consideration of the paper on the position of women within SNCC, written by white activists Mary King and Casey Hayden for presentation at the Waveland conference in November 1964. Initially taken as evidence that SNCC had been a sexist organization, it has increasingly been reevaluated as a document that could only have been written by women who had worked in the less sexist atmosphere of SNCC and whose sense of their own potential had been nourished by the participatory democracy that was a distinctive feature of SNCC's managerial style.[11]

In the wake of Carson's work, the most significant synoptic study of SNCC is Wesley Hogan's *Many Minds, One Heart: SNCC's Dream for a New America* (2007). It too is primarily an intellectual history that details the evolution of both SNCC and its white student contemporary organization, Students for a Democratic Society (SDS). The democratic education that SNCC members acquired was essentially experiential. At its heart was the recognition that freedom was realized through participation and undercut by deference to experts or other habits that diminished participation. Formal education and status did not warrant anyone additional influence in the SNCC vision of democratic politics that valued the lived experience above all else. Hogan laments the fact that this vision of participatory democracy never became the culturally dominant one, but she believes that it was preeminent within SNCC and was a key characteristic of belonging to it. In her view, this outlook could only be acquired with time and through patience and a willingness to listen. This was why the influx of summer volunteers in 1964 constituted such a problem for SNCC. Concerned that some of the newcomers "didn't have a SNCC orientation," Dona Richards warned that the group needed to "be particular as to people we attract." Her then husband, Bob Moses, wondered aloud at the Waveland retreat of November 1964 about how to identify "the good people."[12] This raises the methodological challenge of how to count those who were in SNCC but not of it.

Certainly, Hogan's work illustrates how different individuals and groups in SNCC had different experiences. The Waveland clash between the hard-liners and those they castigated as the "Freedom High" group was the consequence in her view of the irreconcilability of the Atlanta office outlook typified by Forman and the local organizing tradition embodied in Charles Sherrod, Charles McLaurin, and indeed Bob Moses himself. Where Carson largely accepted Forman's account of this struggle to create a revolutionary organization, Hogan champions the cause of his opponents, who believed that investing in local activities was the best way to strengthen SNCC. However, the division between the central office and local projects meant that too little guidance was given to the summer volunteers who wished to stay in Mississippi. In Hogan's view this led to "the abandonment of SNCC's democratic ethic and the drift away from the close, mutually supportive relationships between SNCC staff and local people."[13]

Another account of SNCC is offered by Andrew Lewis in *The Shadows of Youth* (2009). To illustrate SNCC's fragility in the autumn of 1960, he quotes office secretary Jane Stembridge: "SNCC was not coordinating the Movement. . . . We were not sure, and still aren't, what SNCC is." Within eighteen months, however, the group's vanguard character as a "band of brothers" had crystallized. Measured in terms of field activists, Lewis estimates that SNCC, with about fifty full-time organizers, was by 1963 already the largest civil rights organization in the South. In his assessment, some of its long-standing members, like John Lewis and Marion Barry, had changed their roles even before Freedom Summer, so that they were less frequently on the front line. As a result of SNCC's growth, Lewis declared, "responsibilities had become more segmented and the line between field work and office work more clear." The organization's increase in size had "strained the intimacy and loose organizational structure of the earlier years that had fostered a trust and camaraderie that made consensus easier." Like Carson and Hogan, Lewis saw the Freedom Summer influx as damaging the organization's esprit de corps and raising the fundamental question, "Did being a member of SNCC still mean the same thing as it had two years before?" By the time of the Waveland retreat, he concluded, the organizational structure that had served a small, close-knit group was no longer sustainable.[14]

Change within SNCC is therefore fully acknowledged within the historiography, but the deterioration of the organization after 1964 is the first point at which its size and its recruitment of individuals who do not fit into the existing group culture are perceived as serious problems. Prior to the 1964 Freedom Summer, scholars broadly regard SNCC as a remarkably coherent group characterized by powerful shared experiences. The only caveat in this orthodoxy is the recognition that by 1963 certain individuals had become more involved in the Atlanta office (notably James Forman) or with fund-raising outside of the South (such as Marion Barry and John Lewis). Prior to this development, it is conventionally assumed that people joining SNCC stayed with it and shared its values. Whether this is an accurate picture is open to question, however.

Using the records of eight conferences held by SNCC between Raleigh in April 1960 and Atlanta in April 1963, one can identify 891 attendees (see fig. 5.1).[15] Some of these, like Ella Baker and Howard Zinn, were adult advisers, but the majority were students. Whether adult adviser or student, 779 individuals attended just a single SNCC event in the period up to April 1963, and in most cases played no further visible part in the larger history of the movement.[16] Eighty-nine of them attended a total of two meetings, but only fourteen attended three meetings. There were only a handful of perennial attendees: four attended four meetings, and five attended five.

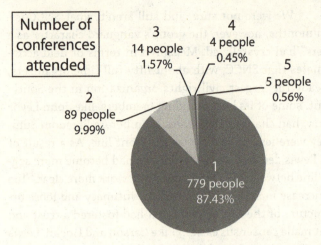

Figure 5.1. Source: The Student Nonviolent Coordinating Committee [SNCC] papers, 1959–72, (Sanford N.C.: Microfilming Corporation of America 1982) reel 11.

Several recurring names are well established in SNCC's history. More than anyone else, Ella Baker's repeated presence at SNCC meetings positioned her to be its leading mentor in the first years of its existence. She connected the students to a tradition of activism that stretched back to the Popular Front of the 1930s and had a web of contacts from her time as NAACP branch director. Almost as regular in her attendance was the much younger Connie Curry, a white woman who linked SNCC to the liberal fringes of Cold War dissent through the National Student Association (NSA), which had lost many of its southern college branches in the wake of the *Brown* decision. Now working for the NSA's Southern Student Human Relations Project in Atlanta, she traveled to Raleigh with Baker.[17] These early meetings, held not just at Raleigh but in Atlanta, Nashville, and Chapel Hill, had to rely on small grants or the ability of individuals to pay their own way. This ensured that the Atlanta conferences in 1960 and 1963 attracted more students from the Atlanta area and that the Nashville conference in 1962 similarly attracted more from its own locality. Nevertheless, students who committed to SNCC at Raleigh and became its early leaders, like Henry Thomas, Charles McDew, Lonnie King, Marion Barry, Bernard Lafayette, Bernard Lee, Charles Sherrod, Jim Bevel, Diane Nash, Julian Bond, and Marvin Robinson, were regulars at later conferences.[18] In contrast, the likes of Clarence Mitchell III and David Collins Forbes lack a profile in movement studies commensurate with their repeated presence because they forged local careers in Baltimore and Raleigh, respectively.[19]

What is equally striking, however, and yet more consistent with a broader pattern with regard to involvement in newly insurgent social movement organizations, is that many attending the original meeting in Raleigh did not continue to feature at SNCC conferences.[20] The overwhelming majority (85) of the 127 confirmed names at the conference do not reappear. Of the Greensboro Four, whose February lunch-counter protest launched the sit-in wave, only Ezell Blair appears on the attendee list in Raleigh, and his name did not feature at later conferences. Others, such as prominent Nashville activists Peggy Alexander and Paul LaPrad, were more important in their local movement center than within SNCC per se. Still others, exemplified by Howard Shipman of Alabama State in Montgomery and Muriel Quarles of Morgan State in Baltimore, seemingly attended the Raleigh conference on the basis of local involvement in sit-ins but then stepped back from the movement.[21]

The Raleigh conference was clearly intended to identify a cadre of student leaders who would seek to maintain the momentum of the sit-in movement. By April 1960 this was already starting to abate, and it threatened to dissipate entirely once the academic year ended and students dispersed from college towns across the South. The Atlanta meetings held in May and August 1960, which were partly intended to ensure that student activism continued, attracted a dedicated core of activists from the original conference. Since these gatherings were by invitation or nomination, they were much smaller than the Raleigh conference and aimed to be as representative of the southern centers of activism as possible. The May 13 event drew Marian Wright and Lonnie King from Atlanta, Major Johns and Marvin Robinson from Baton Rouge, Clarence Mitchell from Baltimore, Henry Thomas from Washington, D.C., Irving Dent from Jackson, Mississippi, Bernard Lee from Montgomery, Marion Barry from Nashville, Charles McDew from Orangeburg, South Carolina, Virginius Thornton from Petersburg, Virginia, David Forbes from Raleigh, and Lucius Bryant and Charles K. Steele Jr. from Tallahassee. In the third meeting, in August, Lee, Mitchell, Barry, Forbes, King, and Thomas were joined by Frank James of Arkansas, Angeline Butler of Tennessee and South Carolina, and Edward B. King Jr. of Kentucky and Virginia—the last two presumably being recorded as representing two states on the basis of their home and college addresses.[22]

Equally evident by the August 1960 meeting was the appearance of a definite SNCC staff presence. Henry Thomas and Jane Stembridge were designated "secretary" and "office secretary," respectively, and Robert Moses, the organization's first field secretary, was labeled simply as

"SNCC." Owing to his commitment to service in the field, however, Moses was not consistently available to attend staff conferences prior to 1963. His absence suggests how much SNCC was defined by local dynamics rather than by central planning. Another figure strongly associated with SNCC, James Forman, was an irregular attendee after taking up his post as SNCC executive secretary in August 1961, which necessitated his involvement in fund-raising and northern liaison activities. The presence of observers from the NSA, Curtis Gans and Donna McGinty—the latter attached, like Curry, to its "Southern Project"—showed how the sit-ins had captivated student radicals across the country and foreshadowed the involvement of New Left groups in the coming year as the Freedom Rides ratcheted up student militancy.[23] Before this phase of the struggle emerged, SNCC showed that it had weathered the threat posed by the summer break in organizing another large conference of student activists on October 14 in Atlanta, where the temporary committee was made permanent.

Significantly, three-quarters of the 254 Atlanta registrants were new to SNCC gatherings. Only 64 individuals, including adult figures such as Ella Baker, Martin Luther King, and James Lawson, had been present at the inaugural Raleigh meeting. Some of the student returners would play a key role in SNCC's development in the coming year, notably Jim Bevel, Bernard Lafayette, and Charles Sherrod, whose involvement confirmed the importance of sit-in experiences in Nashville and elsewhere for generating further activism. SNCC would also draw strength from the influx of newcomers, who included Casey Hayden (alias Sandra Casson), Tom Hayden, Tim Jenkins, Jim Monsonis, Joanne Grant, and Charles Jones.[24] These individuals would have long-standing careers as activists, but the presence of increasing numbers of white students associated with the emergent SDS and African Americans from northern centers foreshadowed some of the tensions that would emerge over both voter registration as a goal and nonviolent direct action as a method.

The Freedom Ride experience of the summer of 1961, which crystallized the character of early SNCC, simultaneously reflected and ended the dominance of the Nashville cadre. Using Ray Arsenault's roster of Freedom Riders, I have identified forty-eight individuals who participated in at least one Freedom Ride and attended at least one SNCC event among the eight events sampled between April 1960 and April 1963. This underlines my primary finding that the vast majority of individuals who attended SNCC events did not remain active within SNCC or emerge as nationally acknowledged protest figures more generally. Of the SNCC conferees who were also Freedom Riders, however, only eight are recorded as having attended the Raleigh conference, and only one (Leon Rice) essentially resurfaced during the Freedom Rides, having not attended since Raleigh and having no recorded SNCC involvement in the post–Freedom Ride period leading up to April 1963.

With a larger registration of 254 people, the SNCC Atlanta conference of October 1960 produced a proportionately larger number of Freedom Riders (19). Examination of attendance at the organization's major conferences after the Freedom Rides to see whether involvement led more people to SNCC meetings in 1962 and 1963 reveals 19 individual Freedom Riders listed at the November 1962 gathering (attended by 196 people in total) and 20 Freedom Riders at the much bigger April 1963 event (where total attendance was 328). Collectively, therefore, there was a limited and largely unvarying level of involvement in the Freedom Rides by people who attended earlier or later conferences. However, examination of the individual cases throws greater light on the complex relationship between SNCC activism and the Freedom Rides.

Among the students who had attended the 1960 Raleigh conference, for instance, and later participated in the Freedom Rides were Jim Bevel, Bernard Lee, and Henry Thomas, all of whom moved away from SNCC during 1962 and 1963. Bevel, with his then wife Diane Nash, had stayed in Mississippi following his release from Parchman prison, but despite working on voter registration in his home state, he remained more committed to the nonviolent direct-action strategy that would take him ultimately to the SCLC, which had always been Bernard Lee's real base. A constant at SNCC meetings prior to the Freedom Rides, the Howard University–based Hank Thomas, like John Lewis, was drawn into the CORE-sponsored original rides rather than arriving as part of the SNCC reinforcements sent to Birmingham. In early 1962 he was involved in CORE-sponsored demonstrations in Huntsville, Alabama, but was never again as heavily involved with SNCC. In contrast, Bernard Lafayette and Charles Sherrod returned from their experience of the Freedom Rides primed to take their commitment to nonviolence into SNCC's new priority activity of voter registration in Alabama and southwest Georgia, respectively, and become even more committed to the organization.

In fact, some of the Albany registrants at the 1962 SNCC meeting, such as Joy Reagon, may more accurately be described as recruited via the Albany campaign that began in late 1961 (to test this Georgia city's compliance with the Interstate Commerce Commission rulings on integrated bus and train stations) rather than being seen as Freedom Riders in the more usual sense, since they did not take buses toward Mississippi. This is not to question the significance of the Freedom Rides to SNCC's development, however. Involvement in them enhanced its profile, which did much to generate the influx of newcomers at Atlanta and other conferences.[25]

Conforming to the usual pattern, nearly three-quarters of the 196 people attending the November 1962 meeting were newcomers to SNCC conferences. What was increasingly different, however, was their state affiliations. The combination of Robert Moses's field work and the significance of the state as the effective terminal point of the Freedom Rides made Mississippi a key area for SNCC by the end of 1962. The influx of new people from new centers is especially apparent in relation to the Magnolia State. With only a token presence in the 1960 conferences, and that mainly due to Moses's initial visit during the summer, it was more widely represented in 1962 and 1963. By November 1962, familiar names from SNCC's Mississippi projects, such as Hollis Watkins, Lester McKinnie, and Sam Block, had appeared. By April 1963 the 31 conference attendees associated with southwest Georgia were outstripped by the 59 from Mississippi. It was also in this period that the likes of Ruby Doris Smith, Prathia Hall, and Joyce and Dorie Ladner figured in the conference lists. The involvement of these African American women illustrated SNCC's willingness to afford its female members greater responsibility and leadership roles than was the case in other civil rights organizations. However, the central fact remains that SNCC attracted new people far more than it retained the old. At the November 1962 meeting, 146 new individuals attended who did not show at the April 1963 meeting in Atlanta. In total, only 32 were present for both these meetings. Unsurprisingly, therefore, of the 332 who came to Atlanta, 284 were not recorded at previous meetings.

The April 1963 conference program has a separate listing of SNCC staff, which is divided into the Atlanta office (10), the New York office (2), field workers (32), and the 4 Freedom Singers. This 48-strong contingent is clearly an underestimate of SNCC membership, but it underlines the perception that SNCC was, most of all, a "field" organization. This list is preceded by a section headed "members of the coordinating committee," which may be interpreted as the conference coordinating committee, although it includes such familiar names as Marion Barry, Worth Long, and Lester McKinnie, none of whom appears on the staff list.[26] This committee also includes figures such as Gloria Richardson of the Cambridge movement and Benjamin Van Clark of the Savannah movement, which reaffirms that SNCC was always more about responding to local needs than developing a centralized strategy.[27]

To conclude, the central fact about SNCC's experience as an organization between 1960 and 1963 was that its fleeting members were far more numerous than its genuine veterans and stalwarts. The common impression formed of SNCC was that it represented a vanguard with a special solidarity born of a shared experience of activism and that this unique quality was undermined by the influx of "outsiders" during the Freedom Summer of 1964.[28] My argument, in contrast, is that an influx of outsiders was precisely what SNCC was used to. This feature reinforced SNCC's protean nature as an organization that was defined fundamentally by what it was doing locally. It also underlined why SNCC was hostile to coordination long before becoming skeptical about nonviolence.

Distrustful of the strategic dictates of any central committee, SNCC was largely focused on day-to-day tactics. It was this daily experience that forged the special bonds among small groups of people, many of them local volunteers who did not go beyond their local work. The damage inflicted by Freedom Summer had less to do with the arrival of newcomers into a bonded clan and more to do with their failure to go away once the summer was ended. It was at that point that they truly intruded into the local units that formed the SNCC constellation. SNCC had coped with newcomers throughout its existence, primarily by a process of attrition. The turnover of personnel should be a key fact in our interpretation of the organization, and it supports the proposition that SNCC was different by 1964, not primarily because individuals had been radicalized by experience, which did occur, but because the organization was largely composed of different people. While previous accounts properly record the impact of these experiences on figures like Stokely Carmichael and James Forman, we need also to acknowledge that the new mood in SNCC in 1964–65 attracted new people, and that those who came into and then disappeared from the movement are also a part of the story.

Notes

1. Charles W. Eagles, "Towards New Histories of the Civil Rights Era," *Journal of Southern History* 66 (November 2000): 815–48.

2. This is evident in studies of Mississippi: John Dittmer, *Local People: The Struggle for Civil Rights in Mississippi* (Urbana: University of Illinois Press, 2003); and Charles Payne, *I've Got the Light of Freedom:: The Organizing Tradition and the Mississippi Freedom Struggle* (Berkeley: University of California Press, 1995).

3. For studies of mentor figures, see Barbara Ransby, *Ella Baker and the Black Freedom Movement: A Radical Democratic Vision* (Chapel Hill: University of North Carolina Press, 2003); (on Lawson and the Nashville group) David Halberstam, *The Children* (New York: Fawcett Books, 1999); and Howard Zinn, *SNCC: The New Abolitionists* (Boston: South End Press, 1964). Among autobiographical accounts are those of the radical trio: Stokely Carmichael with Ekwueme Michael Thelwell, *Ready for Revolution: The Life and Struggles of Stokely Carmichael (Kwame Ture)* (New York: Scribner, 2005); James Forman, *The Making of Black Revolutionaries* (Seattle: University of Washington Press, 1997); and Cleveland Sellers with Robert Terrell, *The River of No Return: The Autobiography of a Black Militant and the Life and Death of SNCC* (Jackson: University of Mississippi Press, 1990). Also very important are the personal accounts of moderates, notably John Lewis with Michael d'Orso, *Walking with the Wind: A Memoir of the Movement* (Boston: Mariner Books, 1999). Arguably, the key figure in SNCC developments between 1962 and 1965 is considered in Eric Burner, *And Gently He Shall Lead Them: Robert Parris Moses and Civil Rights in Mississippi* (New York: New York University Press, 1995). Among the women of SNCC, only one is the subject of a book-length study: Cynthia Fleming, *Soon We Will Not Cry: The Liberation of Ruby Doris Smith Robinson* (Lanham, Md.: Rowman & Littlefield 1998).

4. Andrew B. Lewis, *The Shadows of Youth: The Remarkable Journey of the Civil Rights Generation* (New York: Hill and Wang, 2009), 111.

5. Clayborne Carson, *In Struggle: SNCC and the Black Awakening of the 1960s* (Cambridge: Harvard University Press, 1981), 136–45, 199–204.

6. Emily Stoper, *The Student Nonviolent Coordinating Committee: The Growth of Radicalism in a Civil Rights Organization* (Ph.D. diss., 1968; Brooklyn: Carlson, 1989), 96–97.

7. Burner, *And Gently He Shall Lead Them*, 198.

8. See James Laue, *Direct Action and Desegregation, 1960–1962:Towards a Theory of the Rationalization of Protest* (Ph.D. diss., 1965; Brooklyn: Carlson, 1989); Martin Oppenheimer, *The Sit-In Movement of 1960* (Ph.D. diss., 1963; Brooklyn: Carlson, 1989); Maurice Pinard, Jerome Kirk, and Donald Von Eschen, "Processes of Recruitment in the Sit-in Movement," *Public Opinion Quarterly*, 33 (Autumn 1969): 355–69; Donald Von Eschen, Jerome Kirk, and Maurice Pinard, "The Conditions of Direct Action in a Democratic Society," *Western Political Quarterly* 22 (June 1969): 309–25; and Herbert H. Blumberg, "Accounting for a Nonviolent Mass Demonstration," *Sociological Inquiry* 38 (January 1968): 43–50.

9. A good sample of the journalism that publicized SNCC in the mainstream media is collected in Clayborne Carson, ed., *Reporting Civil Rights: American Journalism: Volume 1, 1941–1963*, and *Volume 2, 1963–1973* (New York: Library of America, 2003). Carson has also edited a compilation of SNCC's own publication, *The Student Voice: 1960–1965* (Westport, Conn.: Greenwood Press, 1990). In addition the movement was reported by the Southern Conference Education Fund's monthly newspaper, *The Southern Patriot*, and by the similarly left-leaning *Freedomways*. Two Atlanta-based journalists, Pat Watters and Reese Cleghorn, provided vivid coverage of SNCC's voter-registration work in *Climbing Jacob's Ladder: The Arrival of the Negroes in Southern Politics* (New York: Harcourt, Brace, 1967).

10. John Neary, *Julian Bond, Black Rebel* (New York: William Morrow, 1971).

11. "The Position of Women in the Movement," November 1964, Student Nonviolent Coordinating Committee Papers [hereafter SNCC Papers] (Sanford, N.C.: Microfilming Corporation of America, 1982), reel 12. The discussion over the paper's significance largely begins with Sara Evans, *Personal Politics: The Roots of Women's Liberation in the Civil Rights Movement and the New Left* (New York: Vintage, 1980).

12. Wesley Hogan, *Many Minds, One Heart: SNCC's Dream for a New America* (Chapel Hill: University of North Carolina Press, 2007), 253.

13. Ibid., 215.

14. A. B. Lewis, *The Shadows of Youth*, 82, 111, 127, 148, 173, 182–83.

15. The details of the SNCC conferences can be found in the SNCC Papers, Group A, Atlanta Office Series V, SNCC Conferences 1960–1964, reel 11.

16. The majority of names do not appear in the indexes of main monographs on SNCC, nor are they listed on websites such as www.crmvet.org.

17. Curry has given her own account of her involvement in "Wild Geese to the Past," in Constance Curry et al., *Deep in Our Hearts: Nine White Women in the Freedom Movement* (Athens: University of Georgia Press, 2000), 3–35.

18. Howard University student Hank Thomas is best known for his Freedom Rides participation; see Ray Arsenault, *Freedom Riders: 1961 and the Struggle for Racial Justice* (New York: Oxford University Press, 2006), 145–47. South Carolina State's Charles McDew succeeded Marion Barry at the Atlanta SNCC conference of 1960 and was SNCC chairman until 1963. Lonnie King and Julian Bond were prominent members of the Atlanta student movement; Lafayette, Bevel, and Nash were key members of the Nashville group; and Bernard Lee from Alabama State in Montgomery was very much SCLC's representative within SNCC.

19. Mitchell, the son of a noted NAACP lobbyist, committed himself early to a political career in Maryland, first in the state assembly (1963–66), and then in the state senate (1967–86). See http://politicalgraveyard.com/families/16038.html. A well-known clergymen, Forbes is pastor of Christian Faith Baptist church in Raleigh, North Carolina. See David Cecelski, "David Forbes: The Birth of SNCC," Southern Oral History Project, http://ibiblio.org/sohp/research/lfac/N&O/6.5b23-David_Forbes.html.

20. For the dynamics of social movements, see Mario Diani and Doug McAdam, eds., *Social Movements and Networks: Relational Approaches to Collective Action* (New York: Oxford University Press, 2003).

21. Paul LaPrad, "Nashville: A Community Struggle," in *Freedom Ride*, ed. James Peck (New York: Grove Press, 1962), 82–88. Peggy Alexander is often seen in photos of the Nashville sit-ins with Diane Nash.

22. Spelman student Marian Wright Edelman has given some account of her early connections with SNCC in *Lanterns: A Memoir of Mentors* (New York: Harper, 2000). Her Morehouse colleague Lonnie King has not written a memoir, but she organized the fiftieth anniversary of the Atlanta student movement, having also served as the head of the local NAACP chapter. For the Atlanta movement more generally see David Harmon, *Beneath the Image of the Civil Rights Movement and Race Relations: Atlanta, Georgia: 1946–1981* (New York: Garland, 1996). For Johns and Robinson, two students

expelled from Southern University in Baton Rouge for demonstrating, see Dean Sinclair, "Equal in All Places: The Civil Rights Struggle in Baton Rouge, 1953–1963," *Louisiana History* 39 (Summer 1998): 347–66. Angeline Butler describes her recruitment into the Nashville movement in an oral history available online at http://digital.library. nashville.org/item/?CISOROOT=/nr&CISOPTR=190.

23. For interactions between SNCC and the New Left see Hogan, *Many Minds, One Heart.*

24. Largely due to her later involvement in the drafting of the paper on women's roles within SNCC, Casey Hayden figures in most SNCC histories. See, in particular, Evans, *Personal Politics.* Her own account of her time in SNCC, "Fields of Blue," is in Curry et al., *Deep in Our Hearts,* 333–76. Her former husband, Tom Hayden, published *Reunion: A Memoir* (New York: Random House, 1988). Tim Jenkins, vice-chairman of the NSA, was the driving force behind the August 1961 Atlanta conference, which he hoped would transform SNCC from "an amorphous movement to an organization" (see Hogan, *Many Minds, One Heart,* 64, 100). Monsonis was a founding member and national secretary of SDS. The late Joanne Grant wrote for the *National Guardian* in New York and helped to publicize movement activities nationally. Charles Jones had been active in Charlotte, North Carolina, and would shortly be among the protesters in Rock Hill, South Carolina, who chose "jail—not bail." He also helped Charles Sherrod and Cordell Reagon in their work in Albany, Georgia, in late 1961.

25. There is still no full-length study of the Albany movement, nor of figures such as Jim Bevel and Charles Sherrod, who deserve sustained attention as exemplars of the movement's different facets. For Albany, see Robert E. Luckett Jr., "Charles Sherrod and Martin Luther King: Mass Action and Nonviolence in Albany," in *The Human Tradition in the Civil Rights Movement,* ed. Susan M. Glisson (Lanham Md.: Rowman & Littlefield, 2006), 181–98.

26. A student at Philander Smith College in Little Rock, Arkansas, Worth Long eventually became Alabama project director in the run-up to the 1965 Selma campaign. Tennessee State student Lester McKinnie became a stalwart of the Mississippi movement.

27. For Gloria Richardson and the Cambridge movement, see Peter Levy, *Civil War on Race Street: The Civil Rights Movement in Cambridge, Maryland* (Gainesville: University of Florida Press, 2003). Benjamin Van Clark and the Savannah protests generally are less covered in the scholarly literature, but see Stephen Tuck, *Beyond Atlanta: The Struggle for Racial Equality in Georgia, 1940–1980* (Athens: University of Georgia Press, 2001).

28. For a good summary of the constellation of forces at work within SNCC after the disappointment of the Mississippi Freedom Democratic Party's 1964 Democratic National Convention challenge, see Hogan, *Many Minds, One Heart,* chapter 10.

6

SNCC's Stories at the Barricades

SHARON MONTEITH

As the freedom struggle reached new heights in the summer of 1963, literary critic Granville Hicks commented, "All around the fringes of the movement, and on both sides of the barricades, magnificent dramas are taking place."[1] Interviewing civil rights workers around that time for his book *Who Speaks for the Negro?* (1965), Robert Penn Warren adjudged that James Forman of the Student Nonviolent Coordinating Committee (SNCC) was living "intensely, I should guess, and painfully, in a strange drama of compulsion, bitterness and hope. This is what makes him demanding to the imagination."[2] Civil rights activists had already become folk heroes, mythologized in freedom songs such as Phil Ochs's "Freedom Rides," grippingly photographed by Danny Lyon, and idealized in Howard Zinn's on-the-ground study of the "new abolitionists." Their experiences were recounted in oral history projects, some published in the era of activism like Warren's and others after its end. These emphasize the dual roles of time and memory and the psychological effects of organizing for those who battled for the African American franchise. Missing from sources that contribute to the history of SNCC, however, are participant-fictions, the depictions of activism that survive in narrative fiction written by members of SNCC.

Georgia congressman and SNCC chairman (1963–66) John Lewis declared at the end of his 1998 memoir, "There is no way to describe how palpable the fear was among black people living in the South just thirty and forty years ago. I'm talking about raw fear."[3] However, local people who rose above this pervasive sense of dread were re-imagined in short stories and novels that convey SNCC's position in the vanguard of support for independent black politics in the South and something of the regard in which its activists held rural folk. The visceral terror that organizers themselves endured while embedded in local communities is also explored. In short, the strange and compulsive drama to which Robert Penn Warren and Granville Hicks referred and the fear of racial terrorism that John Lewis remembers were being represented imaginatively by individuals who were influential in shaping SNCC's guiding principles and by others who lived out these ideals at the barricades. Poetry by organizers and volunteers is sometimes used illustratively in histories and appears in memoirs, but the stories SNCC folk wrote have not received the attention they deserve—either as sustained imaginative writing that is revealing of grassroots efforts to realize SNCC's strategic goals or as immediate responses to the violence and stress that broke some organizers, damaged others, and left local people and summer volunteers dead.

This essay considers what two examples of these forgotten fictions tell us about SNCC. The first is a book-length manuscript, "Thin White Line," written by SNCC executive secretary (1961–66) James Forman. This depicts the student politics that drove organizers like the author into the southern civil rights movement. The second is a published short story by SNCC staffer and strategist Michael Thelwell (later Ekwueme Michael Thelwell) that dramatizes one night in the life of a field secretary organizing local politics. These are only two from among a tranche of poems, stories, and novels written by SNCC staff who dedicated years to the struggle and by student volunteers who gave a summer to the cause.

In civil rights scholarship, "nonfiction" sources found in archives or personal recollections like memoirs and oral history constitute the traditional basis for the evidence that builds historiography. As in other fields of historical study, there is a privileging of an "objective," detached approach in which "the knower" is made distinct from what is known and fact is differentiated from its imaginative representation. It is a challenge to shift the discussion to include the cultural dimension of protest.[4] Much can be gained, however, from also examining some of the more "subjective" and reflexive sources that help to illuminate the moral and political vision of a key personality such as Forman, the existential issues with which organizers such as Bob Moses contended in envisioning a movement philosophy,[5] and, not least, the mood and feel of the southern freedom movement. So passionate were many of the activists that it is unsurprising that they should explore their experience aesthetically.

As James M. Jasper posits when formulating "the art of moral protest," a lens that focuses on culture and creativity may help us judge the goals of social movements as well as their methods.[6] This is made evident when reading Forman's manuscript in the light SNCC's inception and staff debates about the efficacy of direct-action protest as set against voter-registration activities. Francesca Polletta, one of the few social scientists to recognize the significance of storytelling in social movements, has complicated traditional objectivism in this context through inclusion of SNCC among her case studies.[7] Outlining some of her earliest ideas on the subject, she noted that stories are important in describing the origins of a movement: "When does protest begin? When does one become an activist? These questions are unanswerable in an objective manner. . . . Narratives allow for this to be explained in personal ways that shed better light on the dialogue and activities that precede the establishment of formal movement organizations."[8]

Forman's "Thin White Line" functions as a fulcrum through which to explore multiple forms of political commitment and activist agency. Its political backdrop includes his experience of covering the Little Rock school desegregation crisis for the *Chicago Defender* in 1958, when he stayed with local civil rights leaders Daisy and L. C. Bates, and of supporting Fayette, Tennessee, sharecroppers living in a tent city after being evicted from their tenancies for registering to vote in 1960. Working as a reporter in Little Rock, he would claim later, "heightened my consciousness for the need of a mass-based organization," and the novel would contain what he hoped was "a detailed definition of the kinds of organization needed."[9]

Many SNCC workers remember Forman's repeated exhortations that they should "write it all down." Significantly, the metaphors he used to express the group's ideologies have found their way into the titles of organizational histories and activist memoirs. In the course of a single speech at a retreat in Waveland in November 1964, for example, he warned that if an interracial brotherhood still figured in its goals, SNCC had to decide "if the circle will be unbroken," a phrase that recalled the gospel song. He also expressed concerns that a loss of internal cohesion would prove the source of "a river of no return," thereby leading to SNCC's demise. At the end of his speech, Forman suggested that he needed to take some time for himself to work on a book titled "A Band of Brothers: A Circle of Trust," which would be "a personal history of SNCC."[10] He then reminded staff, "All of us have our little histories within us and I would wish that all of us could set them down on paper."[11]

Forman would not publish his autobiography, a collective history of SNCC finally titled *The Making of Black Revolutionaries*, until 1972.

However, he had served his writing apprenticeship on the unpublished novel, which he clearly had in mind when he told Robert Penn Warren in March 1964, "I have never understood art for art's sake."[12] He would excerpt sections from the novel as stories in *High Tide of Black Resistance and Other Political and Literary Writings* (1967). Possessing a title that balanced the political with the literary and content that blended Forman's early journalism, speeches, and journal entries with his fiction, this volume embodies the eclectic mix of genres through which SNCC may be best understood.

"Thin White Line" is a catalyst for Forman's personal development into a civil rights organizer. He *imagines* his way into the movement. Having worked on this story ten or twelve hours a day for a year, Forman had envisaged his way to his next stage of personal development by the fall of 1959. As he recalled in his autobiography, "I knew I was definitely going South in the near future to build a revolutionary youth organization and to write about the struggle of black people as I participated in it."[13] Forman's novel should be read as a prototypical movement fiction. Set in the years from 1952 to 1956, it was written mostly while he was studying for a B.A. in Public Administration at Chicago's Roosevelt University, where he became president of the student body and a delegate to the 1956 National Student Association. The manuscript was completed in 1959 and revised over a longer period to include four almost-complete drafts.

The novel, Forman said, was written in the form of "a great wish extension." "After putting many of my experiences in novelistic form," he explained to Warren, "I had the hero going South to develop a mass movement using nonviolence as a tactic."[14] This description of Paul, the character evidently based on him, offers an explanation of what Forman derived from the experience of writing. Indeed, his literary aspirations may be read back through his political career as an activist.

At first sight it may seem odd that the narrative is framed by a white character, Tom Blake, based on a student Forman met at Roosevelt, as all his characters are to some extent. When "Thin White Line" opens in 1952, Tom is a white Baptist minister preparing to speak to his southern congregation. Described in Forman's opening paragraph as a "nonconformist," Blake seeks to initiate social change in his small Tennessee community.[15] This twenty-three-year-old father of two speaks out when members of his church allow Jewish children to be taunted at Sunday school and again when a Catholic worshipper is made unwelcome. He fears Christianity has "a split personality" because his church remains racially segregated; though ambivalent about how best to address this, he is determined to bridge the gap between Christian ideals and the racialized reality they shore up in the South. Forman would later describe the black church as "a ready-made protest organization."[16] The alternative focus in his fiction on the white church and the responsibility of a white man of God may be read as presaging his appeal to white churches in May 1969 for reparations in recognition of their historic role in the perpetuation of southern racism.

In this early work, however, the characterization of the minister-turned-student is much less rigid than Forman's appeal for reparations would suggest. Oppositions and ambiguities lie at the heart of the novel. It explores the white southern liberal's position as misfit or outcast. Tom Blake eventually quits the ministry and the South in despair over the consequences of his mild efforts to bridge the racial divide. Even a song festival where blacks and whites will be seated separately leads to threatening letters and fear for his family's safety. The black minister with whom he plans the event is then killed in a car bomb. Tom subsequently fails to intervene when a black man is pistol-whipped by his own church deacon, who is also the town's sheriff. The outcome of all this is that Blake loses his faith. Broken by his failure to change the town, he heads for Chicago and a new start. Forman then turns his attention to black students struggling to find a way to align their student politics and the evolving freedom struggle. Two of these characters are reflections of his own experience: Ted is a creative writer using his friends as material for stories, and Paul feels compelled to travel into the South.

Although "Thin White Line" is a discursive novel of ideas that sometimes reads like a series of speeches, it is an imaginative exploration of the extent to which student politics extended beyond university campuses in the 1960s. What one character calls "the American color complex" (278) underpins the ways in which student protagonists use interracial relationships as a means to explore themselves racially as well as sexually, either in Co-Operative House or at the Cosmopolitan Club, where political positions are debated. Co-Operative House is a nucleus of SNCC's vision of a beloved community: "By all standards of conventional dress and thought, these Negro and white students . . . breaking bread together were extremely unconventional" (165). Another character muses that it may be easier to build a militant organization than to alter existing patterns of thought and behavior (157). Reflecting this, SNCC would discover that building and sustaining an interracial community in the heart of segregationist Mississippi was indeed a precarious enterprise, not only because of the affront their "beloved community" represented to segregationists but also because of the pressures on black and white individuals alike to repel the racial history they were taken to represent. Mississippi field organizer Bob Moses articulated what he deemed a concomitant challenge to the larger movement project as to "whether SNCC could integrate itself . . . and live as a sort of island of integration in a sea of separation." However, the image may now be read back through Forman's manuscript, in which Paul describes Chicago's Hyde Park as holding out against racial change, "an oasis of segregation amidst an island of integration" (372).[17]

Paul acts as a catalyst for other characters in envisioning what whites as well as blacks can do to hasten racial change. This is particularly important in his evolving commitment to join the freedom struggle in the South, bequeathing the fight for civil rights in Chicago to "that rebel from Texas, Tom Blake" (410). Paul wants to be a teacher and a leader; he believes he is prepared to die for "the Black Cause" (210). However, Forman distributes many of the ideas that would underpin SNCC's goals rather than making Paul his only mouthpiece. Thus, Ted—black and Illinois-born like Forman—feels personally violated by a democracy that does not allow African Americans in the South to vote: "it's frightening . . . it affect[s] the inside of a man, his whole being, his outlook . . . we pussyfoot with the very essence of that government [and] we don't protect them when they try to register" (402).

Despite the political machinations of Mayor Daley's Chicago and the everyday evidence of racism in this northern city, the things that most incense Forman's student intellectuals focus their attention on the South, such as the murder of fourteen-year-old Chicago resident Emmett Till in Mississippi in 1955 and the "Bilbo-Eastland-Talmadge crew" of segregationist politicians. Their most fervent political hopes must first be realized in the South: "the right to vote for Southern negroes, a chance for Northern negroes to move out of the black belt, a right to work for all negroes" (155–56). Giving expression to this once he is established in Texas, Paul writes his friend Ted, an apprentice novelist, "You will find all the dramatic material in the movement you need to become a good writer. And we need you here" (429).

Any ambitions Forman had to publish his novel were set aside when on February 1, 1960, the sit-in movement took off. Others who would join SNCC were slower to recognize the students as the catalyst they were for a new social movement. Julius Lester, a student at Fisk University in 1960, recalled that he read the news of the sit-in on the back page of his newspaper "with less interest than I did the evening's television listings." Stokely Carmichael, SNCC chairman in 1966–67, was also disdainful of sit-ins until he met some of those involved in May 1960.[18] Forman, however, had already imagined the movement that the student protests would engender and that he would be instrumental in building: "History was enacting what I had advocated in the novel. . . . It was all down there on paper, the suffering, the hope, the plan. It was only left for me to write the ending with my own life in the South."[19]

At the close of his 1964 account, Howard Zinn allows that SNCC's radicalism was expressed in "odd bits of conversation which reflect not a precise doctrine but an emotion . . . not an ideology but a mood," and muses that "moods are hard[er] to define. They are also hard[er] to imprison."[20] Forman attempted to write a novel of ideas in which "the acid test of evaluating a person is their stance on civil rights" (395). He tends to evaluate rather than limn out his characters' moods. As writers of fiction, civil rights workers were neophytes, but through his young protagonists—southern and northern, white and black, men and women— Forman succeeded in conveying the "mood" and "temperament" that would contribute to SNCC's political ethos. Reading the novel alongside what would be his first published book, *Sammy Younge Jr.* (1968), subtitled *The First Black College Student to Die in the Black Liberation Movement*, provides affirmation that Forman's writing captures something of the mood that inaugurated SNCC and also that which presaged its end. In "Thin White Line" he imagines what nonviolent protest will demand of its proponents, and in *Sammy Younge Jr.* he marks an ideological break with tactical nonviolence.

Forman would later assess the period through which student revolutionaries, like his fictional characters Paul and Ted, would pass in his collective memoir *The Making of Black Revolutionaries*, originally published in 1972. However, the day-to-day experience of organizing in the South would be explored more effectively by others, including Michael Thelwell, a SNCC field secretary in 1963–64 and then a SNCC strategist based primarily in the Washington, D.C., office as director of the Mississippi Freedom Democratic Party (MFDP) in 1964–65. Forman insisted that SNCC field secretaries write detailed reports for organization files. In Julian Bond's recollection, Forman also wanted the reports to contain "lyrical descriptions of exactly how an organizer goes about his or her work."[21] A seasoned writer of such reports, Thelwell transformed their style and content into a thought-provoking short story. This intensified Forman's metaphor of the thin white line, tightening as it was stretched taut to guard white supremacists against the freedom struggle, in its descriptions of field secretaries living and working "on the fine line between life and death in the back roads of the South."[22]

In an open letter to the journal *Freedomways* in 1962, Julian Bond wrote, "SNCC is working in the South in areas no other civil rights group has ever been to, with farmers, domestics, laborers, and people who really want to be free."[23] He reiterated this proud definition of one of SNCC's original goals some forty years later: "While organizing grassroots voter-registration drives, SNCC workers offered themselves as a protective barrier between private and state-sponsored terror and the local communities where SNCC staffers lived and worked."[24] In "The Organizer," Thelwell depicts a field secretary who embodies the "protective barrier" to which Bond refers but who suffers in a state of shock as he struggles to manage the immediate aftermath of a racist murder at the heart of the community he serves. His story may be read as extrapolating from reports on a spate of bombings in McComb, a small town in the southwest corner of Mississippi, and as a direct response to the bombings of September 20, 1964, described by Mendy Samstein in *The Student Voice* (SNCC's periodical) as "The Murder of a Community."[25]

Born in Jamaica, Thelwell moved to the United States in 1959 and became a member of the Nonviolent Action Group (NAG) at Howard University, where he also edited the student magazine, *The Hilltop* (1962–63). After gaining his B.A. in Literature in 1964, he enrolled in the graduate writing program at the University of Massachusetts–Amherst in 1965. His collected writings detail the SNCC shift from civil rights to black nationalist politics in which he was a participant. In addition to his own publications, he co-wrote strategic essays with Stokely Carmichael and Lawrence Guyot and collaborated with Carmichael on his posthumously published autobiography.[26] Thelwell's later activism was mainly channeled into intellectual work after co-founding the W.E.B. DuBois Department of Afro-American Studies at the University of Massachusetts in 1969. Ironically, realization that he had never taught classes on the movement in all his years as a professor of African American studies only came at a SNCC reunion in 1987. He had, he acknowledged, "subconsciously recused myself from the subject for reason of previous involvement." When Thelwell began to teach movement history in an interdisciplinary program, he used the short stories he had published in the 1960s as course material. Students responded positively to these, he noted, because "rather than [being] post-facto reconstructions and analyses, they were of the time."[27]

An archetypal example of the stories Thelwell wrote, "The Organizer" depicts SNCC's model of fieldwork in the rural South through a project director worn down and conflicted by what is expected of him. It is the most detailed and evocative fictional distillation of this role. Thelwell allows, "I never had the pleasure of organizing in the black community in the South; I organized, as it were, in the corridors of power."[28] Nevertheless, he succeeds in conveying in a story of a single Mississippi night what was extraordinary about the quotidian struggle against the forces of massive resistance. His protagonist is embedded in the black community of Bogue Chitto, a setting that imbues "The Organizer" with fear and foreboding. Located thirteen miles northeast of Philadelphia, Mississippi, it was notorious at the time of writing as the swamp location of the burned-out station wagon that Michael Schwerner, James Chaney, and Andrew Goodman had been driving when they were abducted and murdered at the beginning of the Council of Federated Organizations' Freedom Summer project of 1964, for which Thelwell recruited volunteers.

The conspiratorial violence of the countermovement that killed Schwerner, Chaney, and Goodman continued to be visited on black communities. In his story, Thelwell celebrates the extraordinary valor of local people united and militant in their desire for change and explores how organizers could be transformed by the communities they served. The main character, Travis Peacock, feels a stronger kinship with bombing victim Jesse Lee Hightower and his family than with his natural family, who now seem to him "shadowy figures leading barren and futile lives in their northern suburb" (8). He becomes twisted with rage that his civil rights organization must exploit Hightower's murder in the press and on the television news. The character in "The Organizer" who guides Peacock through this process is clearly modeled on James Forman, who is described as "big shaggy, imperturbable, bearlike . . . always scrambling to keep the organization afloat, to keep the cars running, the rent paid."[29] Renamed Truman, he is depicted as the calm, firm voice on the phone from the head office in Atlanta, the organization's "true man," who reminds the grief-stricken and guilty Peacock that if SNCC is to make a difference and to stop bombings like that which killed Hightower, it must make the murder public and dramatize its effects. Through Peacock and Truman, Thelwell portrays the tension understood by each that balancing the community's needs and the movement's far-reaching goals entailed enormous personal sacrifice.

Travis Peacock is representative of the small cadre of black field secretaries who began working in the rural South as early as 1961. His name may be an amalgam of Jimmie Travis, who narrowly survived being shot while working for SNCC in Greenwood in 1963, and Willie (later Wazir) Peacock, who worked on voter registration throughout northeastern Mississippi and notably in Greenwood. However, Thelwell's project director clearly stands in for a larger community of organizers, including Sam Block and Lawrence Guyot in Greenwood, Mississippi, and Charles Sherrod in southwest Georgia—and, because the story echoes an actual bombing that occurred in McComb, Jessie Harris, who was project leader in that community with Mendy Samstein and others in 1964. An associated problem for the historian reading the story is that this composite character will obscure the differences between organizers' experiences in very different southern locales. However, Peacock's symbolic function in the story illustrates the three rules by which all organizers were expected to live. As enumerated by Thelwell, they are: first, never let the community know you are afraid; second, remember that the organizer is always responsible; and third, the organizer must publicize racist murders for maximum political, moral, and financial effect. "The Organizer" is an object lesson for SNCC field-workers in its depiction of the test faced by Peacock with regard to upholding the "first rules" of organizing and dealing with the "secret fear of every organizer" that one of the people you work with closely will be murdered.

Thelwell dramatizes black Bogue Chitto as a complex place with rich and carnivalesque language. Its inhabitants are shrewd and undeterred, and derive strength from bitter ironies understood and shared. They deduce from the sheriff's reports that church burnings are committed by "a mysterious and very active arsonist called 'Faulty Wiring.'"[30] Community elders attempting to register to vote are repeatedly told that the office has closed. "That's alright honey," one of them declares, "Us done waited a hunnard years, be plumb easy to wait some more" (17).

The threat of white violence is ever-present and eventually becomes real. Enraged by Hightower's murder, a crowd of blacks faces down Sheriff Hollowell and his deputies. Peacock intervenes not only to avoid further bloodshed but also to maneuver the locals into dispersing without losing face. Accordingly, he taunts the sheriff whose gun is trained on his back: "Why bad ass Bo Hollowell's standin there shakin jes lak a dawg trying to shit a peach stone."[31] A narrative aside is telling: "That cracked people up, real laughter, vindictive and punitive to the lawman, but full, deep and therapeutic to the crowd" (18). In risking the sheriff's trigger finger, Peacock puts himself in the line of fire to protect the community, and only on returning to the Freedom House does he allow anger, grief, and fear to wash over him. Jerome Smith, a Congress for Racial Equality (CORE) worker in 1964, described that feeling as the "jump-off point." "All the fear," he declared, "was never in the moment itself. It was always after, when you'd think about what you'd done, what you'd been through, and tremble."[32]

Thelwell offers the first literary representation of the civil rights organizer as steadfast but anxious and exhausted. Alone at night in the Freedom House while his team is in Atlanta for a meeting, Peacock shakes with fear when the telephone rings and must steel himself to withstand the taunts of "Nigger, yo' subjeck to bein blowed up" (6). He has to make his fieldwork matter despite the odds, a taxing goal described by Bob Moses in a report of February 1963: "You dig into yourself and the community and prepare to wage psychological warfare; you combat your own fears about beatings, shootings, and possible mob violence; you stymie by your own physical presence the anxious fear of the Negro community . . . that maybe you *did* only come to boil and bubble and then burst."[33] Peacock fortifies himself with moonshine; he frets and worries; he exhibits symptoms similar those of a shell-shocked veteran of war. But he stands beside the community even as he exploits its tragedy and personifies what Moses identified on SNCC's fifth anniversary as "SNCC people" who try "to move within the boundaries of fear . . . even though afraid."[34]

Thelwell's southern movement fiction has a visceral immediacy, a quality that, in hindsight, he feels "reek[s] of the stench of the struggle" but also, as this passage illustrates, of the terror that workers sought to manage.[35] For some SNCC workers the fear their work engendered returns in the rush of memory, as in Lawrence Guyot's 2004 description of fieldwork, in which he slips tellingly into the continuous present tense: "It was just part of the fabric. In order to do anything in Mississippi, you must first deal with the question of fear. You either transcend it or move beyond it. And that's what you did."[36] Thelwell's interweaving of past and present tenses represents that tension as he stands listening to his own breathing once the caller hangs up: "Somehow that final click is the most terrifying part. As long as you can feel that there is a human being on the other end, despite the obscenity and the threats, you have some contact. . . . Peacock began to regret his decision not to go to the meeting. . . . Where did his responsibility end?" (6).

While SNCC would later be celebrated, even mythologized, there was a risk in the late 1980s that what young organizers had achieved in their tireless work for voter registration in the South would be forgotten. They appeared to be remembered more often for what had happened to them post-SNCC.[37] Thelwell's story commemorates SNCC and the communities it sought to serve at the moment they were caught in the crosshairs of racial terrorists and complicit local lawmen. However, it also reflects what participants in the struggle saw as "real stories." Julius Lester's 1964 journal recorded similar tales of bravery by those who lost their jobs for trying to register to vote or taking white and black civil rights workers into their homes, leading him to speculate that "courage is the norm in Mississippi."[38]

Thelwell's story affirms that the freedom struggle was not the sole preserve of young activists. Mature plain folks were deeply involved in it too. They included women like Fannie Lou Hamer, a granddaughter of slaves who rallied to SNCC's project in 1962 after being evicted from her plantation home for attempting to register to vote, and Annie Devine, who quit her job selling insurance to work full time for CORE in 1964. Thelwell knew both of them through his work with the MFDP, and they are embodied in the character of Mama Jean, "the first to go across the river to try to register to vote" (7). Mama Jean may be even more closely read as a version of Aleynne Quinn, who owned a popular café in McComb that fed civil rights workers for free and whose house was bombed in retaliation. Mendy Samstein adjudged her "a towering figure of strength."[39] In "The Organizer," Mama Jean's café is threatened with closure for her activism. "If she broke," Peacock muses, "the community would crumble overnight" (7). But she stays strong, while Peacock vomits his fear, believing he will be judged only as "the stranger who brought death among them." She is the person to whom he clings and who voices the lines that Fannie Lou Hamer made her own when telling the preacher who would retreat before the forces of Jim Crow: "ah'm sick an tard of bein' sick an' tard of yo' selling the folks out" (16).[40] It is she who galvanizes Peacock to "adopt the accent of the folk" and to adapt her words to commune with the crowd surrounding Sheriff Hollowell, but she also helps him to contain it. "Yeah, mah brothahs an' sistuhs," Mama Jean declares, "that cracker know we sick an' tard, thet we sick an' tired o' *bein' sick an' tard*" (19).

Thelwell's story crystallizes in a single episode the tensions that persisted for organizers embedded in small southern communities. Peacock is forced to enact in practice what he has accepted in principle—the murder of a man he loves must be exploited, and the pain that follows hard on Hightower's death must be packaged. He finally acknowledges that Hightower's widow has "a great face. Be great on a poster or TV" (27).

Such fictions contribute directly to the story of SNCC, and, indeed, rediscovering them also necessitates tracing individual movement histories. While David Halberstam followed the few civil rights workers he knew best in *The Children* (1998), and Wesley Hogan allows that her 450-page study has twenty SNCC people "standing in" for more than four hundred participants, this kind of recovery research contributes to a reconsideration of not only the most renowned of SNCC staff such as Forman but also those like Thelwell who excelled in a peripatetic role.[41]

The contribution fiction makes to telling SNCC's stories should not be underestimated. In 1966, the year Thelwell published "The Organizer," the first Black Writers conference met at Fisk. At this gathering, Forman initiated a discussion of the relationship of the writer to the struggle. He worried that creative writers had written little about the freedom movement, describing them as "out of touch," but he also expressed the hope that SNCC could promote what he called "a fruitful dialogue between artists and activists."[42]

"The Organizer" exemplifies that kind of dialogue if read as an emotive fictionalization alongside Mendy Samstein's 1964 factual "city of terror" report on McComb. Samstein began his piece for *The Student Voice* by allowing that "it is hard for someone who has not lived in . . . the Negro community in McComb . . . to understand the reality behind the two bombings of September 20." He deploys literary strategies in appealing to his readers, ventriloquizing the anguish the black community feels with each bombing: "Whose house, who is dead? It's not mine. Then who? My neighbor, my friend—my mother, my brother, my son, or maybe SNCC again. Who?"[43] Thelwell depicts the bleak hopelessness that stretches before Hightower's widow and the rage that blazes in her eyes, even despite herself, as she answers the sheriff's perfunctory questions about the bombing that left her husband dead. By having Peacock load a shotgun in the Freedom House, he shows that armed defense was never far behind SNCC's tactical nonviolence: "He . . . longed for the swift liberating relief of wild, mindless, purging violence, ending maybe in death. But survival, what of that? Suppose he was one of the survivors. It was a nightmare that had hovered in the back of his consciousness ever since he had joined the movement—yet he saw himself limping away from the burning town, away from the dead and maimed, people to whom he had come singing songs of freedom and rewarded with death and ashes. The organizer is always responsible" (14).

Samstein closed his report in *The Student Voice* with an exposé of the "cover-up" of "the real story," with police telling the press that three thousand black people took to the streets of McComb, a claim authenticated by Mike Wallace (on CBS's Morning News), even though the entire population of McComb barely touched that number. "And so," Samstein opines, even in the face of its media coverage, "the story of the murder of a community goes untold."[44] In the more expressive as well as reflective mode of the short story, Thelwell portrays the effects of the bombing. The story closes with Peacock planning another community meeting to follow hard on his sleepless night.

"The Organizer" was reprinted in a yearbook of short stories in 1968 and in an African journal special issue edited by Chinua Achebe in 1974. It has even been collected in Thelwell's "essays in struggle," *Duties, Pleasures, and Conflicts*, published in 1987 with an introduction by James Baldwin. Like other participant-fictions, however, it has received no attention from cultural historians or literary scholars. The entire genre has lacked scholarly examination in large part because such works were overlooked by literary critics when the civil rights movement was at its peak. This omission reflected reductive judgments that disregarded fiction considered "political." *Civil Rights in Recent Southern Fiction*, a brief survey published in 1969 by James McBride Dabbs, typified neglect of works by movement activists. It described works by Lillian Smith, Elizabeth Spencer, Ellen Douglas, and Ann Fairbarn, among others. However, Dabbs cites only one example of participant literature, doing so with evident ambivalence in the final section of his survey, titled "Some Other Writers." He commends *I Play Flute* (1966), the verse collection of SNCC's first office secretary, Jane Stembridge, for communicating "the immediacy of life," but is uncomfortable about the aesthetics of the activist poet. "The great temptation to a poet involved in the movement," he warned, "is to become passionate about it, a propagandist for the cause, not a celebrant of life." Accordingly, Dabbs expresses preference for the work of another poet whose lack of personal involvement in the freedom struggle imbued his work with "the solid endurance of art."[45]

Some critical attention has been paid to activist-authored novels and stories written in the late 1970s and 1980s that convey a hard-won awareness of movement losses and gains through the perspective of hindsight.[46] However, there is a widely held misperception in scholarly circles that the first civil rights fictions were written after the movement had run its course. Richard H. King cites the earliest works as novels by Alice Walker and Rosellen Brown, published in 1976 and 1984, respectively, and Christopher Metress does not mention 1960s fictions in his essay on the "long" civil rights movement in literary history.[47] There is evidently a truncated critical sense of the temporal range of southern movement fiction which attention to participant-fictions seeks to address.

*　*　*

To a young Barack Obama, about to graduate from college and begin work as a community organizer on Chicago's South Side in the early 1980s, the civil rights movement seemed to exist in "grainy black-and-white" as "a series of images, romantic images, of a past I had never known. . . . SNCC workers standing on a porch in some Mississippi backwater trying to convince a family of sharecroppers to register to vote." In hindsight he feels that such images helped to formulate his plans: "They told me (although even this much understanding may have come later, is also a contract, containing its own falsehoods) that I wasn't alone. . . . Communities . . . expanded or contracted with the dreams of men—and in the civil rights movement those dreams had been large."[48]

The visual images Obama reflected on were those of television news footage and photojournalism, and documentaries such as *Eyes on the Prize*, which was first screened in 1986. These will remain dominant forms though which the imagery—and the mythology—of the movement circulates. Nevertheless, the stories that SNCC wrote at the time were, as Thelwell judged twenty years on, "directly rooted in the day-to-day grittiness of the Movement."[49] He had attempted to convey something of "the very texture of reality intensified" (xiii), and a passage toward the end of "The Organizer" conveys in both political and metaphysical terms why Thelwell should have written such a story. Travis Peacock works in the national office before he begs SNCC's organizing staff to let him work in the field. His role in the national office has been that of a communications officer, writing up incidents like the murder of Jesse Hightower: "He had written hundreds of coldly factual reports of burnings, bombings, and murders. And the 'statements,' how many of these had he written, carefully worded, expressing rage, but disciplined controlled rage, phrases of grief balanced by grim determination, outrage balanced by dignity, moral indignation balanced by political demands. Every time it was the same, yet behind those phrases, the anger and the sorrow and the fear were real" (22).

In the short-story form, Thelwell gets behind reports like Samstein's in *The Student Voice* and those abstracted in *News of the Field*, another of SNCC's newsletters. He reconfigures a form and a discourse expected to seem balanced and objective while acting as "propaganda," reports defined in a SNCC working paper as "interpretive pieces which tell our story to those outside the movement, which pinpoint the issues that our action is directed toward."[50] In "The Organizer," Thelwell not only provides an object lesson but forges a shift in the real by shaping quotidian violence and pain aesthetically, as an activist but also as an "artist of grief" (22), a term that resonates with other fictions written by organizers and summer volunteers.[51]

In 1983, Obama espoused the importance of mobilizing "black folks" at the grass roots and the significance of what he called the "sacred stories" of those people he organized every day in the Altgeld Gardens public housing project, "stories full or terror and wonder, studded with events that still haunted or inspired them."[52] A number of these stories returned Obama to the civil rights era—and indeed, when read alongside *The Making of Black Revolutionaries*, they recall Forman's depictions of Chicago's South Side. A similar effect occurs when reading Thelwell's work. In 1986 James Baldwin judged that engagement with his stories was like "facing someone who has, in his hands, some crucial sections of the jigsaw puzzle of which you have in your hands some other sections."[53] In not studying SNCC's fictions, as written by Forman, Thelwell, and so many others, it is plain that we miss a significant element of movement history as envisaged by its participants.

Notes

The author would like to thank James Forman Jr. and Chaka Forman for permission to quote from their father's papers.

1. Granville Hicks, *Saturday Review*, August 3, 1963.

2. Robert Penn Warren, *Who Speaks for the Negro?* (New York: Vintage, 1966), 188.

3. John Lewis with Michael D'Orso, *Walking with the Wind* (New York: Simon and Schuster, 1998), 463.

4. Television documentaries and news programs are discussed by Sasha Torres in *Black, White, and in Color: Television and Black Civil Rights* (Princeton: Princeton University Press, 2003). The role of photography is explored in Leigh Raiford, *Imprisoned in a Luminous Glare* (Chapel Hill: University of North Carolina Press, 2010). I examine exploitation movies as the first form in which racial violence aimed at SNCC was dramatized on screen in "Exploiting Civil Rights: Pulp Movies in the 1960s," in *American Cinema and the Southern Imaginary*, ed. Deborah Barker and Kathryn B. McKee (Athens: University of Georgia Press, 2011), 194–216.

5. See, for example, Sharon Monteith, "The Bridge from Mississippi's Freedom Summer to Canada: Pearl Cleage's *Bourbon at the Border*," in *Cultural Circulation: Canadian Writers and Authors from the American South—A Dialogue*, ed. Waldemar Zacharasiewicz (Vienna: Austrian Academy of Arts and Sciences, 2011), which includes discussion of the influence of Albert Camus's writing on Bob Moses.

6. James M. Jasper, *The Art of Moral Protest: Culture, Biography, and Creativity in Social Movements* (Chicago: University of Chicago Press, 1999), 14.

7. Francesca Polletta, *Freedom Is an Endless Meeting: Democracy in American Social Movements* (Chicago: University of Chicago Press, 2002) and *It Was Like a Fever: Storytelling in Protest and Politics* (Chicago: University of Chicago Press, 2006).

8. Francesca Polletta, "Contending Stories: Narrative in Social Movements," *Qualitative Sociology* 21, no. 4 (1998): 419–46.

9. James Forman, *The Making of Black Revolutionaries* (Seattle: University of Washington Press, 1997), 113; originally published as *The Making of Black Revolutionaries: A Personal Account* (New York: Macmillan, 1972).

10. The phrase would be "brothers and sisters" in "Letter to my sisters and brothers"; preface, *The Making of Black Revolutionaries*, xxi–xxiii.

11. Forman's Speech at Waveland, Appendix E, Wesley C. Hogan, *Many Minds, One Heart: SNCC's Dream for a New America* (Chapel Hill: University of North Carolina Press, 2007), 275–76. See Cleveland Sellers, *The River of No Return: Autobiography of a Black Militant and the Life and Death of SNCC* (1973), 115; Cheryl Lynn Greenberg, ed., *A Circle of Trust: Remembering SNCC* (New Brunswick, N.J.: Rutgers University Press, 1998); and "Will the Circle Be Unbroken?" the audio history of southern civil rights campaigns 1940–70 produced by the Southern Regional Council.

12. Forman in Warren, *Who Speaks for the Negro?* 173.

13. Forman, *The Making of Black Revolutionaries*, 113–14.

14. Forman in Warren, *Who Speaks for the Negro?* 173.

15. James Forman, "Thin White Line," Draft A, James Forman Papers, Manuscript Division, Library of Congress, Washington D.C. Subsequent citations will be given parenthetically.

16. Forman, *The Making of Black Revolutionaries*, 53.

17. Bob Moses in Henry Hampton and Steve Fayer, eds., *Voices of Freedom: An Oral History of the Civil Rights Movement from the 1950s through the 1980s* (New York: Vintage, 1995), 183.

18. Julius Lester, *All Is Well: An Autobiography* (New York: William Morrow, 1976), 68; Stokely Carmichael in Warren, *Who Speaks for the Negro?* 397.

19. Forman, *The Making of Black Revolutionaries*, 116.

20. Howard Zinn, *SNCC: The New Abolitionists* (1964; Cambridge, Mass.: South End Press, 2002), 273–74.

21. Julian Bond, foreword to Forman, *The Making of Black Revolutionaries*, xi.

22. Forman, *The Making of Black Revolutionaries*, 289.

23. Julian Bond, "The Southern Youth Movement," *Freedomways* 3 (1962), reprinted in Esther Cooper Jackson with Constance Pohl, eds., *The Freedomways Reader: Prophets in Their Own Country* (Boulder, Colo.: Westview Press, 2000), 71.

24. Julian Bond, "SNCC: What We Did," *Monthly Review* 52, no. 5 (2000), http://monthlyreview.org/001001bond.php.

25. Mendy Samstein, "The Murder of a Community," *The Student Voice*, September 23, 1964, 2–3.

26. Stokely Carmichael and Ekwueme Michael Thelwell, *Ready for Revolution: The Life and Struggles of Stokely Carmichael* (New York: Scribner, 2003). Thelwell may be

best known to some readers for *The Harder They Come* (1980), his novelization of the 1972 Jamaican-set movie that starred Jimmy Cliff.

27. Michael Thelwell, *Duties, Pleasures, and Conflicts: Essays in Struggle* (Amherst: University of Massachusetts Press, 1987), xi.

28. Thelwell quoted in Greenberg, *A Circle of Trust*, 153.

29. Michael Thelwell, "The Organizer," in *Duties, Pleasures, and Conflicts*, 24. Subsequent citations will be given parenthetically. Descriptions of Forman as a reassuring presence abound, as do depictions of him as bearlike, "a large man with the stature and disposition of a bear" (Sellers, *River of No Return*, 47).

30. This is the same grim humor one finds in Thelwell's essays documenting voter-registration work, as when a Natchez judge is known as "Necessity" because of Horace's observation that "Necessity knows no law."

31. The tactics recall Dick Gregory's performances and routines in the South in support of SNCC and the movement.

32. Jerome Smith, "The Jump-Off Point," in *My Soul Looks Back in Wonder: Voices of the Civil Rights Experience*, ed. Juan Williams (New York: Sterling, 2004), 63.

33. Bob Moses, VEP report, February 1963, in Pat Watters and Reese Cleghorn, *Climbing Jacob's Ladder: The Arrival of Negroes in Southern Politics* (New York: Harcourt and Brace, 1967), 159.

34. "Questions Raised by Bob Moses," *The Movement*, April 1965, 1.

35. Thelwell, *Duties, Pleasures, and Conflicts*, xi.

36. Guyot quoted in John Blake, *Children of the Movement* (Chicago: Lawrence Hill Books, 2004), 80.

37. For example, in 1980 SNCC volunteer Dennis Sweeney murdered Democratic congressman Allard Lowenstein, one of the key planners marshaling volunteers for Mississippi's Freedom Summer project in 1964. Newspapers cited brutal violence during Freedom Summer as the trigger for Sweeney's psychological breakdown, and three books that explored the toll the movement took on Sweeney were published in the decade. SNNC's first chairman, Marion Barry, was the first prominent civil rights activist to become chief executive of a major American city, but his initial tenure as mayor of Washington, D.C. (1979–91), was marred by his arrest for drug use in 1990 and subsequent sentencing to a six-month prison term.

38. Julius Lester, journal entry, July 11, 1964, Biloxi, Mississippi, reprinted in *All Is Well*, 112.

39. Samstein, "The Murder of a Community," 2.

40. Fannie Lou Hamer's grave in Ruleville, Mississippi, is situated on cooperatively held African American–owned land. The headstone reads, "Fannie Lou Hamer, Oct 6 1917–March 14 1977," with an inscription, "I am sick and tired of being sick and tired."

41. Hogan, *Many Minds, One Heart*, xxx.

42. David Llorens, "Writers Converge at Fisk University," *Negro Digest*, June 1966, 54–68, quote on 65.

43. Samstein, "The Murder of a Community," 2.

44. Ibid., 3.

45. James McBride Dabbs, *Civil Rights in Recent Southern Fiction* (Atlanta: Southern Regional Council, 1969), 140–41.

46. See, for example, Sharon Monteith, "Revisiting the 1960s in Contemporary Fiction: 'Where Do We Go from Here?'" in *Gender and the Civil Rights Movement*, ed. Peter Ling and Sharon Monteith (New York: Garland, 1999), 215–38; Christopher Metress, "Making Civil Rights Harder: Literature, Memory, and the Black Freedom Struggle," *Southern Literary Journal* 40, no. 2 (2008): 138–50.

47. Richard H. King, "The Discipline of Fact/The Freedom of Fiction?" *Journal of American Studies* 25 (August 1991): 171–88; Metress, "Making Civil Rights Harder."

48. Barack Obama, *Dreams of My Father: A Story of Race and Inheritance* (Edinburgh: Canongate, 2007), 134.

49. Thelwell, *Duties, Pleasures, and Conflicts*, xiii.

50. Mary King, "Working Paper, November 1964," reprinted in appendix 1 of her *Freedom Song: A Personal Story of the 1960s Civil Rights Movement* (New York: Morrow, 1987), 562.

51. I examine these stories in *SNCC's Stories: Fiction, Film, and the Southern Freedom Struggle of the 1960s* (forthcoming).

52. Obama, *Dreams from My Father*, 190.

53. James Baldwin, introduction to Thelwell, *Duties, Pleasures, and Conflicts*, xviii–xix.

7

From Beloved Community
to Imagined Community

SNCC's Intellectual Transformation

JOE STREET

The development of the Student Nonviolent Coordinating Committee (SNCC) following the 1964 Mississippi Summer Project has traditionally been presented in terms of institutional decline and intellectual regression. Many historians of the civil rights movement express regret at SNCC's subsequent trajectory, noting its failures and growing irrelevancy as it moved from integrationism through Black Power advocacy to demise as a FBI-informant-ridden rump.[1] Emily Stoper ascribes SNCC's decline to the increasing tension between its identity as a redemptive organization (in her words, its "sect-like qualities") and its political program.[2] Clayborne Carson also points to internal disarray and dissension as key factors in the organization's decline, placing them alongside its growing alienation from its southern rural roots and a growing predilection for rhetoric and ideology over activism and practice. Yet Carson also notes that much of SNCC's posturing in the mid- to late 1960s articulated positions and ideas that coalesced during and through the activist experience.[3] This insight opens up the possibility for a reinterpretation of SNCC's history between the conclusion of the 1964 Mississippi Summer Project and the decision to expel SNCC's remaining white members in 1967. During this period, an influx of new activists—black and white—helped to transform the organization in terms of both personnel and ideology. Analysis of SNCC's changing concept of community reveals that its transformation was in many respects logical and directly related to its activist experience, rather than merely being a narrative of decline.

After the Summer Project period, SNCC moved away from its devotion to the concept of a "beloved community" ideal of interracial harmony toward a conceptualization more attuned to Benedict Anderson's notion of an "imagined community" defined by racial identity. For Anderson, a nation is much more than a geographical entity defined by physical borders. As envisioned by him, it is a community of like-minded individuals who, though they may lack direct knowledge of each other, are united by belief in their common bonds with fellow nationals. The absence of personal contact requires them to forge these links in an imagined capacity. In other words, national identity rests on the assumption of *shared values* and, equally, of *distinctiveness* from other nationalities that is almost entirely created in the mind. A true community, on the other hand, tends to be defined through direct contact between its members.[4]

Anderson's concept has great utility for the study of racial nationalism. In departing from the traditional understanding that nations are closely linked to the concept of the nation-state, it enables deeper evaluation of how transnational and multinational groups define themselves. Racial nationalists express deep affinity with those who share the same race. These racial characteristics (most obviously color) also provide a simple method of exclusion. Black nationalists in the United States often referred to African Americans as a "nation within a nation," both to unite the black community and to separate it from white America.[5]

This notion of an "imagined community" can be applied to SNCC's history. The organization's early years were characterized by fierce personal bonds between its activists. As SNCC grew larger and more unwieldy in the mid-1960s, however, it became increasingly fractious. This loss of a sense of community was one of the key factors in SNCC's decline. Another was the concomitant rise in black nationalist sentiment among some SNCC activists, who felt strong bonds with fellow blacks but grew increasingly mistrustful of the organization's white members. Where the beloved community was defined by participation in SNCC's work, the imagined community was defined by blackness. In this sense, Charles Payne is correct to argue that the "basic metaphor" for SNCC's interpersonal relationships developed from "family" to "nation," but this contention needs further refinement, particularly with regard to the meaning of these core terms.[6]

James Forman famously referred to SNCC as a "band of sisters and brothers." In its early years, however, the organization is better defined as a community bound together by a shared sense of purpose and anti-hierarchical structure. Regardless of their frequent arguments, this was a community of like-minded individuals in the truest sense of the term. The bonds between individual members were forged through common experiences and beliefs.[7] Payne's application of the term "nation" to SNCC in its later stages of development needs Anderson's interpretation for it to be fully appropriate within the context of the group's history. Moreover, the transition between different notions of community is less jarring than that from "family" to "nation." Anderson's theory is extremely useful, therefore, for pinpointing how interpersonal relations within SNCC developed. More importantly, it suggests that SNCC's shifting notion of community is crucial for an understanding of the organization's intellectual and social development.

SNCC and the Beloved Community

The notion of community was at the heart of SNCC from its outset. The group's founding statement avowed that "the redemptive community supersedes immoral social systems."[8] Infused with Christian ideals of nonviolence, this declaration reflected the influence of the Nashville group of student activists in the early SNCC. In their credo, the redemptive suffering and moral superiority of SNCC activists would engender a new era of racial harmony that Methodist minister James Lawson, the Nashville group's mentor, termed the "beloved community." According to Diane Nash, one of the Nashville students prominent in the early SNCC, the beloved community constituted "a climate in which all men are respected as men, in which there is appreciation of the dignity of man and in which each individual is free to grow and produce to his fullest capacity." For fellow Nashville student and future SNCC chair John Lewis, it was "nothing less than the Christian concept of the kingdom of God on earth."[9]

The notion that SNCC itself had to practice the beloved community in order to re-create it in the wider society was vitally important. As Ella Baker counseled, the students needed not only to explore the civil rights protests that were immediately before them but also see their whole lives as catalysts for change.[10] The organization's future was hotly debated at the founding Raleigh conference of 1960. When a delegate called for discussion of the group's "goals, philosophy, future, and structure," Lawson responded that its philosophy had to be settled before consideration of its goals.[11] Clearly, the Nashville cohort believed that the community *of* SNCC was as important as the community it hoped to bring about.[12] This understanding of the close relationship between SNCC's organizational practice and its philosophical goals remained a salient feature of its internal debates throughout its existence. Indeed, this interplay was similar to that of certain Republican militias and communities during the Spanish Civil War. Here, people debated long and hard about whether to impose hierarchies in order to win the war or to practice the sort of society they were fighting for during the war. It may well be significant that neither these militias nor SNCC was successful in achieving its aims.[13]

The Nashville group's influence—particularly its religious faith—waned after SNCC shifted focus from direct action to voter registration in 1962. Some of its members moved away from the organization, while others drifted back to education.[14] Yet its insistence that SNCC be practiced and lived as much as anything else remained central to the organization. The ideal and experience of "being" SNCC forged very strong personal bonds between its activists. The common experience of redemptive suffering, philosophical debate, and simply living as SNCC activists held them together and was arguably fundamental in establishing their unity of purpose. For Cleveland Sellers, this defined the activists as "*SNCC people . . . bound together in a community of common commitment.*"[15]

The voting-rights protests in McComb, Mississippi, in October 1961 offered vivid proof of this. Bob Zellner was marching alongside Bob Moses and Charles McDew when they were set upon by a mob. As Zellner was being beaten by the white segregationists, Moses and McDew moved to his side to help absorb the punches. "I would remember this moment as the time of bonding—a brotherly male bonding as fierce, I suppose, as any welded in war," he recalled. This solidarity gave Zellner "a most pleasant feeling of security, serenity and absolute joy."[16] Howard Zinn later spoke of this as the "magical social effect" of working in SNCC.[17]

Far from being momentary, this feeling extended into almost every pore of SNCC's body. As Francesca Polletta notes, many staff meetings were structured around group reports rather than individual ones, which encouraged group discussion and ensured that individuals were not singled out. Furthermore, there remained a sense that each person's opinion was to be respected. While the freedom to speak often ensured that SNCC meetings lasted well into the night, it also bonded individuals to each other and to the organization. As Muriel Tillinghast noted, the decisions made in SNCC meetings were frequently about how individuals would live their lives—and there was no way that these decisions could be made by a simple majority vote.[18]

The notion of a beloved community was central to SNCC's philosophy through 1966, but this did not mean that dissent was stifled. Even Zinn's laudatory account of SNCC's early history hints at the tensions that were not far from SNCC's surface. He presented these internal struggles as "the aches of progress, the inevitable and welcome signs that people are meeting for the first time, and that through a transition which brings occasional bursts of hostility, people are learning to live with one another." It is clear, however, that there were disagreements about SNCC's philosophy, and the application of this philosophy to the South, throughout its life.[19]

The SNCC policy that African Americans and whites should work in their respective racially defined communities was one bone of contention.[20] During preliminary work in Mississippi, Bob Moses—who was no nationalist—operated exclusively with blacks. This was not only because of the dangers that whites would bring to his work but also because it was considered beneficial for the black organizers to be in charge (not least in order to gain vital leadership experience). Yet white activists found white communities so unreceptive that it was deemed pointless at best and dangerous at worst to maintain racially separate projects. This led to white and black members working together in African American communities. The resultant tensions came to a head during discussions in November 1963 of the planned 1964 Mississippi Summer Project.

Some black activists decried white volunteers' tendency to assume leadership roles in interracial projects. In their view, the pernicious effect of integration also resulted in SNCC reinforcing rather than replacing traditional structures of black deference and white superiority. Though aware that the black-only movement had not been as effective as hoped, Moses acquiesced to the decision that all Summer Project directors be black but urged the use of white volunteers as project workers, a position treated with scorn by some of those present.[21] When this plan reached SNCC's Executive Committee, those in favor of bringing large numbers of whites to Mississippi were the organization's most experienced activists. Crucially, it took the intervention of Moses to win acceptance of the proposal at the January meeting of the Council of Federated Organizations (COFO), an umbrella organization responsible for many of Freedom Summer's logistics. Tensions over these issues were to intensify over the coming years.[22]

SNCC's Community in Practice

The experiences of SNCC's staff often revealed how difficult it would be for the beloved community to be created and lived. This was especially evident during the 1964 Summer Project. SNCC activists, particularly the African American southerners, grew increasingly sensitive to the psychological and social impact of whites working in the black community. According to SNCC freedom school coordinator Liz Fusco, the Summer Project represented an acceptance that what could be done in Mississippi "could be deeper, more fundamental, more far-reaching, more revolutionary than voter registration alone. . . . [It was] a decision to enter into every phase of the lives of the people of Mississippi."[23] This applied not only to the local people but also to the project's volunteers and staff.[24]

Like freedom school students, teachers were encouraged to broaden their horizons and look beyond their immediate surroundings. Many began questioning what brought them to Mississippi, whether middle-class whites could truly understand what it meant to be black, and why many African Americans no longer trusted white liberals.[25] This process brought to the surface many of the strains that were to contribute to the organization's demise and revealed the difficulties and tensions inherent in attempting to bring about the beloved community. With staff living in the local community, the Summer Project effectively attempted to integrate part of the state. Racial tension was apparent even at the orientation sessions, with white volunteers commenting that they found the regular SNCC staff insular and difficult to engage with. Conversely, the naïveté of the excitable white volunteers appalled many staff members.[26] For Sally Belfrage, these competing visions of the beloved community— whites feeling that it was natural, blacks that it was earned—resulted in part from the growth of racial pride among the black workers.[27]

As Wesley Hogan argues, however, another issue was also significant. Thrust into an unprecedented situation with sparse training, white volunteers nudged face-to-face interracial relationships much higher up on the list of things SNCC had to address. First, these volunteers had little or no experience of negotiating interracial etiquette prior to the summer of 1964. Second, enough of them brought a college-educated arrogance to taint the group as a whole. These two factors prompted some COFO staffers to conclude that white volunteers did not or could not show adequate respect for local Mississippians.[28]

This (albeit well-meaning) lack of understanding was apparent at the Holly Springs freedom school, where Pam Parker rhapsodized in letters home about her "girls," two of whom were mothers in their twenties.[29] Others became inculcated with SNCC's spirit rather than remaining on the outside looking in. Gren Whitman, a white Summer Project volunteer who later joined SNCC's staff, soon concluded that although the beloved community was a laudable and inspiring aim, it was not necessarily realistic in the situations that faced SNCC workers. At this juncture his outlook broadly reflected SNCC's unofficial stance on nonviolence and perhaps its own attitude toward the beloved community.[30]

While whites were welcomed into SNCC's ranks during the Freedom Summer, their role in the movement remained under debate, as evidenced by the presence of Robert F. Williams's memoir-cum-treatise, *Negroes with Guns* (1962), on the freedom school curriculum. Williams's ambivalence about white involvement became increasingly influential with black SNCC activists. Two of these were arrested while in possession of thousands of copies of his regular newsletter, *The Crusader*, for distribution in Mississippi's black community. In his book Williams argued that the African American struggle was being blunted by white liberals who urged nonviolence: "It is because our militancy is growing that they spend hundreds of thousands of dollars to convert us into pacifists." Accordingly he concluded, "We must direct our own struggle, achieve our own destiny."[31] Holding even more trenchant views on this score by 1964, Williams anticipated much of SNCC's future rhetorical stridency. White liberal supporters of the movement had become "ofay liberals" whose African American associates were now "coward Judases." "These self-righteous moralists," Williams charged, were deceiving and brainwashing "obsequious Negroes into believing that they have been divinely commissioned to introduce the superior conduct of latent masochism to a violently wicked jungle."[32]

The concept of the beloved community came under further scrutiny after the Summer Project. Matters were not helped by the embarkation of eleven key activists on a restorative trip to Africa during September 1964, which unwittingly contributed to the organization's turmoil. In their absence SNCC's organizing initiatives faltered. Almost as important, a number came home with political lessons from their experience on the mother continent. John Lewis and Fannie Lou Hamer were profoundly affected by the daily sight of black people in positions of authority. James Forman found confirmation for his sense that the African American freedom struggle was directly linked to those of black peoples in Africa. Influenced by conversations with Malcolm X, Lewis returned to the United States with a similar conviction.[33] The broadening of their perspectives anticipated the shift by some SNCC activists toward fuller identification with the worldwide black community.

The request of more than eighty (mostly white) volunteers to remain in Mississippi after the Summer Project was part of the reason that Courtland Cox called for a staff meeting in October. He was concerned that the "racial and class composition" of SNCC would be "significantly alter[ed]."[34] Discussion over a planned Black Belt Project produced tensions between those, such as Forman, who advocated a more bureaucratized structure for SNCC and those who tended to follow the more freewheeling style of organizing associated with Bob Moses' approach to organizing. This disagreement revolved around the same issue discussed in 1960: should SNCC live out the society that it wished to bring about? The plan to involve only African American students in the Black Belt Project indicated that SNCC now anticipated the division of this society along racial lines in the short and medium term.[35] It furthermore suggested that the lived experience of southern civil rights activism was causing an estrangement from the beloved community ideal.

Papers submitted for consideration at the following month's staff conference at Waveland, Mississippi, highlighted the tension between experience and ideal. Whereas Charles Sherrod entreated his comrades to avoid becoming fixated on the race issue, SNCC Alabama state director Silas Norman argued that the "ethnic relationship" bonding black people together simply could not be entered into by whites. In Sherrod's opinion, if such a polarized view of race was accepted, it would undermine SNCC's capacity to "be the new society" and would bring about its downfall.[36] Harking back to the debates of 1960, his reasoning was echoed by some white members. Mike Miller, from SNCC's San Francisco Bay Area operation, for example, noted that the organization could not claim to be building the beloved community if it allowed race to be used as a reason to disavow arguments proposed by its white members. Speaking for many of these, he urged that SNCC should be the model for the community it hoped to develop nationwide. Like Sherrod, Miller also warned that racial essentialism could threaten the organization's existence.[37] The concerns over race and nationalism even infected the discussion of sexual discrimination, with many black staff members rejecting the claims in Casey Hayden and Mary King's memo on women in the movement on grounds of the authors' racial identity. Stokely Carmichael even claimed that the very attempt to raise the issue of sexual discrimination was, in effect, an attempt to derail the African American struggle.[38]

The characteristically inconclusive conclusion at Waveland confirmed that the beloved community was no longer at SNCC's core and suggested that Norman was correct to warn that SNCC's size was a danger to its continued survival.[39] As a number of SNCC veterans pointed out, the decision-making process was reliant on everybody knowing and trusting each other. By this time, however, most of the participants in SNCC meetings were more like strangers. Because of SNCC's expansion—in terms of both personnel and geographical spread—the personal bonds between members became less central to its identity. Small wonder, then, that Stokely Carmichael observed a serious internal problem of "old vs. new staff" and that John Lewis lamented SNCC's loss of the "closeness and cohesiveness" that characterized its early days.[40] The new obligation of staff members to submit regular reports on their work—in effect having to justify their existence—furthered fractured SNCC's community. Without the intimacy and trust of old, activists were less likely to continue working according to traditional practice. Also of concern was the growing bitterness of many African American veterans toward whites and their increasing skepticism that the races could be brought together on an even footing. Clearly, SNCC's concept of community was changing as much as its physical community.[41]

Imagining a Community

Even though SNCC was far from adopting the imagined nationalist community as a political ideology at this point in its history, certain nationalist tenets are observable in its organizing initiatives following Freedom Summer. In January 1965, Barbara Simon suggested that SNCC establish a cultural arm to reinforce the notion that blacks had a separate culture from whites and to emphasize the African roots of African American heritage. She was particularly keen that black nationalist groups should have a role in such an agency.[42] In August, Judy Richardson established a residential freedom school that was to involve one hundred black students drawn in equal numbers from the urban North and rural South. The school would run for one session in each of these geographical settings, with the intention of strengthening cultural bonds between the two student groups. This project was intended to encourage understanding that the problems faced by the black populations in the two regions were essentially similar. Its long-term goal was to aid in the creation of a national black community that was not divided along urban-rural and sectional lines. This attempt to unify such diverse black communities represented a shift toward a nationalist position that aimed to intensify racial bonds and promote a conception of the African American community as a nation within a nation.[43]

At the personal level, the rise of nationalist ideas in SNCC caused further tension. John Lewis rather bitterly noted that activists like Stokely Carmichael were quick to adopt nationalist poses even though they had lived more integrated lives before joining the organization. Attributing this to feelings of self-consciousness wrought by their integrated lives, he recalled Bob Mants pointing out at a SNCC meeting: "A Southern Negro doesn't need to wear a sign saying he's black. We don't need to wear Afros to show that we are black. We *know* we are black."[44] Carmichael's shift was not simply due to psychological concerns, however. It was directly related to his experiences in the integrationist movement, notably the treatment meted out to activists at demonstrations by white supremacist police officers.[45] The failure of the movement to address this injustice directly led to Carmichael's adoption of Black Power in June 1966 and a more strident position regarding race.

This occurred shortly after Carmichael was elected as SNCC chair in place of Lewis. The latter claimed to be mainly popular with SNCC veterans, who had developed personal bonds of trust and respect, rather than with newer members, whose heads were full of Frantz Fanon and Malcolm X rather than Gandhi or Thoreau. More accurately, his base consisted of the integrationist veterans, such as Bill Hansen or Charles Sherrod (both of whom were absent from the vote to elect Carmichael), since his rival also had solid backing from SNCC veterans, including James Forman, and former members of the Howard University–based Nonviolent Action Group, with whom Carmichael had worked for a number of years.[46] Even though Lewis was by now adamant that the civil rights movement had to be "black controlled, dominated and led," his close personal association with moderate elements of the integrationist movement, especially Martin Luther King Jr., rendered his continuing leadership of SNCC unpalatable to the radicals and the newer members of the organization. Others felt that it was just time for a change or that, in the words of Ernest McMillan, SNCC needed more "uncompromising, assertive and bold leadership."[47]

Large numbers of SNCC's new members came with somewhat different expectations and assumptions from those who had joined in the organization's formative years. Whereas their forebears' experience was informed by the optimism of the early integrationist movement, theirs was defined by SNCC's mid-1960s struggles with the Democratic Party and other civil rights groups. They disdained the federal government's inaction in response to the deaths of three Summer Project workers in 1964 and considered Lyndon Johnson's appropriation of the civil rights anthem "We Shall Overcome" a cynical ploy. They had witnessed SNCC veterans become embittered at the failure of the American establishment to grant African Americans even basic rights. They had watched civil rights moderates attempt to blunt SNCC's radicalism, as evidenced by the censoring of parts of John Lewis's planned speech at the 1963 March on Washington. SNCC's radical shift, combined with its increasing focus on rhetoric, attracted more recruits who found the organization's militancy appealing and who had even fewer links to its roots in biracial protest. Drawn to SNCC in part by Carmichael's oratorical flights of fancy, these activists wanted SNCC to attain purity through cleansing itself of white influences rather than through pursuit of an interracial ideal. Julius Lester, who joined the staff in 1966, articulated the radical vision in stating forthrightly that the beloved community was now "irrelevant." For him, the black community should simply turn its back on white America and instead look to Africa in order to reconnect with the wider black community and hence rediscover its racial identity.[48]

Distressingly for many veterans, new members were more than happy to verbalize their rejection of SNCC's traditions. At one staff meeting, Fannie Lou Hamer, one of the organization's bravest and most committed activists, was berated by some neophytes for being "no longer relevant" and not at their "level of development."[49] Her long years of political struggle meant nothing to these activists who had joined SNCC direct from the campuses. Firebrands in SNCC's Chicago office built on Julius Lester's insistence that black people needed to take control of their lives. They entreated the African American population to "fill [them]selves with hate for all white things" while "learning to think Black." For them, SNCC had become a human rights organization that "belong[ed]" to all black peoples who were oppressed by the white man.[50] It would be simple to suggest that this development was the consequence of generational shifts within the organization, but deeper forces were at play. These new activists were, according to James Forman, highly educated and literate, and sneered at less educated staffers such as Hamer. Though not better educated than some veterans, notably Forman and Moses, the newcomers still considered their conception of the situation more advanced than the practice-based ideas of the veterans. More importantly, lack of personal bonds made the new members less inclined to support older activists. This adds weight to the notion that commitment to the beloved community was based more on personal bonds than on philosophy.

Members from the new Atlanta Project, who worked in the overwhelmingly African American area of Vine City, were most forceful in articulating nationalist sentiments and rejecting the idea of a beloved biracial community. Most of these staff members were recent SNCC recruits. Roughly half were northern, and a number had been involved in nationalist groups prior to joining SNCC. Many were college- rather than "field"-educated, but all were convinced that whites could not relate to any aspect of the African American experience. In the eyes of the Atlanta organizers there could not be a truly biracial community, for whites inevitably stymied black initiative and independence, not least because they had been party to the near-colonial dominance of black America. For them, SNCC's attempt to bring about a post-racial community was unrealistic and resulted in the organization becoming a "closed society," alienated from the community it purported to be organizing. This was an almost ironic reversal of SNCC's previous openness, since the organization was never as closed as when it proposed to exclude whites. Quite simply, Black Power to the Atlanta Project meant a more exclusive, separatist SNCC.[51]

The Atlanta Project experience convinced participants that SNCC's original policy of having only blacks working in the black community was right. They elevated this belief into a central organizing principle, leavened with elements of Malcolm X's thought.[52] Bill Ware, a local organizer with Pan-Africanist sympathies, argued vehemently that the emotional bonds uniting black people were more important than any ties that whites had with the black struggle, both in the United States and worldwide. For him, whites were only able to enter this struggle on an intellectual level, which precluded their full involvement. Their participation might be principled, but it was based on an "esthetic . . . [rather than] a human basis. . . . They cannot participate where anger . . . revenge . . . hate . . . are necessary." In Ware's view, whites could not "negate their history" and would by definition blunt the revolutionary edge of the black movement.[53] Accordingly, the Atlanta Project's notion of community was racially specific. By now, too, even long-term SNCC activists held similar views. Ivanhoe Donaldson, for example, argued that SNCC had to understand nationalism if it was to prosper in the late 1960s, and Charles Cobb stated that African Americans "should aspire to a sense of nationhood" among themselves rather than taking any responsibility for redeeming the United States.[54]

While Carmichael later became closely associated with certain nationalist tenets, he was a crucial bulwark against SNCC's nationalists in his early months as SNCC chair.[55] At a fall 1966 press conference, when questioned on the issue of whites in SNCC, he threw his arms around future Yippie Abbie Hoffman and stated, "Abbie's in SNCC, he's white and he's beautiful," thus confirming the importance of personal bonds.[56] More convincingly, he resisted entreaties to expel whites from the organization. While many of Carmichael's statements on other issues seemed to reflect the position of the Atlanta Project, it is notable that at this point he kept his distance from their essentialism.[57] The personal bonds that he had developed with many fellow activists surely influenced this reticence. Final confirmation that SNCC had become a black-only organization came in May 1967, however. Bob Zellner applied to be given full voting rights in SNCC while organizing in the New Orleans white community, an idealistic attempt to continue working for the organization to which he had devoted much of his adult life. Though his petition was doomed to fail, the discussions surrounding his request showed that remnants of the beloved community continued to inform SNCC's decision-making process. Many newer members argued that to keep Zellner on would be against the organization's racial policy, but James Forman pleaded that Zellner should be given special dispensation because the two men were close friends. The personal bonds that Zellner had forged through more than five years of activism and the respect that black SNCC veterans such as Forman had for white organizers with his experience were clearly still strong enough to underwrite a challenge to the organization's new nationalist commitment.[58]

Ultimately, the refusal to approve Zellner's petition signified SNCC's final transformation from an inclusive to an exclusive group. Where once it had accepted anybody's help, regardless of their political affiliations or race, it now explicitly rejected white members. Thus SNCC conformed to Anderson's understanding that nations, or imagined communities, are defined as much by what and whom they exclude as they are by what and whom they include.[59] With many of the organization's African American integrationists departed, expelled, or merely exhausted, SNCC became dominated by those who considered the community of blackness more realizable than an integrated beloved community. This constituted a final and irrevocable rejection of SNCC's earlier approach to community building. Where once the organization had prized the personal bonds that emerged through the organizing experience, it now elevated theoretical notions of racial solidarity and identification, thus reifying the divide between the races. Yet it also ensured that one thing remained constant in SNCC's life—the organization would live out the kind of community it hoped to bring about.

SNCC's early activists started with a notional commitment of bringing about a beloved community, but three factors resulted in the waning of this ideal. First, as James Forman noted, SNCC's radicalization was a consequence of "direct experience."[60] Through this, many activists, such as Stokely Carmichael, gradually came to the conclusion that the beloved community was an outmoded, sentimental, even specious goal. Second, SNCC attracted more new organizers than its original working practices could absorb. Initially its decision-making process could rely on a common sense of purpose among the staff. Unanimity could be achieved relatively easily when SNCC was a small group, most of whose members knew each other personally. By 1964, however, the staff was so large that many of those present at meetings did not know each other, much less have strong personal bonds. Accordingly, the effort to achieve unanimity at meetings became a painful, frustrating, and ultimately pointless process. The sheer size of SNCC resulted not only in the fracturing of its community but also its sense of itself *as* a community.

Finally, SNCC's radicalization developed a self-perpetuating momentum as the organization attracted newer, more radical members who lacked personal bonds with veteran organizers. The newcomers' ties were more likely to be with their fellow radicals and with radical ideology, as demonstrated in the abuse of Fannie Lou Hamer in 1966. Cleveland Sellers's expulsion further highlighted the momentum of this process. His adversaries considered themselves SNCC veterans even though they had not joined the organization until after Carmichael's election as chair. Himself adjudged a radical in the mid-1960s, Sellers was now considered too moderate to continue working for the organization.[61] The bonds that the later radicals forged were more with black people than they were with "SNCC people." By the time of Sellers's expulsion, this meant not only having black skin but also being able to "think Black." The imagined community of blackness offered SNCC's new nationalists a world of certainty that obviated the need to engage with, let alone work alongside, whites. As a result, the beloved community became a relic of a bygone era in civil rights protest.

Notes

1. Richard H. King, for example, laments that "the history of SNCC was genuinely tragic . . . [and] inexorable." King, *Civil Rights and the Idea of Freedom* (Athens: University of Georgia Press, 1992), 140. See also Adam Fairclough, *Better Day Coming: Blacks and Equality, 1890–2000* (London: Penguin, 2001), 310–14, 315–16; and Taylor Branch, *At Canaan's Edge: America in the King Years, 1965–68* (New York: Simon & Schuster, 2006), 573–74, 606–7, 611, 612.

2. Emily Stoper, "The Student Nonviolent Coordinating Committee: Rise and Fall of a Redemptive Organization," *Journal of Black Studies* 8 (September 1977): 17 (quotation), 19, 23.

3. Clayborne Carson, *In Struggle: SNCC and the Black Awakening of the 1960s* (Cambridge: Harvard University Press, 1981), 287, 299–300.

4. Benedict Anderson, *Imagined Communities: Reflections on the Origin and Spread of Nationalism*, rev. ed. (1983; London: Verso, 1991), 1–7.

5. This idea can be traced back through generations of nationalists. See Robert S. Levine, *Martin Delany, Frederick Douglass, and the Politics of Representative Identity* (Chapel Hill: University of North Carolina Press, 1997), 60.

6. Charles M. Payne, *I've Got the Light of Freedom: The Organizing Experience and the Mississippi Freedom Struggle* (Berkeley: University of California Press, 1995), 365.

7. James Forman, speech at Waveland conference, November 1964, in Wesley C. Hogan, *Many Minds, One Heart: SNCC's Dream for a New America* (Chapel Hill: University of North Carolina Press, 2007), 276; James Forman, *The Making of Black Revolutionaries*, new ed. (Seattle: University of Washington Press, 1997), 307. See also Peter Ling's "SNCCs: Not One Committee, but Several" in this volume.

8. "Student Nonviolent Coordinating Committee Founding Statement," http://www.crmvet.org/docs/sncc1.htm.

9. Diane Nash, "Inside the Sit-ins and Freedom Rides: Testimony of a Southern Student," in *The New Negro*, ed. Mathew Ahmann (New York: Biblio and Tannen, 1969), 45 (quotation), 60; John Lewis with Michael D'Orso, *Walking with the Wind: A Memoir of the Movement* (New York: Simon & Schuster, 1998), 76–78, quote on 78. See also Carson, *In Struggle*, 21.

10. Barbara Ransby, *Ella Baker and the Black Freedom Movement: A Radical Democratic Vision* (Chapel Hill: University of North Carolina Press, 2003), 245–46.

11. Carson, *In Struggle*, 23

12. Mary King, oral history in *A Circle of Trust: Remembering SNCC*, ed. Cheryl Lynn Greenberg (New Brunswick, N.J.: Rutgers University Press, 1998), 26. See also Charles McDew oral history, ibid., 35.

13. George Esenwein and Adrian Shubert, *Spain at War: The Spanish Civil War in Context, 1931–1939* (London: Longman, 1995), 125–29, 145–49.

14. Carson, *In Struggle*, 24–25.

15. Cleveland Sellers with Robert Terrell, *The River of No Return: The Autobiography of a Black Militant and the Life and Death of SNCC* (Jackson: University Press of Mississippi, 1990), 54.

16. Bob Zellner interview with Anne Romaine, Anne Romaine Papers, Southern

Folklife Collection, University of North Carolina, Chapel Hill, 2.1.2 (Mississippi Freedom Democratic Party), folder 73, 10–11.

17. Howard Zinn, *SNCC: The New Abolitionists* (Boston: Beacon Press, 1964), 185.

18. Francesca Polletta, *Freedom Is an Endless Meeting: Democracy in American Social Movements* (Chicago: University of Chicago Press, 2002), 79, 83–84; see 69–85 for decision making in SNCC's projects.

19. Zinn, *SNCC*, 167–68. See also differing responses to the question "Did you feel that there was a beloved community in SNCC?" from SNCC members Ernest McMillan and Gren Whitman. McMillan saw this beloved community in almost all aspects of SNCC life; Whitman did not. Ernest McMillan, response to author's questionnaire, March 23, 2010; Gren Whitman, response to author's questionnaire, March 16, 2010, both in author's collection.

20. Forman oral history in Greenberg, *Circle of Trust*, 79.

21. Carson, *In Struggle*, 96–97, 98–99; Zinn, *SNCC*, 186.

22. Carson, *In Struggle*, 99–101.

23. Minutes of SNCC Executive Committee, December 27–31, 1963, Student Nonviolent Coordinating Committee Records, Library of Congress, microfilm reel 3, frames 0305–0324 [hereafter SNCC Records]; Liz Fusco, "Freedom Schools in Mississippi, 1964," 1 (quote), ibid., reel 39, frame 0005. See also "Mississippi: Structure of the Movement, Present Operations, and Prospectus for This Summer," 1964, 3, ibid., reel 6, frame 0049.

24. "Prospectus for the Summer," c. 1964, 2, Howard Zinn Papers, State Historical Society of Wisconsin [hereafter SHSW], box 2, folder 12; Charles Cobb, "Prospectus for a Summer Freedom School Program," December 1963, reprinted in *Radical Teacher* 40 (Fall 1991), 36; John Dittmer, *Local People: The Struggle for Civil Rights in Mississippi* (Urbana: University of Illinois Press, 1994), 258; Payne, *I've Got the Light of Freedom*, 42; Stokely Carmichael with Ekwueme Michael Thelwell, *Ready for Revolution: The Life and Struggles of Stokely Carmichael (Kwame Ture)* (New York: Scribner, 2003), 302.

25. SNCC handout, "Basic Question: What Are Freedom Schools for and What Do You Want from Them," n.d. [c. 1964], Lise Vogel Papers, SHSW.

26. Carson, *In Struggle*, 112–13.

27. Sally Belfrage, *Freedom Summer* (Charlottesville: University of Virginia Press, 1990), 81.

28. Hogan, *Many Minds, One Heart*, 173.

29. Pam Parker, "Freedom School Report," July 18, 1964, SNCC, reel 68, frames 0432–0434 (Papers of the Mississippi Freedom Democratic Party). See also McMillan response to author's questionnaire.

30. Whitman and McMillan responses to author's questionnaire; Carmichael, *Ready for Revolution*, 307.

31. Joe Street, *The Culture War in the Civil Rights Movement* (Gainesville: University Press of Florida, 2007), 87–88; SNCC staff meeting transcript, June 9–11, 1964, 15, Zinn Papers, box 2, folder 7; Robert F. Williams, *Negroes with Guns* (1962; reprint, Detroit: Wayne State University Press, 1998), 75, 78 (quote), 79.

32. Carmichael, *Ready for Revolution*, 303; *The Crusader*, January 1963, 3 (first and second quotes); *The Crusader*, February 1964, 3 (third quote), box 16, Social Action

Vertical File [hereafter SAVF], SHSW. It is unclear which editions of *The Crusader* were being carried. The quotes are representative of Williams's writing between the January 1963 and May–June 1964 issues.

33. Harry Belafonte oral history in *Voices of Freedom: An Oral History of the Civil Rights Movement from the 1950s through the 1980s*, ed. Henry Hampton and Steve Fayer (London: Vintage, 1990), 206; Carson, *In Struggle*, 136; Lewis, *Walking with the Wind*, 295–97, 310; Forman, *The Making of Black Revolutionaries*, 407–11. For a moving and insightful view of the impact of the Africa trip on some of those left behind see Roy Shields Jr., "Overall Report, Southwest Georgia," February 1965, esp. 1–2, SAVF, box 47.

34. Carson, *In Struggle*, 137

35. Forman, *The Making of Black Revolutionaries*, 416–17; Payne, *I've Got the Light of Freedom*, 367–68.

36. Silas Norman, "What Is the Importance of Racial Considerations in the SNCC Staff?" paper presented for Waveland, n.d., Charles Sherrod Papers, reel 1, segment 23, SHSW; Charles Sherrod, "From Sherrod," paper presented for Waveland, n.d., ibid., reel 1, segment 23.

37. Mike Miller, "RE: Questions Raised for National Staff Meeting," n.d., Sherrod Papers, reel 1, segment 23; Carson, *In Struggle*, 144–45.

38. Carson, *In Struggle*, 147–48, 325 n. 32.

39. Silas Norman, "Some Basic Considerations for the Staff Retreat," Mary King Papers, SHSW, box 1. Note that Wesley Hogan's history of SNCC effectively ends with the Waveland conference. Hogan, *Many Minds, One Heart*, 226–34.

40. Polletta, *Freedom Is an Endless Meeting*, 95–96, 107 (Carmichael quotation); Lewis, *Walking with the Wind*, 301; Forman, *The Making of Black Revolutionaries*, 418–19, 422–24; Mary King, *Freedom Song: A Personal Story of the 1960s Civil Rights Movement* (New York: William Morrow, 1987), 438–39, 449–50, 484, 486. This is also reflected in COFO, where tensions between the "come here" and "been here" staff members (the former were normally white northerners, the latter black southerners) hindered the organization's progress after 1965. See Hogan, *Many Minds, One Heart*, 223.

41. Polletta, *Freedom Is an Endless Meeting*, 110–11; Carson, *In Struggle*, 144.

42. Barbara Simon, "Proposal for a Cultural Arm of SNCC," January 5, 1965, SNCC Vine City Papers, SHSW, box 1, folder 8 [hereafter Vine City].

43. Judy Richardson memo to SNCC Executive Committee, "Re: Residential Freedom School," September 1964, SNCC Records, reel 3, frame 0367; "Prospectus for Residential Freedom School," n.d., attachment to memo to SNCC staff, May 29, 1965, 1, SAVF, box 47; "Southwest Georgia SNCC Newsletter," February 28, 1965, 2, SNCC Records, reel 37, frame 0352; Judy Richardson, "Report on Residential Freedom School," August 1965, ibid., reel 35, frames 0077–0082.

44. Lewis, *Walking with the Wind*, 306–7.

45. Carmichael's first "Black Power" speech, in Greenwood, Mississippi, late on June 16, 1966, focused on his outrage at his frequent arrests: "This is the twenty-seventh time I have been arrested—and I ain't going to jail no more! . . . The only way we gonna stop them white men from whuppin' us is to take over. We been saying

freedom for six years and we ain't got nothin.' What we gonna start saying now is 'Black Power!'" Carmichael, *Ready for Revolution*, 507.

46. Lewis, *Walking with the Wind*, 364, 382–85; Sellers, *River of No Return*, 188; Carson, *In Struggle*, 235. One might also point to the influx of young black students in 1965 in the wake of the Southern Christian Leadership Conference's usurping of the local campaign movement in Selma, Alabama. They were as likely to have been shaped by Lewis's refusal to toe the SNCC line as by Lewis himself. See Carson, *In Struggle*, 162.

47. Lewis, *Walking with the Wind*, 365; Forman, *The Making of Black Revolutionaries*, 455; Carmichael, *Ready for Revolution*, 479–82; McMillan response to author's questionnaire.

48. Julius Lester, "The Angry Children of Malcolm X," *Sing Out*, October/November 1966, in *Black Protest Thought in the Twentieth Century*, ed. August Meier, Elliott Rudwick, and Francis L. Broderick, 2nd ed. (Indianapolis: Bobbs-Merrill, 1971), 469–84, quote on 483.

49. Forman, *The Making of Black Revolutionaries*, 476.

50. Lester, "The Angry Children of Malcolm X," 483; Chicago SNCC, "We Want Black Power," in Meier et al., *Black Protest Thought*, 487, 488.

51. Untitled position paper in Atlanta Project files, n.d., SNCC Records, reel 37, frames 0561–0568 (quote on fo564); Bill Ware, "By Bill Ware," c. 1966, 1–2, Vine City, box 1, folder 11; John Churchville, "An Analysis of the Civil Rights Movement," ibid., box 1, folder 11. "The Nitty-Gritty: The Reasons Why," n.d., Vine City, box 1, folder 8, goes some way to explaining why the Atlanta Project wanted to be all black. See also untitled position paper, spring 1966, ibid., box 1, folder 6. The Atlanta Project also allied itself with an element of Pan-Africanist thought through its proposed Community Store: see "The Necessity for Southern Urban Organizing," 6, ibid., box 1, folder 8.

52. Churchville's "Analysis" references Malcolm X's house Negro/field nigger analogy, his ideas concerning the widening of the struggle to encompass human (as opposed to civil) rights, and his early insistence that all whites were tainted by racism.

53. Ware, "By Bill Ware," 2. St. Clair Drake and his own service as a Peace Corps volunteer in Ghana were earlier influences on Ware. Drake had also exerted great influence over James Forman's view of the political implications of African liberation struggles. Carson, *In Struggle*, 192–95; Hasan Kwame Jeffries, *Bloody Lowndes: Civil Rights and Black Power in Alabama's Black Belt* (New York: New York University Press, 2009), 190; Forman, *The Making of Black Revolutionaries*, 83, 483.

54. Ivanhoe Donaldson, "We Need to Radically Confront America," *The Movement*, July 1966, in *The Movement, 1964–1970*, ed. Clayborne Carson and the staff of the Martin Luther King, Jr. Papers (Westport, Conn.: Greenwood Press, 1993), 136; Cobb, remarks at SDS national conference, summer 1966, ibid., 7.

55. Note his notorious speech at the February 17, 1968, "Free Huey" rally organized by the Black Panther Party at the Oakland Auditorium. Transcript: Pacifica Radio/ UC Berkeley Social Activism Sound Recording Project at http://www.lib.berkeley.edu/ MRC/carmichael.html.

56. Abbie Hoffman, "SNCC: The Desecration of a Delayed Dream," *Village Voice*, December 15, 1966: 6; Lewis, *Walking with the Wind*, 382.

57. Stokely Carmichael, "Power and Racism," *New York Review of Books*, September 1966, reprinted in *Stokely Speaks: Black Power Back to Pan-Africanism*, ed. Ethel N. Minor (New York: Vintage, 1971), 27–28.

58. Excerpts from transcript of May 1967 staff meeting in Danny Lyon, *Memories of the Southern Civil Rights Movement* (Chapel Hill: University of North Carolina Press, 1992), 176, 178–81 (note that Zellner vehemently defended Forman's right to a rest at the Waveland conference in November 1964, ibid., 162); Carson, *In Struggle*, 216–17, 240–42; Sellers, *River of No Return*, 194–97; Forman does not discuss this episode in his memoirs. The warm bonds between Julian Bond and former integrationists Ruth Howard and Curtis Hayes also found expression at a chance meeting in Washington, D.C., in the late 1960s. See David Llorens, "Julian Bond: 'Down by the Lake, Shootin' Fish,'" *Ebony*, May 1969, 70.

59. Anderson, *Imagined Communities*, 7.

60. Forman, *The Making of Black Revolutionaries*, 396.

61. Sellers, *River of No Return*, 250. Carson (*In Struggle*, 294) notes that the identifiable staff consisted overwhelmingly of members who had joined since 1966.

8

The Sit-Ins, SNCC, and Cold War Patriotism

SIMON HALL

On April 20, 1960, a *New York Times* editorial commented that the sit-ins currently sweeping across the South represented a "cry . . . for justice and democracy . . . that cannot be stifled, that must and will be heard, and that all the citizens of this democracy can ignore only at our and the free world's peril."[1] It was not alone in viewing the protests through the wider context of America's Cold War struggle against Communist totalitarianism. Segregationists rather predictably blamed Communists and fellow travelers for disrupting the (white) South's cherished way of life.[2] The nation's political leaders, well aware that their counterparts in the Soviet Union were only too happy to seize on incidents of racial discrimination for purposes of discrediting America's claims to free-world leadership, depicted the sit-ins as being in keeping with America's democratic traditions and emphasized that such expressions of dissent would not be tolerated in the Soviet bloc.[3] Surprised by the sudden outburst of nonviolent direct action, established civil rights leaders also placed the demonstrations within the broader Cold War fight to defend and extend democracy. On April 16, 1960, National Association for the Advancement of Colored People (NAACP) executive director Roy Wilkins proclaimed that the student sit-ins were "redeeming . . . [America's] promise of life, liberty, and the pursuit of happiness for all under government by the consent of the governed." The veteran civil rights leader continued, "We owe them and their white student cooperators a debt for rearming our spirits and renewing our strength as a nation at a time when we and free men everywhere sorely need this clear insight and this fresh courage."[4]

This essay explores the use of Cold War patriotism—the fusing together of rhetorical appeals to Americanism (especially the nation's founding ideals of freedom, liberty and equality) with arguments that the country's Cold War leadership was compromised by Jim Crow racism—from the sit-ins through the early years of the Student Nonviolent Coordinating Committee (SNCC). It then examines how and why this tactic was replaced mid-decade with expressions of solidarity with Third World revolutionaries. Finally, it analyzes this organization's long-standing interest in the international dynamics of the black freedom struggle in the United States.

SNCC's Invocation of Cold War Patriotism

Appealing to America's founding ideals and laying claim to the citizenship rights enunciated in the Constitution had long been central features of black protest. However, the onset of McCarthyism during the 1950s, which dramatically narrowed the space for political dissent and caused serious problems for civil rights organizations and their trade union allies, made strategies of patriotic protest particularly attractive.[5] Moreover, America's desire to win influence over newly independent nations in Africa and Asia to aid its global struggle against Communist expansion offered civil rights activists a valuable opportunity. In arguing forcefully that segregation and the denial of citizenship rights to blacks at home compromised America's free-world leadership and exposed the gap between its ideals and its practice, civil rights leaders were able to exercise a degree of leverage that encouraged the federal government to take action.[6] "Cold War patriotism" thus became a central feature of black protest during the postwar era.

In 1947, for example, in testimony before President Harry Truman's Committee on Civil Rights, the head of the NAACP's Legal Defense Fund, Thurgood Marshall, argued that the systematic denial of constitutional rights to black southerners was "undoubtedly the greatest indictment of our American democratic form of government" and, as such, an obstacle for America's global leadership.[7] Eight years later, in his first major speech as a civil rights leader, Martin Luther King Jr. told a mass meeting of the Montgomery Improvement Association that the bus boycotters were motivated by a "love for democracy and . . . [a] deep-seated belief that democracy transformed from thin paper to thick action is the greatest form of government on earth." He also roused his audience by claiming that "certainly, certainly, this is the glory of America, with all of its faults. This is the glory of our democracy. If we were incarcerated behind the iron curtains of a Communistic nation, we couldn't do this. If we were dropped in the dungeon of a totalitarian regime, we couldn't do this. But the great glory of American democracy is the right to protest for right."[8] Two years later, in the aftermath of the Little Rock school desegregation crisis, Roy Wilkins argued that the decision of Arkansas governor Orval Faubus to use troops to prevent black children from entering Central High School had "dealt a stab in the back to American prestige as the leader of the free world and presented our totalitarian enemies with made-to-order propaganda for use among the very nations and peoples we need and must have on the side of democracy."[9]

The young civil rights activists of the early 1960s drew on this tradition. A spirit of patriotism infused the early sit-ins, whose leaders claimed that eliminating segregation would boost the international fight against Communism. In Greensboro, the cradle of the protests, the end of the first week of sit-ins climaxed on Saturday, February 6, 1960, with hundreds of students participating in demonstrations. They included the North Carolina Agricultural and Technical College football team, who, armed with small American flags that had been distributed in advance by movement leaders, "formed a flying wedge" that moved through gangs of white hecklers to enable civil rights activists to reach the lunch counters.[10] Speaking at a packed rally in a Greensboro church that same month, legendary Birmingham, Alabama, civil rights leader Fred Shuttlesworth declared, "We don't want token freedom. We want full freedom." He urged his listeners to be ready "to go to jail with Jesus" if necessary to "remove the dead albatross of segregation that makes America stink in the eyes of the world."[11]

Shortly afterward, in Atlanta, Georgia, the Committee on Appeal for Human Rights launched its sit-in movement with a statement, drawn up by students from six colleges from across the city, that appeared in the March 9 edition of the *Atlanta Constitution*. In remarks intended for both "the citizens of Atlanta" and "the world," it demanded "those rights which are inherently ours as members of the human race and as citizens of these United States" and stated "clearly and unequivocally that we cannot tolerate, in a nation professing democracy and among people professing Christianity, the discriminatory conditions under which the Negro is living today in Atlanta, Georgia—supposedly one of the most progressive cities in the South."[12] America, this statement continued, was "fast losing the respect of other nations by the poor example which she sets in the area of race relations." It concluded with a declaration that "we plan to use every legal and non-violent means at our disposal to secure full citizenship rights as members of this great Democracy of ours."[13]

The sit-in movement led directly to the founding of SNCC at Shaw University in April 1960.[14] An iconic and inspirational organization, it was committed to participatory democracy, the building of local organizations, and the development of indigenous leadership. Like the sit-in activists, SNCC utilized Cold War patriotism to advance the cause of civil rights. Just weeks after being formed, it sent letters to candidates for office in the forthcoming elections demanding the right to be "first-class citizens of our homeland," urging that America "*be* a democracy," and insisting that racism had to be eradicated if the United States was to "remain a force in the preservation of freedom throughout the world."[15]

In the new organization's most powerful assertion of Cold War patriotism, a SNCC delegation led by group chairman Marion Barry addressed the Platform Committee of the Democratic National Convention at Los Angeles in July 1960.[16] It called on the Democratic Party to pledge to speed up the pace of school desegregation, pass fair employment legislation, ensure black voting rights in the South, and protect civil rights demonstrators from segregationist violence.[17] In his speech before the committee, Barry invoked America's founding ideals, asserted SNCC's own patriotism, and argued forcefully that meaningful progress on civil rights was of critical importance to the ultimate success of the nation's Cold War mission. "In a larger sense," he avowed, "we represent hundreds of thousands of freedom loving people, for whom our limited efforts have revitalized the great American dream of 'liberty and justice for all.'"[18] Refuting former president Harry Truman's unfounded charge that the sit-ins were, in some unspecified way, "engineered by the Communists," Barry asserted that participants in the civil rights movement were united in their belief in "the dignity of the individual, our hope in the democratic form of government, and our devotion to our homeland."[19]

The SNCC leader concluded his presentation with a rousing invocation of Cold War patriotism:

> On July 4, 1776, the Continental Congress, adopting the Declaration of Independence . . . created a new potential for life and liberty. On July 16, 1945, the explosion of the first atomic bomb at Alamogordo, New Mexico, created the possibility of death and enslavement. We stand today between these great turning points in history, saying that America cannot fail in its responsibility to the free world. We must be strong. Civil defense and economic power alone will not ensure the continuation of democracy. This democracy itself demands the great intangible strength of a people able

to unite in a common endeavor because they are granted a common dignity. This challenge cannot be met unless and until all Americans, Negro and white, enjoy the full promise of our democratic heritage—first class citizenship. Dedicated to this end, we, the students of America, must continue our movement.[20]

Cold War patriotism also featured prominently in an editorial carried on the front page of the SNCC newspaper, *The Student Voice*, in its March 1961 issue. Inspired in part by the recent addition of non-white states to the United Nations (Cambodia, Cameroon, Chad, Nigeria, Somalia, Senegal, and the Republic of the Congo, along with several other newly independent nations that joined in the autumn of 1960), this proclaimed that America was "at a crossroads." It was now time for the nation, "and particularly our Southern states," to "recognize our responsibility to the world, to mankind, and to ourselves by ridding the country of the cancer that is segregation." Given the urgency of world events—including decolonization and the "deepening crisis in Laos"—the United States had to "purge itself of the rabies of racism . . . only bold forthright action can square America's racial practices with the coveted role of world's champion advocate of democratic human rights."[21]

Two months later, during the Freedom Rides, SNCC administrative secretary Edward B. King Jr. sent a telegram to President John F. Kennedy urging decisive leadership to halt the appalling white supremacist violence that the interracial activists had encountered and to enforce the recent U.S. Supreme Court ruling (in *Boynton v. Virginia*) requiring interstate transport facilities to be desegregated. King pointed out that "at a time, in the history of our great nation, when we are telling the people of Asia, Africa, Latin America and the free world in general that we desire to be friends, Negro Americans continue to be assaulted by the Southern reactionaries." SNCC called on the president to "speak to the American people on the issue that Negro Americans are, in fact, first-class citizens of this nation; that they are as such, entitled to exercise all rights and privileges guaranteed by the Constitution. . . . And finally, that your high office issue a firm and unequivocal statement in support of the right of free travel for all citizens without interference by any segment of the American people."[22]

SNCC also deployed Cold War patriotism to protest the expulsion on February 11, 1963, of ten students from Arkansas AM&N College in Pine Bluff for taking part in a sit-in demonstration at a Woolworth's store. The following day, the anniversary of Abraham Lincoln's birth, the organization's chair, Charles McDew, sent telegrams to Kennedy and Arkansas senator J. William Fulbright. The one to the president urged him to "examine the local situation in Pine Bluff" and "consider our image abroad when Senator J. W. Fulbright of Arkansas presides over the Senate Foreign Relations Committee, and at the same time, in his own home state, students are being denied a state-supported education solely because they are taking the words of Abraham Lincoln and the spirit of our democracy seriously." The one to Fulbright asked him to "reconcile this action in your home state with the image of our country abroad and tell us whether we can have world justice while American students suffer because they believe in the American creed: that all men are created equal."[23]

The SNCC-inspired Mississippi Freedom Democratic Party (MFDP) similarly resorted to Cold War patriotism during its ultimately unsuccessful effort to win official recognition at the 1964 Democratic National Convention in Atlantic City. On June 28, in a statement before the Minnesota state convention of the Democratic Farmer-Labor Party in St. Paul, Mississippi native Dewey Greene urged support for the MFDP challenge. The twenty-three-year-old activist from the delta town of Greenwood declared that "every day we allow Mississippi racists to deny constitutionally guaranteed rights to the Negro citizens of Mississippi, America suffers. We cannot call for freely elected governments around the world when we do not have a freely elected, democratic government in the state of Mississippi." Greene urged Minnesota Democrats to support the effort to "make Mississippi a more democratic and a better place to live for its one million Negro citizens."[24]

SNCC's Critique of Cold War Imperialism

SNCC's commitment to Cold War patriotism during the first half of the 1960s contrasts sharply with its approach later in the decade when it denounced America's military involvement in Vietnam, condemned the United States as a racist, imperialist power, and proclaimed solidarity with non-white liberation struggles across the Third World. On January 6, 1966, for instance, SNCC issued a statement opposing the Vietnam War, criticizing America's claim to be fighting for the "freedom" of the Vietnamese as "deceptive," and decrying it for "pursuing an aggressive policy in violation of international law." Challenging the broader Cold War mission of the United States, it also charged that "our country's cry of 'preserve freedom in the world' is a hypocritical mask behind which it squashes liberation movements which are not bound and refuse to be bound by expediency of U.S. Cold War policy."[25] A few weeks later, speaking at a Memorial Dinner of the Council for American-Soviet Friendship, SNCC chair John Lewis declared that "our government's role in Vietnam horrifies us and shames us. . . . We want the Vietnamese people to run their own country."[26]

SNCC's rhetoric grew even more acidic as the fighting in Vietnam dragged on. A statement released in April 1967, on the eve of the spring mobilization antiwar protests, described the conflict as "brutal, immoral and racist" and declared that it formed "part and parcel of an American foreign policy which has repeatedly sought to impose the status quo by force on non-white peoples struggling from liberation from tyranny and poverty."[27] Speaking in September 1968 in Bratislava, Czechoslovakia, at an international conference that brought together American antiwar protesters and representatives of the North Vietnamese and National Liberation Front (Vietcong), John Wilson expressed SNCC's "solidarity and unquestionable support" for the Vietnamese "struggle for national liberation and self-determination." He also denounced U.S. imperialism and aggression, disparaging "White America" as a "mad dog" that needed to be disposed of.[28]

SNCC's internationalist perspective was not restricted to Vietnam. At a staff meeting in May 1967 the organization's newly elected officers (including H. Rap Brown as chairman and Ralph Featherstone as program secretary) explained that SNCC was "interested not only in Human Rights in the United States, but throughout the world; that in the field of International Relations, we assert that we encourage and support the liberation struggles of all people against racism, exploitation, and oppression." The black struggle for freedom in the United States was viewed as "an integral part of the world-wide movement of all oppressed people, such as in Vietnam, Angola, Mozambique . . ."[29] In the aftermath of the Arab-Israeli Six-Day War, a group of SNCC activists published a highly controversial (and according to its critics, anti-Semitic) article that offered unqualified support to the Palestinians, condemned Zionism, and accused Israeli Jews of imitating the Nazis by "tak[ing] over Palestine," committing "some of the same atrocities against the native Arab inhabitants," and "completely dispossess[ing] the Arabs of their homes, land and livelihood."[30]

In July 1967, former SNCC chairman Stokely Carmichael began a four-month international tour (which included visits to Great Britain, Cuba, the Soviet Union, China, North Vietnam, Algeria and Guinea) that furnished him with numerous opportunities to meet with revolutionaries and statesmen (including Fidel Castro, Ho Chi Minh, Sekou Touré, and Kwame Nkrumah), denounce American foreign policy as "racist" and "imperialist," and pledge solidarity with non-white peoples.[31] Speaking at an international conference in Havana, for example, Carmichael proclaimed, "We share with you a common struggle . . . our [common] enemy is white Western imperialist society. Our struggle is to overthrow this system that feeds itself and expands itself through the economic and cultural exploitation of nonwhite, non-Western peoples—of the Third World."[32]

In August 1967, SNCC pledged its support to the African National Congress's revolutionary armed struggle against South Africa's apartheid regime. It urged black Americans to boycott General Motors (which was a heavy investor in South Africa) and to prepare "psychologically for the day when we may all have to go to fight in South Africa" (it even mooted the possibility that black Vietnam veterans might form a "Black International" that would "FIGHT OR DIE FOR THE LIBERATION OF THE MOTHER COUNTRY").[33]

In conjunction with its avowals of internationalism, SNCC rejected the language of Americanism. In October 1966, for example, during a speech in Berkeley, Carmichael responded to suggestions that blacks simply wanted a piece of the American pie by explaining that "the American pie means *raping* South Africa, *beating* South America, *raping the Philippines, raping every country you've been in* . . . [I] don't want to be *part* of that system!"[34] Moreover, SNCC increasingly viewed black Americans as a "colonized people within the United States" and as "Overseas Africans." In contrast to its members' expressions of devotion to their American "homeland" in 1960, the organization now described Africa as "OUR HOME."[35] A SNCC statement issued in August 1967 to mark the second anniversary of the Watts riot of 1965 starkly illustrated the abandonment of patriotism. Characterizing the Fourth of July as "the white man's Independence Day," this statement emphasized that black Americans were slaves "before July 4th [1776], on July 4th and after July 4th" and had been defined "as three-fifths of a person" by the Constitution, "that great document of democracy." It disparaged expectations that black Americans should celebrate national holidays, "salute the white man's flag, and sing the white man's national anthem" for being "as ridiculous as thinking that we will achieve our own independence under an economic and political system whose existence depends upon oppression, exploitation and the resultant degradation, poverty, and racism we have been subjected to." Instead, SNCC called on blacks to celebrate the anniversary of the Watts riot and honor its "Burn, Baby, Burn" slogan as "our Declaration of Independence . . . signed . . . with Molotov cocktails and rifles."[36]

The Making of SNCC's Black Internationalism

In accounting for SNCC's abandonment of Cold War patriotism, one must consider the wider context in which this development occurred. As Doug McAdam has argued, "the experience of confronting American racism in all its savagery" was a radicalizing one.[37] During the first half of the 1960s, as SNCC labored to bring freedom to some of the most inhospitable regions of the Deep South, its activists learned some sobering lessons about white America. They came to realize that the federal government was not prepared to deploy marshals or use the FBI to protect them from white racist violence. They discovered that the national media and white northerners took more notice when a white activist was killed than when a black one was. And they learned that idealism and principle often came a poor second to hard-nosed political calculation in the priorities of their liberal Democrat allies. The 1964 Democratic National Convention in Atlantic City, where the MFDP failed in its bid to unseat the racist state regulars, was a particular cause of disillusionment on this score. One activist, Joyce Ladner, described it as the "end of innocence."[38]

The experience of SNCC field secretaries was also an important factor in the organization's change of outlook. As Zoharah Simmons (Gwendolyn Robinson) remarked, "There's nothing like being dragged into a paddy wagon and thrown into the lock-up you know . . . this stuff changes you . . . and I guess I do think it was a radicalizing process because it changed my life completely."[39] In similar vein, SNCC leader James Forman avowed that five years of struggle had changed many individuals from being "idealistic reformers to full-time revolutionaries. And *the change had come through direct experience*."[40] This process helps to explain why SNCC, an organization founded on the ideals of interracialism and nonviolence and committed to the creation of the "beloved community," came, by the mid-1960s, to embrace black separatism, abandon nonviolence, and adopt a fiercely critical position regarding U.S. foreign policy.[41] It was also a critical factor in the abandonment of Cold War patriotism.

SNCC activists referred to their own experiences of civil rights organizing when justifying their attacks on U.S. foreign policy. At a staff meeting held in Atlanta on November 29, 1965, Charles Cobb declared that the organization's opposition to the war in Vietnam was influenced by knowing "too much about this country." Courtland Cox similarly asserted that the "only thing the U.S. knows about Freedom is how to lie about it (after five years of work we know this)."[42] Reflecting such sentiments, the SNCC statement of January 6, 1966, emphasized the U.S. government's failure to uphold the law, guarantee basic citizenship rights, and protect civil rights workers in the South. It proclaimed that the United States was "no respecter of persons or law when such persons or laws run counter to its needs and desires. We recall the indifference, suspicion and outright hostility with which our reports of violence have been met in the past by government officials." Drawing on its activists' experience, SNCC declared that "our work, particularly in the South, taught us that the United States government has never guaranteed the freedom of oppressed citizens."[43] Speaking a few weeks later, John Lewis elaborated on his organization's opposition to the war in Vietnam: "How could we fight for . . . free elections in Alabama and Mississippi and ignore the U.S. role in Vietnam to deprive the Vietnamese of this right? How could we remain silent when the U.S. government sent marine divisions to Vietnam and Santo Domingo to protect 'freedom and democracy' and we have yet to see *one* federal agent protect us or any of the Negroes with whom we work?"

While SNCC's abandonment of Cold War patriotism and embrace of a radical Third World internationalism constituted an important feature of its shift toward Black Power, the organization's interest in Africa and the wider world was not new. The African independence movement, itself led by college-trained activists, was an inspirational model for many of the early African American student protesters. Moreover, Africans studying at black colleges in the United States in 1960 often urged their American counterparts to show the same level of aggression in pursuit of freedom as those engaged in the liberation struggle at home.[44] Indeed, as Fanon Che Wilkins has argued recently, "SNCC's internationalism was far more organically rooted in the organization and the experiences of its members" than historians have usually cared to acknowledge, and it is clear that an active interest in, and engagement with, the wider black world was apparent from the moment of SNCC's founding.[45] In his keynote speech at the Shaw University inaugural meeting, for example, Nashville activist James Lawson told the assembled activists that the sit-ins had enabled students to "speak powerfully to their nation and world." Contrasting the slow pace of racial progress in the United States with the decolonization of the mother continent, he declared, "All of Africa will be free before the American Negro attains first-class citizenship."[46] Another featured speaker at Raleigh was Alphonse Okuka, a Kenyan studying at Antioch College, whose presentation focused on the "radical implications of the 'African struggle.'"[47]

Reaffirming SNCC's early interest in developments in Africa, members of the Nonviolent Action Group (NAG), its Howard University affiliate, participated in a picket of the South African embassy in Washington, D.C., on December 9, 1962. A spokesperson explained, "Just as we are concerned with segregation in our country, we are also concerned with inhumanity wherever it appears in the world."[48] This long-standing interest in Africa was illustrated further by John Lewis's speech at the August 1963 March on Washington. In criticizing the proposed civil rights bill's failure to "help thousands of black citizens who want to vote," he declared, "'One man, one vote' is the African cry. It is ours, too. (It must be ours)."[49] On December 12, 1963, in a message congratulating Jomo Kenyatta on his country's independence, John Lewis and James Forman described the Kenyan liberation struggle as "an inspiration for all freedom struggles."[50] Nine days later SNCC activists had a meeting in Atlanta with Kenyan Home Affairs minister Oginga Odinga, who was visiting the city on a State Department–organized nationwide tour following his acceptance of Kenya's seat at the United Nations. This took place at the Peachtree Manor, one of the city's few desegregated hotels, where they presented the minister with gifts, "sang freedom songs, and chanted 'Uhuru.'" Afterward, two of the group were refused service when attempting to get coffee at the segregated Toddle House eatery. As a consequence the entire SNCC delegation staged a sit-in, which resulted in seventeen arrests. Condemning U.S. race relations as "very pitiful," Odinga observed that America "practices segregation—which is what we are fighting in Africa."[51]

SNCC's early interest in Africa reached its peak in September 1964, when a delegation of eleven activists (including John Lewis, James Forman, Bob Moses, Julian Bond, and Fannie Lou Hamer) visited Guinea. As well as providing an opportunity for some much-needed relaxation in the aftermath of Freedom Summer, the experience of observing a society in which black people held power proved a thoroughly inspiring one. As Fannie Lou Hamer explained, "I saw black men flying the airplanes, driving buses, sitting behind big desks in the bank and just doing everything that I was used to seeing white people do."[52] While the rest of the delegation returned home on October 4, John Lewis and Donald Harris stayed on to visit Liberia, Ghana, Zambia, Kenya, Ethiopia, and Egypt, where they met with African statesmen and student leaders and African American expatriates. They also had a chance encounter in Nairobi with Malcolm X.[53] According to historian Fanon Che Wilkins, the Africa trip exposed SNCC's leaders to "a larger world infused with new possibility and hope, thus solidifying Africa's symbolic and political importance to struggles for freedom in the United States." It also provided "international validation for the rising militancy that was challenging civil rights hegemony in the United States."[54]

Reflecting on the Africa trip in remarks to a SNCC staff meeting in February 1965, Lewis avowed that he was "convinced more than ever before that the social, economic, and political destiny of the black people of America is inseparable from that of our black brothers of Africa." He continued, "It matters not whether it is in Angola, Mozambique, Southwest Africa, or Mississippi, Alabama, Georgia and Harlem, USA. The Struggle is one [and] the same. . . . It is a struggle against a vicious and evil system that is controlled and kept in order for and by a few white men throughout the world." In his credo, black people around the world had a shared goal: "The cry in the dependent countries of Africa is still One Man One Vote. It is a cry for Freedom, Liberation, and Independence. It is a cry of People to have some control over their political destiny. The cry of SNCC is essentially the same, for it is a cry to liberate the oppressed and politically denied black people of this country." Lewis evinced a palpable excitement at the international dimension of the freedom struggle. "We are caught up," he proclaimed, "with a sense of destiny with the vast majority of colored people all over the world who are becoming conscious of their power and the role they must play in the world."[55]

Lewis's analysis of the global interconnections and shared interests of the black freedom struggle led him in some radical directions. This was particularly striking in view of the widely held perception of him as the keeper of the flame of integration and interracialism within SNCC in an era of rising Black Power. According to Lewis, SNCC's mission was to create "pockets of power and influence" that would enable black people in rural areas, slums, and ghettos to effect real change. Lewis also contended that in order to liberate the black masses "the civil rights movement must be black-controlled, dominated, and led."[56] While acknowledging that "there are many white people in this country who are victims of the evils of the economic and political system," he asserted that "this country is a racist country. The majority of the population is white and most whites still hold to the master-slave mentality." The SNCC leader had some harsh words too for white liberals. He accused them of failing to understand that black people did not simply wish to "'fit in' to white society, exactly as it is," but rather sought a more fundamental reshaping of the nation's political and economic system and wider society and culture. With the recent experiences of Atlantic City still all too raw, Lewis was blunt in predicting that liberals would "sell us down the river for the hundredth time" in order to preserve their own "material comforts and congenial relations with the establishment."[57] Heralding the change in SNCC rhetoric and strategy over the next two years, these comments vindicate the notion that developments in the second half of 1964—the Mississippi summer project, the MFDP challenge at Atlantic City, and the trip to Africa—constituted the critical turning point in the organization's evolution.

Conclusion

From its origins in the sit-in movement, SNCC had conceived of the black freedom movement as part of a broader, global struggle for racial justice and equality. During its early years, a commitment to the wider decolonization struggle operated alongside the prominent use of Cold War patriotism as a rhetorical tool. Using the emergence of newly independent black nations in Africa primarily as inspiration for its own domestic struggle against institutionalized white supremacy, SNCC argued that progress toward racial justice at home would strengthen America's international fight against the expansion of Communist influence and power, and it invoked the language of Americanism when demanding civil rights reforms. By the mid-1960s, however, this approach had broken down. Radicalized and increasingly disillusioned as a result of their experiences of trying to effect meaningful change in the American South, disturbed by what appeared to be an increasingly unnecessary, unjustified, and brutal military intervention in Vietnam, and influenced by the growing groundswell of Pan-African and Black Power ideology, SNCC activists came to embrace a more militant internationalism that emphasized global solidarity among non-white peoples and condemned U.S. foreign policy as racist, expansionist, and imperialistic.

In the final analysis, the changes in SNCC's approach to international affairs forms part of the wider story of its radicalization and decline.[58] The organization's jettisoning of Cold War patriotism, a rhetorical device that combined powerful moral suasion with steely pragmatism, did not occur in isolation. By the mid-1960s SNCC's commitment to nonviolence and interracialism had broken down, its leaders increasingly used language that was both militant and decidedly anti-American, and almost everyone connected with the organization roundly denounced liberal politicians and liberalism. While these developments are understandable, there is little doubt that they damaged SNCC's ability to attract wider public and political support, decimated its fund-raising capabilities, and left the organization vulnerable to attack from both external critics and rivals within the civil rights movement.

Notes

1. "Some New Red Herring," *New York Times*, April 20, 1960, 38.

2. See, for example, Jack L. Walker, "Sit-Ins in Atlanta: A Study in the Negro Revolt," in *Atlanta Georgia, 1960–1961: Sit Ins and Student Activism*, ed. David J. Garrow (Brooklyn: Carlson, 1989), 67; and Claude Sitton, "Sit-In Campaigns Spread in a Year," *New York Times*, January 29, 1961, 64.

3. See Anthony Lewis, "President Advises South to Set Up Biracial Talks," *New York Times*, March 17, 1960, 37; "Governor Hails Southern Sit-Ins," *New York Times*, April 13, 1960, 32; and "Kennedy Salutes Negroes' Sit-Ins," *New York Times*, June 25, 1960, 13. It is telling that Kennedy made his remarks before an audience of African ambassadors, at a luncheon to discuss development and economic aid, where he explained further that economic and other assistance would not be enough unless America solved its own racial problems.

4. Roy Wilkins, "The Meaning of the Sit-Ins," address at City Club Forum of Cleveland, April, 16, 1960, in *In Search of Democracy: The NAACP Writings of James Weldon Johnson, Walter White, and Roy Wilkins (1920–1977)*, ed. Sondra Kathryn Wilson (Oxford University Press, 1999), 405–6.

5. Marisa Chappell, Jenny Hutchinson and Brian Ward, "'Dress modestly, neatly . . . as if you were going to church:' Respectability, Class and Gender in the Montgomery Bus Boycott and the Early Civil Rights Movement," in *Gender in the Civil Rights Movement*, ed. Peter J. Ling and Sharon Monteith (New York: Garland, 1999), 70. See also Michael Kazin and Joseph A. McCartin, introduction, in *Americanism: New Perspectives on the History of an Ideal*, ed. Kazin and McCartin (Chapel Hill: University of North Carolina Press, 2006); and Simon Hall, "Marching on Washington: The Civil Rights and Anti-War Movements of the 1960s," in *The Street as Stage: Public Demonstrations and Protest Marches since the Nineteenth Century*, ed. Matthias Reiss (Oxford: Oxford University Press, 2007).

6. There is an extensive and rich literature on this subject. See, for example, Robert Korstad and Nelson Lichtenstein, "Opportunities Found and Lost: Labor, Radicals and the Early Civil Rights Movement," *Journal of American History* 75 (1988): 786–811; Mary Dudziak, *Cold War Civil Rights: Race and the Image of American Democracy* (Princeton, N.J.: Princeton University Press, 2002); Gerald Horne, *Black and Red: W.E.B. Du Bois and the Afro-American Response to the Cold War, 1944–1963* (Albany: State University of New York Press, 1986); Azza Salama Layton, *International Politics and the*

Civil Rights Movement in America, 1941–1960 (Cambridge: Cambridge University Press, 2000); George Lewis, *The White South and the Red Menace: Segregationists, Anticommunism, and Massive Resistance, 1945–1965* (Gainesville: University Press of Florida, 2004); Penny M. Von Eschen, *Race against Empire: Black Americans and Anticolonialism, 1937–1957* (Ithaca: Cornell University Press, 1997); Cheryl Lynn Greenberg, ed., *A Circle of Trust: Remembering SNCC* (New Brunswick, N.J.: Rutgers University Press, 1998), 3.

7. "Statement and Testimony of Thurgood Marshall before President Truman's Committee on Civil Rights, 1947," in *President Truman's Committee on Civil Rights*, ed. William E. Juhnke (Frederick, Md.: University Publications of America Microfilm edition, 1984), 97–98, 100–101.

8. Martin Luther King Jr., Speech at Montgomery Improvement Association mass meeting, Holt Street Baptist Church, December 5, 1955, available at http://www.mlkonline.net/mia.html, accessed December 18, 2009.

9. Roy Wilkins, "The Clock Will Not Be Turned Back," speech before the Commonwealth Club of California, San Francisco, November 1, 1957, reprinted in *American Heritage Book of Great American Speeches for Young People*, ed. Suzanne McIntire (New York: John Wiley, 2001).

10. William H. Chafe, *Civilities and Civil Rights: Greensboro, North Carolina, and the Black Struggle for Freedom* (Oxford: Oxford University Press, 1980), 85.

11. Claude Sitton, "Negro Sitdowns Stir Fear of Wider Unrest in South," *New York Times*, February 15, 1960, in Clayborne Carson, ed., *Reporting Civil Rights: Part One: American Journalism 1941–1963* (New York: Library of America, 2003), 437–38. See also Claude Sitton, "1,000 Negroes Join March in Alabama," *New York Times*, March 2, 1960, 1, 29.

12. Atlanta Committee on Appeal for Human Rights, "An Appeal for Human Rights," in *The Eyes on the Prize Civil Rights Reader: Documents, Speeches, and Firsthand Accounts from the Black Freedom Struggle, 1954–1990*, ed. Clayborne Carson et al. (New York: Penguin, 1991), 117.

13. http://www.crmvet.org/docs/aa4hr.htm, accessed December 13, 2009. See also Julian Bond and Melvin A. McCaw, "Special Report: Atlanta Story," *The Student Voice*, June 1960, 4, in *The Student Voice, 1960–1965: The Periodical of the Student Nonviolent Coordinating Committee*, ed. Clayborne Carson (Westport, Conn.: Meckler, 1990), 4. A statement by the Lane College Student Movement of Jackson, Tennessee, reproduced in the SNCC journal ("An Appeal for Dignity," November 1960), used similar language: "We want to state clearly and unequivocally that we cannot tolerate in a nation professing democracy and among people professing Christianity, the discriminatory conditions under which the Negro is living today in Jackson, Tennessee. . . . [W]e intend to do everything in our power that is legal and nonviolent to secure full citizenship rights and to become as every other American, a full citizen with all the ensuing rights, obligations, and privileges." Carson, *The Student Voice*, 23.

14. For histories of SNCC see, in particular, Clayborne Carson, *In Struggle: SNCC and the Black Awakening of the 1960s* (Cambridge: Harvard University Press, 1981); and Wesley C. Hogan, *Many Minds, One Heart: SNCC's Dream for a New America* (Chapel Hill: University of North Carolina Press, 2007).

15. Draft letter to candidates for office, Student Nonviolent Coordinating Committee Papers [hereafter SNCC Papers], 1959–1972, Subgroup A, Series I, reel 1, Library of Congress, Washington, D.C.

16. Cleveland Sellers with Robert Terrell, *The River of No Return: The Autobiography of a Black Militant and the Life and Death of SNCC* (Jackson: University Press of Mississippi, 1990), 38–40.

17. Howard Zinn, *SNCC: The New Abolitionists* (Boston: Beacon Press, 1964), 36.

18. "Statement submitted by the Student Nonviolent Coordinating Committee to the Platform Committee of the National Democratic Convention, Thursday Morning, July 7, 1960, Los Angeles," 1–2, in Bayard Rustin Papers (microfilm), reel 1, Library of Congress, Washington D.C.

19. "Truman Repeats Charge on Sit-Ins," *New York Times*, June 13, 1960, 20; Zinn, *SNCC*, 37; and "Statement submitted by the Student Nonviolent Coordinating Committee to the Platform Committee of the National Democratic Convention," 3.

20. "Statement submitted by the Student Nonviolent Coordinating Committee to the Platform Committee of the National Democratic Convention," 8.

21. "Across the Editor's Desk," March 1961, in Carson, *The Student Voice*, 35

22. "SNCC Wires President Kennedy," April and May 1961, ibid., 43.

23. "Students Expelled in Pine Bluff after Sit-ins," February 11, 1963, Charles McDew telegrams to President Kennedy, February 12, 1963, SNCC Papers, Subgroup A, Series VII, reel 13.

24. "Statement of Dewey Greene, 23, of Greenwood, Mississippi to the Minnesota state convention of the Democratic Farmer-Labor Party, June 28, 1964, St. Paul," SNCC Papers, Subgroup A, Atlanta Office, 1959–1972, Series XVI, Mississippi Freedom Democratic Party, 1960–1967–Records of the Convention Challenge, 1960–1967, "Public Statements, Apr 4–Aug 22, 1964," reel 41.

25. SNCC, "Statement on Vietnam War," January 6, 1966, in *The New Left: A Documentary History*, ed. Massimo Teodori (London: Cape, 1970), 251–52.

26. "Speech by John Lewis, Memorial Dinner of Council for American-Soviet Friendship," January 26, 1966, SNCC Papers, Subgroup A: Atlanta Office, 1959–1972, Series I: Chairmen's Files, 1960–1969, John Lewis, 1963–1966, Speeches and Public Statements, August 28, 1963–January 26, 1966, reel 2, Library of Congress.

27. "SNCC Statement on the Spring Mobilization to End the War in Vietnam," April 14, 1967, SNCC Papers, Subgroup B: New York Office, 1960–1969, Series II: International Affairs Commission, 1964–1969, Vietnam, April 15–October 22, 1967, reel 52, Library of Congress.

28. Tom Wells, *The War Within: America's Battle over Vietnam* (Berkeley: University of California Press, 1994), 204; statement by John Wilson, Bratislava, Czechoslovakia, n.d. (September 1968), 1–2, SNCC Papers, Subgroup A: Atlanta Office, 1959–1972, Series VII: Research Department, 1959–1969, Vietnam, 1965–July 12, 1968, reel 23. Wilson also argued that "the goals of our struggles are the same and we have the same enemy" (4).

29. *SNCC Newsletter* 1 (June–July 1967): 7, Wisconsin State Historical Society, Madison.

30. Carson, *In Struggle*, 267–69. See also "The Middle-East Crisis," August 15, 1967, 1, SNCC Papers, Subgroup A, Series VII, reel 13.

31. See Carson, *In Struggle*, 273–77.

32. Stokely Carmichael with Ekwueme Michael Thelwell, *Ready for Revolution: The Life and Struggles of Stokely Carmichael [Kwame Ture]* (New York: Scribner, 2003), 589.

33. H. Rap Brown and James Forman to Oliver Tambo, August 27, 1967, and "A Message from Chairman H. Rap Brown," August 28, 1967, 2, SNCC Papers, Subgroup A, Series VII, reel 14.

34. Simon Hall, *American Patriotism, American Protest: Social Movements since the Sixties* (Pennsylvania: University of Pennsylvania Press, 2010), 15.

35. SNCC press release, August 18, 1967, and "A Message from Chairman H. Rap Brown," August 28, 1967, SNCC Papers, Subgroup A, Series VII, reel 14.

36. SNCC press release, August 18, 1967, SNCC Papers, Subgroup A, Series VII, 3 (3), reel 14.

37. Doug McAdam, *Freedom Summer* (New York: Oxford University Press, 1988), 31.

38. For the MFDP see Kay Mills, *This Little Light of Mine: The Life of Fannie Lou Hamer* (New York: Plume Books, 1994); and John Dittmer, *Local People: The Struggle for Civil Rights in Mississippi* (Urbana: University of Illinois Press, 1994).

39. Comments made by Zoharah Simmons at "The Ongoing Radicalization of SNCC and the Movement," a panel session at "'We Who Believe in Freedom Cannot Rest': Miss Ella J. Baker and the Birth of SNCC," National Conference, April 13–16, 2000, Shaw University, Raleigh, North Carolina (transcript in author's possession).

40. See Carson, *In Struggle*, 41–42; James Forman, *The Making of Black Revolutionaries* (Washington, D.C.: Open Hand Publishing, 1985), 395–96 (my emphasis).

41. On the radicalization of the grass roots see Carson, *In Struggle*, esp. 111–29; Simon Hall, *Peace and Freedom: The Civil Rights and Antiwar Movements in the 1960s* (Philadelphia: University of Pennsylvania Press, 2004), 13–22; and McAdam, *Freedom Summer*. See also Anne Braden, "The SNCC Trends: Challenge to White America," *Southern Patriot*, May 1966, 2.

42. SNCC Staff Meeting Minutes, November 24–29, 1965, 22–23, copy in possession of author.

43. Teodori, *The New Left*, 251–52.

44. Carson, *In Struggle*, 16.

45. Fanon Che Wilkins, "The Making of Black Internationalists: SNCC and Africa before the Launching of Black Power, 1960–1965," *Journal of African American History* 92 (Autumn 2007): 469.

46. In Peter Levy, *Let Freedom Ring: A Documentary History of the Modern Civil Rights Movement* (New York: Praeger, 1992), 72, 73.

47. F. C. Wilkins, "The Making of Black Internationalists," 468.

48. "NAG to Picket South African Embassy December 9 in Protest against Policy of Apartheid," December 5, 1962, SNCC Papers, Subgroup A, Series VII, reel 13, and http://www.historicalvoices.org/pbuilder/pbfiles/Project39/Scheme361/african_activist_archive-a0b4l1-a_12419.pdf, accessed June 15, 2010.

49. John Lewis, "A Serious Revolution," speech at the August 1963 March on Washington for Jobs and Freedom, reprinted in Teodori, *The New Left*, 100. Events in Africa also influenced the 1963 "Freedom Vote" in Mississippi, in this case through one of SNCC's white allies. During one of a series of discussions with civil rights leaders across the state, Allard Lowenstein suggested a new tactic for the Mississippi campaign. Recalling his involvement in black South Africa as a political observer and a staff member for Senator Hubert Humphrey in the late 1950s, Lowenstein proposed that Mississippi blacks cast protest ballots on election day. "I remember that I had been in South Africa on election day," he told journalist Milton Viorst. "The African National Congress had called a day of mourning so that blacks would demonstrate their discontent. So I thought, in South Africa, where blacks can't vote, they have a day of mourning but in Mississippi they are supposed to be able to vote. So why not have a day of voting?" See Joseph Sinsheimer, "The Freedom Vote of 1963: New Strategies of Racial Protest in Mississippi," *Journal of Southern History* 55 (May 1989): 223.

50. "Kenya Congratulated," December 16, 1963, in Carson, *The Student* Voice, 93.

51. "Christmas in Jail," December 23, 1963, and "Workers Spend Xmas in Jail," December 30, 1963, in Carson, *The Student Voice*, 95–96, 97, 99.

52. Carson, *In Struggle*, 134 (quote); F. C. Wilkins, "The Making of Black Internationalists," 479–80.

53. Carson, *In Struggle*, 135.

54. F. C. Wilkins, "The Making of Black Internationalists," 483.

55. "Statement by John Lewis, Chairman, staff meeting, February 1965," 1–2, 7, SNCC Papers, Subgroup A, Series VII, reel 2.

56. Ibid., 2.

57. Ibid., 3–4, 2, 6.

58. For SNCC's decline see Carson, *In Struggle*, especially part 3, and Emily Stoper, "The Student Non-violent Coordinating Committee and the Rise and Fall of a Redemptive Organization," in *Social Movements of the Sixties and Seventies*, ed. Jo Freeman (New York: Longman, 1983), chapter 19. For funding see Herbert H. Haines, "Black Radicalization and the Funding of Civil Rights: 1957–1970," *Social Problems* 32 (October 1984): 31–43.

9

From Greensboro to Notting Hill

The Sit-Ins in England

STEPHEN TUCK

On the evening of April 10, 1965, three black men entered the Bay House bar in Bristol, England, and ordered a round of beer. Exactly what happened next is contested. According to the landlord, the group "adopted an offensive attitude from the start . . . [there was] no 'please,' none of the usual courtesies." Nevertheless, he insisted that the barman serve them, "to show consideration to the coloured community." But when the group threatened demonstrations against the pub, the landlord explained later, he had them escorted outside, where they attracted a crowd. The police arrived, and when the three men refused to move on, they were arrested.[1] The black drinkers told a rather different story. The Bay House bar had a reputation for serving white customers only, so they went for a drink to discover whether there was indeed a color bar, and if so, to challenge it. Responding to their request for a beer, the landlord had snapped, "Get it down, then get out." When they refused to be hurried, he called the police and had them arrested.[2]

The group of three drinkers was led by twenty-seven-year-old Paul Stephenson, the son of a West African father and white British mother. He had been the only black child at his school in London, had served in the Royal Air Force, and had studied at Birmingham University before moving to Bristol to work as a youth officer for the City Council. Stephenson also led Bristol's West Indian Development Council, a group that had organized a nationally publicized and successful boycott of the city's buses two years before.[3] A handsome and charismatic speaker, he encountered abuse and approval in almost equal measure from whites—though the well-meaning praise he received was sometimes patronizing, as when one woman declared that she was on his side and mentioned her enjoyment of the *Black and White Minstrel* television show as proof of her racial tolerance.[4]

Though raised in Britain and challenging racial discrimination in that most British of institutions—a pub—Stephenson and his friends were making use of a distinctively American import, a Student Nonviolent Coordinating Committee (SNCC)-style sit-in. And like so many of its American counterparts, the Bristol drink-in had the triple impact of exposing racist practice, prompting liberal embarrassment about such discrimination, and provoking a successful legal challenge to end it. After being thrown out of the pub, Stephenson told the press he "was now satisfied that there was a colour bar on the premises."[5] Britain's best-known quality daily newspaper, *The Times*, insisted that "the charges in this case concern a very rare occurrence in this city, namely, the imposition of a colour bar on licensed premises."[6] Stephenson was brought to trial, but the case was dismissed, as was the barman by his embarrassed employers.

The story of the SNCC-style Bristol drink-in could be retold in cities from the North to the South of England during the 1960s. In June 1963, "freedom pub-crawlers" were refused a drink at the Black Bull and Old Britannia pubs in the Lancashire town of Preston.[7] The following month, twelve West Indian immigrants sat in at an all-white pub in the Midlands town of Wolverhampton, warning, "We will repeat our protest every weekend until the licensee changes his mind."[8] In February 1965, black reporter John Ross led "Operation Guinness" to test pubs in the Lewisham area of south London. After he was denied service at the Dartmouth Arms, protesters marched outside the pub carrying placards with the message "We deplore the colour-bar."[9] In April 1965 in Smethwick, Birmingham, members of the Co-ordinating Committee against Racial Discrimination amassed some two hundred to three hundred "guinea pigs"—black and white volunteers—to test pubs in one of the most notorious racial hot spots in Britain.[10] That same month, supporters of Leicester University's Anti-Racialist Committee took part in three demonstrations in the whites-only lounge at the Admiral Nelson pub (the issue in the Admiral Nelson, as with many of the pubs that were targeted by drink-ins, was that there was one whites-only room in an otherwise integrated premises). In December the Admiral Nelson withdrew the color bar from its lounge.[11]

Thus the protests that started in Greensboro did not just spread like a brush fire through the Carolinas and across the southern states (and to a much lesser extent, to the northern and western states); they also reached across the Atlantic.[12] Moreover, the outbreak of freedom drink-ins in Britain was but one manifestation of a form of protest that had already become an international phenomenon. In Cape Town, South Africa, in late November 1960, there was a nearly carbon copy rerun of the famous sit-in at the Woolworth's store in Greensboro earlier that year. Eight non-white members of the opposition Liberal Party walked into the first-floor restaurant of South Africa's large department store. The flustered white manager and her assistant refused them service and tried to bar their entry, but to no avail. Brushing past them, the group held a half-hour-long sit-in at three adjoining tables. The protesters were taking a considerable risk, as the maximum sentence for non-whites eating at a table with whites in a public place in South Africa was two years in prison. Like their U.S. counterparts, they pointed out before leaving that they were entitled to buy all other goods in the store but could not eat in the restaurant, or in any other downtown dining establishment for that matter. A week later, accompanied by eighteen white supporters, the same group of eight stood in line at a self-service snack counter in another department store. After waiting for an hour without being served, they staged a sit-in at a tearoom upstairs. More restaurant protests followed across Cape Town. As with the American sit-ins, which were often timed to cause maximum disruption ahead of Easter or Thanksgiving, the South African protests were intended to reduce non-white department store shopping in the run-up to Christmas.[13]

Of course, the Greensboro Four and their SNCC successors were not the first activists to protest by sitting in. In the United States itself, labor organizers, especially those of the United Automobile Workers, had made extensive use of this form of collective action in the 1930s.[14] In view of this, the African American student sit-ins against racial exclusion might be seen as part of the international resumption of a tried-and-true protest tactic. However, the chronology of sit-ins suggests that SNCC's campaign in the American South inspired activists in other countries to engage in the new global phase of this style of protest. Great Britain, for example, had not experienced sit-ins against racial discrimination before the 1960s. While South Africa had a turbulent racial history, including the anti-pass-law demonstrations that culminated in the infamous Sharpeville massacre of March 1960, the Cape Town sit-in was the first time that protesters had defied restaurant apartheid since the pro-apartheid National Party had come to power twelve years before.[15]

As the 1960s progressed, activists around the world increasingly used sit-ins to protest causes other than racial discrimination. In 1965 there were demonstrations, dubbed "le sit-in," against English-speaking-only restaurants in the predominantly French-speaking Canadian city of Quebec.[16] The sit-in became a staple tactic for the global student protests of 1968, too. One CIA report reckoned that twenty countries experienced student sit-in-style demonstrations that year, mostly protesting the Vietnam War and demanding greater civil liberties.[17] By this stage, activists around the world were drawing on the high-profile example of New Left protest in the United States and across Europe rather than that of Greensboro (though of course it was the SNCC sit-ins that had provided a model for this).[18]

Even in 1968, however, the American civil rights movement still provided direct inspiration for sit-in style protests abroad. German student leader Karl-Dietrich Wolff, president of the Socialist Student League, had been on an exchange year at a high school in Michigan during the Greensboro sit-ins. "My political development is unthinkable without that year in the United States," he recalled later.[19] British racial equality campaigner Paul Stephenson was similarly influenced by the American civil rights movement. He had traveled across the South in 1964 at the invitation of students belonging to the National Association for the Advancement of Colored People. Stephenson's organization of the 1963 Bristol bus boycott also attested to his deep admiration for Martin Luther King Jr.'s role in the Montgomery bus boycott of 1955–56 and the more recent anti-segregation protests in Birmingham, Alabama.[20]

It was hardly surprising that the American sit-in protests spilled over into Britain and elsewhere. By the 1960s the United States was a net exporter of all types of popular, intellectual, and social movement culture, from Motown to counterculture to anti-Vietnam protest.[21] American news was world news—and never more so than in the case of the civil rights movement.[22] Moreover, two American groups had a vested interest in telling the civil rights protest story abroad. The State Department vigorously promoted a tale of nonviolent protest and progress as part of its Cold War narrative of democracy providing the best forum for resolution of race problems.[23] Meanwhile, U.S. civil rights activists sought publicity abroad to increase the power of their protest back home and to raise funds.

SNCC was at the forefront of this campaign for international awareness for two reasons. More than any civil rights organization, it was perpetually on the edge of going broke; it also needed, and courted, publicity in order to protect members working on voting rights and other projects in the Deep South.[24] SNCC's communication department regularly sent press releases to foreign newspapers, especially those in Western Europe. Organization activists also traveled to Britain in person to address college societies concerned with racial justice issues.[25] SNCC's international operation paid dividends—literally, with the establishment of a British Friends of SNCC group by 1963.[26] The mainstream press (in addition to the black press) in Britain carried regular, often lengthy reports of SNCC protest and the resulting white supremacist barbarity in the rural South.[27]

Already attuned to the anti-apartheid cause, Britain's student population followed news of SNCC with particular interest. On March 2, 1961, SNCC's communication department issued a lengthy press release celebrating the expressions of "solidarity with and moral support of the Negro and white students now serving jail and chain gang sentences in South Carolina and Virginia" by "one hundred thousand university students of Canada and thousands of others in England, Wales and Northern Ireland." The United Kingdom's National Union of Students sent "strongly worded cables" to the governors of both states condemning the incarceration of civil rights protestors. British student activists also engaged in fund-raising activities to help their SNCC counterparts. One such initiative was a traveling photographic exhibit promoting "the most active civil rights group in the Southern States, training and enrolling Negroes in the most backward area of the 'Black Belt.' The posters and photos dramatically show what this all means in practical terms, and . . . it is hoped that money will be collected towards SNCC work."[28]

As SNCC's protests spilled beyond America's borders, they beat a sure path to Britain across an Atlantic bridge joining two countries with common experiences of racial strife. African Americans and black Britons both faced discrimination in white-majority countries proud of their liberal credos in the midst of a Cold War.[29] Tales of the flare-ups over race in both countries seemed almost interchangeable at times: clashes between African American GIs and the police in Leicester, England, and Detroit, Michigan, during World War II; a decade or so later, drink-fueled fights over white women on weekend nights in overcrowded, economically struggling urban areas.[30] What mattered about these common experiences is that British activists—white and black—identified with the struggles of their American counterparts. The U.K.'s black press described racial exclusion from the better jobs and housing in Britain as Jim Crow–style oppression. Meanwhile, those resistant to racial change looked nervously at transatlantic developments. Conservative Member of Parliament Enoch Powell's notorious anti-immigration "Rivers of Blood" speech, delivered to a Conservative Association meeting in Birmingham on April 20, 1968, famously started with a classical reference to Rome: "I seem to see the River Tiber foaming with much blood." He then invoked the rather more contemporary specter of American urban race riots: "The tragic and intractable phenomenon which we watch with horror on the other side the Atlantic but which there is interwoven with the history of the United States itself, is coming upon us here by our own volition and our own neglect."[31]

This transatlantic bridge on race matters was crossed by a wide variety of people. In particular, the most prominent black British activist, Claudia Jones, was schooled in U.S. protest politics. Born in Trinidad in 1915, she moved with her family to New York at the age of eight. In Harlem during the 1930s she joined protests against the death sentence for the Scottsboro Nine. Subsequently prominent in Communist circles, Jones was a Young Communist League organizer, a National Committee member, chair of the National Women's Commission of the Communist Party (where she propounded the idea of the triple oppression of poor women of color), and editor of the "Negro Affairs" column for the party's paper, the *Daily Worker*. Arrested and imprisoned on four occasions for her party activities, she was eventually deported and found asylum in Britain, as was her right as a citizen of the Commonwealth.[32] In London, Jones founded and edited the main protest newspaper, the *West Indian Gazette and Afro-Asian Caribbean News*, which reported anti-racist struggles across the globe, including those in Britain. From her perch at the *Gazette*, Jones was at the heart of virtually every organized protest initiative for racial equality in the U.K. She publicized black campaigns, lobbied allies in Parliament, and welcomed influential African American visitors from the United States, from leading political figures such as W.E.B. DuBois and Martin Luther King to cultural giants such as Paul Robeson, Eartha Kitt, and Sammy Davis Jr.

If Claudia Jones was forced to cross the Atlantic, many others volunteered to make the trip. Taking advantage of the increasing ease of travel to America by midcentury, a goodly number of white British students went to observe the U.S. civil rights movement firsthand. For some subsequently influential individuals, their experiences in the American South during their student years proved something of a rite of passage. Leading broadcaster Anthony Smith and senior *Guardian* foreign affairs correspondent Jonathan Steele both witnessed direct-action protest and the reaction it provoked.[33]

Perhaps no one better exemplified this combination of student mobility and concern for social justice than Constance Lever, the daughter of a somewhat disillusioned ex-Communist university lecturer in Durham, in the north of England. In 1961, while a second-year sociology student at the London School of Economics (LSE), she went to visit relatives in California and bought an unlimited travel Greyhound bus ticket to visit some of the country. She ended up in Monroe, North Carolina, arriving just as militant activist Robert F. Williams and his supporters were arming themselves with guns to face down their racist opponents. This choice of destination was not quite an accident—Lever had been involved in anti-apartheid activity at the LSE, had read a leaflet about Williams and Monroe at the anti-apartheid office, and had written to ask if she could visit for a few days. But it was mostly a chance visit—she thought Monroe might be a cheap place to stay and was unaware that Williams was an African American. Lever arrived at the climax of dramatically unfolding events with some thirty Freedom Riders picketing the center of town daily. Joining them "seemed the most natural thing in the world to do," she recalled. However, the presence of a teenage white woman in support of the protest touched off a riot that led to her arrest. At her subsequent appearance in court, one white man shouted out, "Bet she sleeps with a nigger."[34]

Lever and four black women went on hunger strike in jail. Her relatives in California and England found out and contacted the press, and after the *Daily Mail* called her in prison the story became front-page news in Britain. Back in Durham, Lever's "upset" mother, Anita, told reporters that her "problem" stemmed from the family's recent three-year stint living in Kampala, Uganda. As a result, Constance "has no conception that a black person is any different from a white [person]." Anita Lever promised "to have a long talk with her" when she returned home.[35] If maternal counsel to disengage from the campaign for racial equality was rendered, it had no effect. When back at the LSE, Lever joined a Marxist group involved in challenging housing discrimination. Taking up an academic career, she would later research ethnic and class tensions in Australia. In 2002, Lever joined a campaign in support of some two hundred asylum seekers at the Woomera Detention Center who were on hunger strike against deportation.[36] Lever's story is but one reminder that many social justice activists were not limited by national boundaries or even continental ones. Skipping from Africa to Europe to the United States and back, and then to Australasia, Lever learned and shared ideas at every turn.

Many in Britain who did not manage to travel to the United States still followed events there closely. Landmark moments of American civil rights protest, from the sit-ins and Freedom Rides in 1960–61 to the Birmingham bombings in 1963 and passage of the Civil Rights Act of 1964, dominated the front pages of the British mainstream press as well as those of black newspapers.[37] The visits of Martin Luther King, Malcolm X, and Stokely Carmichael did much to invigorate black British organizations.[38] Every opportunity was taken to demonstrate solidarity with the civil rights movement. The March on Washington for Jobs and Freedom of August 28, 1963, in particular, sparked demonstrations of support around the world. In London, hundreds turned out for a march on the U.S. embassy, carrying placards that proclaimed "US Negroes, your fight is our fight," "Afro-Asians with you," and "Caribbean unity against Yankee imperialism."[39] As the drink-ins in Bristol and elsewhere illustrated, activists in Britain—black and white—borrowed readily from their American counterparts. In another demonstration of this, Black Power advocate Michael de Freitas changed his name to Michael X.[40] Meanwhile, the emergent struggle for racial equality in the U.K. encountered the opposition of organized racist groups, some of which traced their inspiration to the United States. The first reported meeting of the British Klan, in the upstairs room of a Birmingham pub, was held barely two months after the Bristol drink-in (both events being reported in the same issue of Britain's leading race newsletter).[41]

Thus the story of the sit-ins in Britain accords with recent scholarship that seeks to extend the history of the American civil rights movement beyond its traditional national (or regional) framework—a framework that still holds, however, in much of the literature that focuses specifically on SNCC and the sit-ins.[42] America's influence on race struggles abroad was profound. And yet the story of the sit-ins in Britain also shows the limits of this influence, suggesting that the transnational transfer of protest tactics and ideas was anything but a simple, direct, one-way process.

In the first place, British blacks responded to important influences from countries other than the United States. Indeed, it would be hard to overemphasize just how many examples they looked to other than the American civil rights movement. There is a danger that transnational dimensions of U.S. history can focus on American engagement with the world, rather than the interconnections of many national stories of which America's is but one. For example, South African apartheid occupied far more column inches in the British black and white press than the American civil rights movement. The preeminent black British newspaper of the late 1950s and early 1960s was titled *West Indian Gazette and Afro-Asian Caribbean News*, thereby taking in almost every part of the black diaspora other than the United States.

Moreover, black Britons overwhelmingly came from the Commonwealth—especially Jamaica, India, and Pakistan—rather than from the United States, with Paul Stephenson a case in point. Indeed, the surge in Caribbean immigration to Britain during the 1950s was indirectly linked to the U.S. government's imposition of strict quotas on West Indian immigration following passage of the restrictive McCarran-Walter Immigration and Nationality Act in 1952. Thus black and white Britons were predisposed by kinship to look to Commonwealth nations and colonies seeking independence for warning and for inspiration. These provided plenty of both, even on the specific issue of protests against the color bar in public facilities upon which the initial SNCC sit-ins focused. Britain's black and white press covered protests about public segregation of the races in South Africa, the Nyasaland protectorate (which became the independent republic of Malawi in 1964), the Kenya colony (which gained independence in 1963), and New Zealand in the year of the first sit-ins in the United States (in addition to featuring news of nationalist movements and postcolonial developments).[43] More broadly, solidarity protests frequently focused on countries of origin, and above all on South Africa, rather than on the United States.[44] Significantly, the Bristol bus boycott of 1963 was not organized solely to coincide with the civil rights protests in Birmingham, Alabama. Equally significant in its timing was the cricket match between Gloucestershire (the county where Bristol was located) and the touring West Indies cricket team that was pivotal to the development of Caribbean nationalism and independence. "A mere coincidence that," Stephenson would airily tell reporters.[45]

As well as having overseas influences other than the American civil rights movement, British blacks had a story of their own. Black communities in British port cities, including Bristol, developed as early as the eighteenth century. As in America, black Britons experienced color bars during the early twentieth century and became the targets of a series of race riots after World War I.[46] The cities in which freedom drink-ins occurred were mostly hot spots of racial unrest stemming from clashes over housing and employment.[47] Black Britons had developed their own civic and protest organizations and networks long before the U.S. civil rights movement hit the headlines, too. The League of Coloured Peoples, led by medical doctor and Christian leader Harold Moody, was established in 1931. What such activity meant was that American examples—or any overseas examples for that matter—did not simply initiate protest in Britain. Rather, they ran in parallel with existing British activity and thus would be adapted by British activists for their own ends. When the renowned black sociologist and civil rights activist Ralph Bunche visited Britain in 1937, for example, Moody invited him to tea to compare notes.[48]

Moreover, the British story of race problems and protest was no carbon copy of the American story, so U.S.-style tactics could not automatically cross the Atlantic. For example, and perhaps most obviously, there had been no domestic slavery in Britain, and there was only a very small black community before the 1950s. In Britain, people of color found themselves lumped together as one group in the eyes of the dominant white community. In contrast, Asian, Hispanic, and African American groups were perceived as different in the United States and often asserted their differences. Signifying this Anglo-American dissimilarity, one Indian immigrant to Britain complained to an interviewer in the mid-1960s, "When I was in U.S.A., I was not considered as a coloured man."[49]

Furthermore, the trajectory of race issues in the United Kingdom was different from that in the United States. There were outbreaks of anti-black mob violence in the Notting Hill area of London and in Nottingham in 1958, shortly before the American sit-ins began. Opinion was divided as to whether this was the work of Teddy Boy hooligans or the result of deeper societal tensions, but commentators agreed that race was a growing problem.[50] For Britain's black community, the murder of Antiguan immigrant Kelso Cochrane in 1959 became a symbol of racial injustice. They were scandalized that the police treated this as a mugging gone wrong rather than a race-hate crime and brought no one to trial for it.[51] In an effort to preempt further racial trouble (but also to appease the right-wing Monday Club critics of immigration within its own party ranks), the Conservative government enacted the Commonwealth Immigrants Act of 1962 to restrict the influx of non-white newcomers from former colonies. Non-white Britons therefore experienced a deterioration of racial conditions just when African American students were full of optimism about their capacity to bring about racial change in the South. If they were to borrow tactics from abroad, they had to adapt them to their own situation. Accordingly, the march on the U.S. embassy to express solidarity with the March on Washington, where Martin Luther King espoused his dream of an interracial future, prominently featured a picture of Kelso Cochrane and was marked by scuffles.[52]

It is striking that black British activists borrowed remarkably sparingly from the tactics employed by the southern civil rights movement in the classic phase of the freedom struggle from Montgomery (1955–56) to Selma (1965). The Atlantic was a barrier at least as much as it was a bridge with regard to protest techniques in these years. The handful of freedom drink-ins and a single bus boycott represented the sum total of U.S.-style actions in mainland Britain.[53] Furthermore, the drink-ins did not constitute an immediate response to the American example. Paul Stephenson's visit to the Bay House pub in Bristol occurred some five years after the Greensboro Four sat in at Woolworth's. Meanwhile, the Bristol bus boycott was quite different from the Montgomery version a decade earlier—the British protest was undertaken by West Indian bus workers, the American one by black bus riders.

The reason why the sit-ins did not spread like a brush fire across Britain is that U.K. race relations were analogous to those of northern and western cities in the United States rather than the Jim Crow South. By 1960 there were relatively few examples of the color bar in public accommodations in Britain, and these lacked local government support. Indeed, the reason why there were drink-ins in Britain rather than sit-ins—or pray-ins, wade-ins, and play-ins, for that matter—was that no restaurants, churches, pools, and parks were segregated in Britain (at least not legally, though residential clustering and an unwelcoming atmosphere—even in many churches—meant that such public venues remained white-only in practice).[54] Moreover, only a tiny minority of pubs defended the color line when challenged (again, though, many were white-only in custom). Volunteers on the freedom drink-ins often found only bars rather than color bars—not that this deterred volunteering. During "Operation Guinness," black reporter John Ross was served in eleven Lewisham pubs before being turned away by the Dartmouth Arms.[55]

The main issues pertaining to racial equality in Britain—namely, low-paying jobs and low-quality housing—centered on the principle of fair access rather than equal access to public accommodations. So SNCC's early tactics of sit-ins, freedom rides, and mock elections did not really meet the needs of British campaigners. Nor were the American activists who came to live in Britain interested in translating such tactics for use in the U.K. Many of those deported from America, most notably Claudia Jones, had been schooled in the radical left-leaning tradition of focusing on economic rights rather than civil rights. Consequently, her *Gazette* paid close attention to the class aspects of the American movement (and barely mentioned the sit-ins). Meanwhile, visiting high-profile African American civil rights activists recognized that the black struggle in Britain was not against Jim Crow–style segregation. Significantly the NAACP dispatched its labor secretary, Herbert Hill, rather than executive director Roy Wilkins to visit the U.K. after the 1958 riots (and he drew far less attention from black residents of Notting Hill than did Jamaican premier Norman Manley). Meanwhile, Martin Luther King spoke not of segregation in Britain but of the "festering boils" of black neighborhoods that were deteriorating into U.S.-style ghettos.[56]

White supremacist ideas and organizations also did not find an easy transatlantic crossing to Britain. The *Sunday Times* reported on the first public meeting of the Ku Klux Klan in Britain with a mixture of condescension and relief that the audience of just thirteen men and two women was outnumbered by reporters and TV crews (whose presence testified to the hold of the American Klan on the British imagination). The meeting in the upstairs room of a Birmingham pub broke up after just ten minutes when the landlord asked everyone present, including the media throng, to leave. In the end, the British Klan did little more than burn a few crosses and write some poison-pen letters to prominent immigrants.[57] In any case—as with those seeking racial equality—white British hate groups were not dependent on overseas organizational models, since they had a long tradition of their own. Indeed, some resented the implication that they needed American help. Colin Jordan, a prominent neo-Nazi and notorious anti-immigrant campaigner, told reporters, "We ain't nothing to do with this childish organisation."[58]

Thus when British activists gazed across the Atlantic, they looked to examples other than SNCC in its early days. They showed much greater interest in the activities and rhetoric of Martin Luther King and Malcolm X, the latter attracting far more attention in the black British press than he did in its American counterpart. It was only after the rise of Black Power later in the 1960s that SNCC's leaders and program began to resonate strongly with black Britons. With its ideology of an international struggle, its inner-city location, and its focus on the manifestations of everyday discrimination and racism, black British activists found Black Power immediately applicable to their domestic situation.[59] While continuing to draw inspiration from elsewhere, notably the revolutionary protest politics emerging in many parts of the Commonwealth, they borrowed more directly from Black Power than from any other aspect of the American civil rights struggle. With London becoming a major venue for Black Power conferences, British blacks consciously adopted its tactics, rhetoric, and dress codes and welcomed Black Power visitors. Even as they did so, however, they adapted Black Power for their own purposes. In the U.K., Indian and Pakistani immigrants joined West Indian immigrants as equal partners in Black Power activity, thus broadening the remit of this new phase of protest rather more widely than the American version.

However limited the direct impact of the SNCC sit-ins (and indeed the early southern civil rights movement) on black Britain, it was still far greater than the transfer of ideas in the opposite transatlantic direction. Even if not much copied in Britain, civil rights activism in America received wide coverage in the U.K. press. In contrast, Paul Stephenson's bus boycott merited but a single paragraph on page nineteen of the *Chicago Defender*, and the freedom drink-ins received similarly scant mention in the African American media.[60]

Even so, the transatlantic civil rights relationship was not entirely one way. In the World War II era, the African American press and civil rights organizations began looking abroad with new passion and insight, taking particular interest in the colonial struggle for independence in Asia and Africa.[61] Pan-Africanist advocate George Padmore, for example, reported approvingly in 1948 on the NAACP's attempts to link up with British contacts to render mutual aid in the "common struggle on both sides of the Atlantic."[62] As the civil rights movement gained pace, black American leaders used Britain to burnish their statesmanship credentials back home. In December 1964, Martin Luther King's "three-day barnstorming visit to Britain" (as the *Washington Post* described it) included a historic speech from the pulpit of St. Paul's Cathedral, and Malcolm X addressed Oxford University's prestigious debating union.[63] And while African Americans did not follow black British protest in detail, news of the 1958 riots did cross the Atlantic, even reaching segregationist ears. Deflecting a British reporter's question about racial troubles in Arkansas with one of his own, Governor Orval Faubus inquired, "What about that shindy in Nottingham? We have sympathy for you."[64]

Historians have rightly pointed to the success of African independence movements, beginning with Ghana in 1957, as an inspirational impetus for the American sit-ins. As James Baldwin famously put it, "All of Africa will be free before we can get a lousy cup of coffee." However, many SNCC volunteers knew about the Notting Hill and Nottingham riots of 1958. These mattered to them because the racial situation in Britain was actually more analogous to America's than was that in Africa.

Notting Hill did not prompt Watts, and SNCC's transition to Black Power had domestic roots. But for those in SNCC who cared to look abroad in the heyday of the sit-ins, developments in Britain checked any optimism about the progress of race relations in the world and portended trouble for African Americans living in a nation with a liberal credo. No doubt it would have added to the increasing unease of many volunteers in the early 1960s about the limits of nonviolent direct action protest for integration. Later in the decade, what was happening in the U.K. confirmed the diagnosis of SNCC's Black Power advocates who condemned the international system of exploitation for denying economic equality to blacks. As Stokely Carmichael declared on a visit to Britain in 1967, "It is institutionalized racism that keeps the black people locked in dilapidated slums, tenements, where they must live out their daily lives subject to the prey of exploitative slum landlords, merchants, loan sharks and the restrictive practices of real estate agents." "We're talking now about the U.S." he continued, but "you can apply a little of it to London."[65]

Notes

1. "West Indian in Bar Scene, Court Told," *The Guardian*, April 27, 1965, 5.

2. "West Indian Cleared of Charges," *The Times*, May 1, 1965, 14.

3. For Paul Stephenson and the Bristol bus boycott, see Madge Dresser, *Black and White on the Buses* (Bristol: Bristol Broadsides, 1986).

4. "People's Tribune," *The Guardian*, February 27, 1964, 9. See also *Institute of Race Relations Newsletter*, March 1964, 6, and July 1965, 10, available in Nuffield College Archives, Oxford University.

5. "West Indian Cleared of Charges."

6. "Charges Concern Colour Bar," *The Times*, April 13, 1965, 7.

7. "A sign, 'no coloured people served here' over the bar was justified on the grounds that coloured men disturbed the girls." *Institute of Race Relations Newsletter*, June 1963, 9.

8. "West Indians Stage an American Style Sit-In," *Chicago Defender*, July 9, 1963, 4.

9. John Ross, "Operation Guiness," *Flamingo*, February 1965, 9–11.

10. "Watch to Be Kept on Colour Bar Premises," *The Irish Times*, April 9, 1965, 10.

11. Letter, *Flamingo*, April 1965, 2.

12. On the rapid spread of the sit-ins, see Harvard Sitkoff, *The Struggle for Black Equality, 1954–1992* (New York: Hill and Wang, 1993). On the impact of the sit-ins in the North and West, see Thomas Sugrue, *Sweet Land of Liberty: The Forgotten Struggle*

for *Civil Rights in the North* (New York: Random House, 2008), and Quintard Taylor, *In Search of the Racial Frontier: Blacks in the West, 1528–1990* (New York: Norton, 1999).

13. "Store Colour Bar Defied," *The Observer*, November 20, 1960, 1; "Restaurant Colour Bar Campaign," *The Observer*, November 27,1960, 7

14. On the links between sit-ins in the Depression and the 1960s, see Marc Stears, *Demanding Democracy: American Radicals in Search of a New Politics* (Princeton, N.J.: Princeton University Press, 2010). On sit-in-style protests in northern cities in the 1940s, see August Meier and Elliot Rudwick, *Along the Color Line: Explorations in the Black Experience* (Urbana: University of Illinois Press, 2002). On sit-ins in the late 1950s, see Stephen Tuck, *We Ain't What We Ought to Be: The Black Freedom Struggle from Emancipation to Obama* (Cambridge: Belknap Press, 2010).

15. "Store Colour Bar Defied."

16. "Montreal Demonstrators Use New Tactic 'Le Sit-In,'" *The Times*, June 24, 1965, 10.

17. Martin Klimke, *The Other Alliance: Student Protest in West Germany and the United States in the Global Sixties* (Princeton, N.J.: Princeton University Press, 2009), 1.

18. Simon Hall, *Peace and Freedom: The Civil Rights and Antiwar Movements of the 1960s* (Philadelphia: University of Pennsylvania Press, 2005).

19. Klimke, *The Other Alliance*, 104. Wolff had also been influenced by the kindness of African American GIs during World War II. See Martin Klimke and Maria Hohn, *A Breath of Freedom*, (New York: Palgrave Macmillan, 2010), 111.

20. Dresser, *Black and White on the Buses*.

21. See, for example, Stephen Whitefield, *The Culture of the Cold War*, 2nd ed. (Baltimore: Johns Hopkins University Press, 1996); Hans Krabbendam and Giles Scott-Smith, *The Cultural Cold War in Western Europe, 1945–1960* (New York: Routledge, 2004); Jessica Gienow-Hecht, *Transmission Impossible: American Journalism as Cultural Diplomacy in Post-war Germany, 1945–1955* (Baton Rouge: Louisiana State University Press, 1999).

22. Thomas Borstlemann, *The Cold War and the Color Line: American Race Relations in the Global Arena* (Cambridge: Harvard University Press, 2001); Brenda Gayle Plummer, ed. *Window on Freedom: Race, Civil Rights and Foreign Affairs, 1945–1988* (Chapel Hill: University of North Carolina Press, 2001).

23. Mary Dudziak, *Cold War Civil Rights: Race and the Image of American Democracy* (Princeton, N.J.: Princeton University Press, 2002).

24. Dinky Romilly to Anthony Lester, n.d., Series I, "Fund Raising. Adminstrative Files, 1960–1968," Student Nonviolent Co-ordinating Committee Papers, Schomburg Center for Research in Black Culture [hereafter SCRBC], New York.

25. See term cards 1964–66, Jacari file, John Johnson Collection, Bodleian Library, University of Oxford, England.

26. My thanks to Peter Ling for this information.

27. "Sheriff Arrested in Rights Case," *The Observer*, October 4, 1964, 2; George Sherman, "'Gaol Not Bail' for Sitters-In," *The Observer*, October 23, 1960, 9; "Deep South Showdown," *The Observer*, June 4, 1961, 6; "Governor to Bar Negro Students," *The Guardian*, May 22, 1963, 1; Alistair Cooke, "Supreme Court Ends Racial Lull," *The*

Guardian, May 22, 1963, 11; "New Techniques of Protest," *The Observer*, August 25, 1963, 7.

28. By 1965, however, there was only one official "Friends of SNCC" group abroad, in Canada. Other donations seem to have been made on a more ad hoc basis. See "List of Friends of SNCC," box 8, folder 4, Ella Baker Papers, SCRBC.

29. See, for example, "Coloured People in Britain," *The Guardian*, March 12, 1951, 4.

30. David Reynolds, *Rich Relations: The American Occupation of Britain, 1942–1945* (London: Ramboro, 1995); Michael Sewell, "British Responses to Martin Luther King Jr. and the Civil Rights Movement," in *Martin Luther King and the Making of the Civil Rights Movement*, ed. Anthony J. Badger and Brian Ward (Basingstoke: Palgrave, 1996).

31. Andrew Roth, *Enoch Powell: Tory Tribune* (London: Macdonald, 1970), 357. Meanwhile, Klan leaders were proud of their British connections; see W. J. Weatherby, "A Guest of the Ku-Klux-Klan," *The Guardian*, Dec. 3, 1960, 6.

32. Carole Boyce Davies, *Left of Karl Marx: The Political Life of Black Communist Claudia Jones* (Durham, N.C.: Duke University Press, 2008); Marika Sherwood, *Claudia Jones: A Biography* (London: Lawrence and Wishart, 2000). See also Claudia Jones, "The Caribbean Community in Britain," *Freedomways* 4 (Summer 1964): 341–57.

33. Talks by Anthony Smith and Jonathan Steele in "Movement and Memory: The American Civil Rights Movement in England," organized by the author, May 2005, Oxford University.

34. E-mail from Constance Lever-Tracy to author, January 13, 2011; James Forman, *The Making of Black Revolutionaries* (New York: Macmillan, 1972), 190.

35. "English Girl's Mother Upset," *Lexington Dispatch*, August 28, 1961, 1; Francine Stock, "'Why Can't the Hispanics,' Asks the Lady, 'Knuckle Under Our Culture the Way Other Races Did?'" July 23, 2001, http://www.newstatesman.com, accessed March 2010. See also Robert F. Williams, *Negroes with Guns* (New York: Marzani and Munsell, 1962).

36. Constance Lever-Tracy, "Global Warming and Sociology," *Current Sociology* 56, no. 3 (2008): 445–66, http://www.safecom.org.au/1media-250602.htm, accessed January 2011.

37. See, for example, "Negroes Blown Up at Sunday Classes," *The Guardian*, September 16, 1963, 1.

38. See Sewell, "British Responses to Martin Luther King Jr."

39. *West Indian Gazette*, September 1963, 1. On demonstrations around the world, see Tuck, *We Ain't What We Ought to Be.*

40. John L. Williams, *Michael X: A Life in Black & White* (London: Century, 2008).

41. *Institute of Race Relations Newsletter*, July 1965, 6, 10.

42. On the civil rights movement beyond American borders see Dudziak, *Cold War Civil Rights*; Klimke and Hohn, *A Breath of Freedom*; Tuck, *We Ain't What We Ought to Be*; Susan D. Pennybacker, *From Scottsboro to Munich: Race and Political Culture in 1930s Britain* (Princeton, N.J.: Princeton University Press, 2009), 382; Kevin Gaines, *American Africans in Ghana: Black Expatriates in the Civil Rights Era* (Chapel Hill: University of North Carolina Press, 2006); Glenda E. Gilmore, *Defying Dixie: The Radical Roots of Civil Rights, 1919–50* (New York: Norton, 2008); James H. Meriwether, *Proudly We*

Can Be Called Africans: Black Americans and Africa, 1935–61 (Chapel Hill: University of North Carolina Press, 2002).

43. Geoffrey Moorhouse, "Growth of the Maori: Race Relations in New Zealand," *The Guardian*, March 5, 1960, 4; "Tensions in Nyasaland," *The Guardian*, March 24, 1960, 1; "Colour Bar Goes at Leave Centre," *The Guardian*, March 31, 1960, 2; "They Chose Jail to . . ." *West Indian Gazette*, December 1959, 7; "Freedom, Our Concern," *West Indian Gazette*, September 1960, 1.

44. See, for example, Robert A. Skinner, "The Roots of 'Solidarity': Race, Religion and the Social and Moral Foundations of British Anti-apartheid Activism, 1946–58" (Ph.D. diss., University of Sussex, 2004); Special Issue, *Journal of Southern African Studies* 35, no. 2 (2009); Roger Fieldhouse, *Anti-Apartheid: A History of the Movement in Britain, 1959–1994* (London: Merlin, 2005); Elizabeth May Williams, "'Until South Africa Is Free, We Shall Not Be Free!': Black British Solidarity with the Anti-Apartheid Struggle during the 1980s" (Ph.D. diss., University of London (Birkbeck College), 2008.

45. "People's Tribune," *The Guardian*, February 27, 1964, 9. On cricket's significance in fostering nationalism in Britain's Caribbean colonies, see Hilary McD. Beckles, *The Development of West Indies Cricket: The Age of Nationalism* (Kingston, Jamaica: University of the West Indies Press, 1998).

46. Marcus Collins, "Pride and Prejudice: West Indian Men in Mid-Twentieth Century Britain," *Journal of British Studies* 40 (July 2001): 391–418; Jacqui Jenkinson, *Black 1919: Riots, Racism and Resistance in Imperial Britain* (Liverpool: Liverpool University Press, 2008). On the development of black British thought and protest activity before the American civil rights movement hit the headlines, see Hakim Adi, *West Africans in Britain 1900–1960: Nationalism, Pan-Africanism and Communism* (London: Lawrence and Wishart, 1998). For general histories that show the longer development of black British history, see Peter Fryer, *Staying Power: Black People in Britain since 1504* (London: Pluto, 1984); Winston James, "The Black Experience in Twentieth-Century Britain," in *Oxford History of the British Empire: Black Experience and the Empire*, ed. Philip Morgan and Sean Hawkins (Oxford: Oxford University Press, 2004), 347–86; Immanuel Geiss, *The Pan-African Movement* (London: Methuen, 1974); Bill Schwarz, ed., *West Indian Intellectuals in Britain* (Manchester: Manchester University Press, 2003).

47. See, for example, Joseph Street, "Malcolm X, Smethwick, and the Influence of the African American Freedom Struggle on British Race Relations in the 1960s," *Journal of Black Studies* 38, no. 6 (2008): 932–50.

48. Harold Moody to Ralph Bunche, March 17, 1937, Ralph Bunche Papers, General Correspondence, box 10b, SCRBC. See also David Killingray, "'To Do Something for the Race': Harold Moody and the League of Coloured Peoples," in Schwarz, *West Indian Intellectuals in Britain*, 51–68

49. W. W. Daniel, *Racial Discrimination in England* (Harmondsworth, Middlesex: Penguin, 1968), 48.

50. Edward Pilkington, *Beyond the Mother Country: West Indians and the Notting Hill White Riots* (London: I. B. Tauris, 1988).

51. "From a Chapter of W.I.–U.K. History," *West Indian Gazette*, October 1959, 7.

52. *West Indian Gazette*, September 1963, 1.

53. In Northern Ireland, the Civil Rights Association, which campaigned to improve civil rights for the Catholic minority in Ulster, was more directly influenced by the American civil rights movement.

54. On the variety of sit-in-style protest in the South, see Tuck, *We Ain't What We Ought to Be*.

55. "Watch to Be Kept on Colour Bar Premises."

56. "Dr King's Racial Warning to Britain," *The Times*, December 7, 1964, 6.

57. "Ku Klux Klan," *Flamingo*, September 1961, 41.

58. *Institute of Race Relations Newsletter*, July 1965, 5–6.

59. R.E.R. Bunce and Paul Field, "Obi B. Egbuna, C.L.R. James and the Birth of Black Power in Britain: Black Radicalism in Britain 1967–72," *Twentieth Century British History*, http://tcbh.oxfordjournals.org/content/early/2010/11/09/tcbh.hwq047.full, accessed January 10, 2011; Rosie Wild, "Black Was the Colour of Our Fight: Black Power in Britain, 1955–1976" (Ph.D. diss., University of Sheffield, 2008).

60. "Breakthrough in Britain," *Chicago Defender*, August 31, 1963, 19.

61. Penny Von Eschen, *Race against Empire: Black Americans and Anticolonialism, 1937–1957* (Ithaca: Cornell University Press, 1997).

62. George Padmore, "World Views: Britishers Return," *Chicago Defender*, May 22, 1948, 15.

63. "Around the World," *Washington Post*, December 8, 1964, A17.

64. Fenner Brockway, "Racial Discrimination," *Labour Monthly*, February 1957, 61–64; Pilkington, *Beyond the Mother Country*, 135.

65. Stokely Carmichael and Mumia Abu-Jabal, *Stokely Speaks: From Black Power to Pan-Africanism* (Chicago: Chicago Review Press, 2007), 78–91.

Epilogue

Still Running for Freedom

Barack Obama and the Legacy of the Civil Rights Movement

STEVEN F. LAWSON

In a memorable speech delivered before the Lincoln Memorial in Washington, D.C., in 1957, Martin Luther King Jr. urged Congress to enact legislation to restore voting rights to disfranchised African Americans in the states of the South. Repeatedly declaring "Give us the ballot," he anticipated that blacks would use it to obtain full rights as citizens, ensure justice, and guarantee representative government.[1] Three years later, the sit-ins began in Greensboro and spread like wild vines of southern kudzu. These lunch-counter demonstrations, as the longtime activist Ella Baker memorably noted, were concerned with "something much bigger than a hamburger or even a giant-sized Coke."[2] Instead, they sparked the movement against three hundred years of white supremacy with its requirements of black deference and subservience. Nothing less than achieving first-class citizenship and human dignity would satisfy demands for racial equality. Born as a direct-action group to challenge segregation, the Student Nonviolent Coordinating Committee (SNCC) increasingly realized in its second year of operation that the limited number of black voters in the South denied African Americans the political power required for the achievement of civil rights goals.[3] Accordingly, voter registration became the main focus of its activism from 1962 onward. With a powerful civil rights movement in full flow, passage of the Voting Rights Act of 1965 appeared to herald a new day in southern and national politics by opening the way for vastly enhanced black political mobilization in pursuit of racial equality.

The election of Barack Obama as president in 2008 showed, in the words of former Nashville student sit-in leader and SNCC chair John Lewis, now a Democratic congressman for Georgia, "we have come such a distance in such a short time." Obama himself recognized that his political rise owed much to the legacy of the civil rights revolution for which Lewis and so many others had struggled so resolutely. In 2005, speaking at the Georgia congressman's sixty-fifth birthday celebration, Obama, then the Democratic senator for Illinois, remarked, "I'm here because people like John Lewis believed. . . . Feared nothing and risked everything for those beliefs." In further testimony to this debt, the new president signed a commemorative photograph for Lewis at the post-inauguration luncheon, "Because of you, John. Barack Obama."[4]

This essay explores the political legacy of the civil rights movement that helped put Obama in the White House, considers the extent and limitations of the changes that it wrought, and assesses the challenges that Obama faced in carrying it forward.

Having obtained ballot rights, African Americans in both the South and the rest of the nation turned their sights toward the election of blacks to advance their cause in public office. In the remaining years of the twentieth century the number of elected black officeholders nation-wide consequently skyrocketed from less than two hundred in 1965 to more than nine thousand in 2002. The majority of these were located in the South, with the most impressive gains in Georgia, Louisiana, Mississippi, South Carolina, and Texas. Mississippi, which had the lowest number of blacks registered to vote in 1965, had more black elected of-ficeholders (897) than any other state in the nation. At the national level there was a steady expansion of black legislators in the U.S. House of Representatives, with the Congressional Black Caucus counting forty-three members in 2009. Thanks to Democratic control of the 110th (2007–9) and 111th Congresses (2009–11), veteran black lawmakers such as Charles Rangel of New York City, John Conyers of Detroit, and Bennie Thompson of Jackson, Mississippi, held the chairmanships of important House committees. In 2008 the combination of black and white ballots achieved what was inconceivable a generation earlier—the election of African American Barack Obama as president of the United States.[5]

The racial transformation of southern and national politics is evidenced in another way. In 2002 the number of black women officeholders climbed to 3,400, triple the number twenty years earlier. In 2008, eleven black women served in Congress. This trend reflected the growing prominence of women in the electoral process both as voters and candidates. The civil rights movement had empowered black women, who played a critical if often unsung role in the freedom struggle. While men held top leadership positions, women both initiated and provided grassroots support for the protests that transformed the South and the nation. Furthermore, the movement inspired pride in women, thereby encouraging their enhanced political participation that subsequently carried over into the electoral arena.[6]

Black public officials have some notable accomplishments to their name. Their candidacies stimulated increased black political mobilization, and their election provided significant African American access to city halls and county courthouses, where most black officials hold power. They also succeeded in opening up jobs and allocating government contracts to their black constituents, improving the quality of municipal services and reducing racist rhetoric and violence in the process. Reaping tangible and symbolic gains, they helped tear down the psychological and physical barriers that held back African American progress. A retired worker in Tuskegee, Alabama, clearly recognized the difference they made: "Everything's better. In the old days, before black officials ran the county, most black people steered clear of the white enclaves. They used to arrest you over there if you went through, but not any more."[7]

It is important to understand, however, how much African Americans hoped to gain from the right to vote. Like other groups seeking the suffrage before them, most notably women, blacks overestimated the power of the ballot to solve a host of deeply entrenched economic and social problems. With southerners having invested so much time, energy, and ingenuity to keep them away from the ballot boxes, it was not surprising that African Americans prized the right to vote as a principal agency for achieving freedom. James Bevel, one of Martin Luther King's top lieutenants, expressed this belief in very concrete terms during the March 1965 protests in Selma, Alabama, that paved the way for passage of the Voting Rights Act a few months later. Referring to the obstructionist sheriff who battled the demonstrators, he predicted, "If we get out and work [for voting rights], Jim Clark will be picking cotton with my father in about two years." Clark was indeed voted out of office once blacks got the ballot. However, the ballot failed to deliver the more ambitious hopes that King and his followers had invested in it.[8]

Despite impressive successes, blacks remain underrepresented in elective government positions relative to their share of the population. Consisting of around 11 percent of voting-age Americans, they comprised less than 2 percent of the total number of elected officeholders in 2009, when only one African American sat in the U.S. Senate and two served as state governors.[9]

The liberationist effects of the ballot have generally proved inadequate in freeing blacks from the economic distress that they disproportionately endure. The 2000 Census Report showed that the median income for blacks was $29,470, compared with $46,305 for whites. At this time 22.7 percent of African Americans lived in poverty, nearly double the national rate (11.7 percent) and almost three times the rate for non-Hispanic whites (7.8 percent). Significantly. the region with the highest concentration of poverty was the South, where more than half the nation's African American population still lived. Other statistics on racial disparity in wealth were no better. Only 45 percent of black families were homeowners, compared to 74 percent of white families. The continued presence of neighborhood residential segregation throughout the nation had also depressed the value of black homes. The 2000 Census data showed that the median net worth of white homes was $74,900, compared with $7,500 for black households, or roughly ten times less for African Americans. Without doubt the subprime crisis of 2007–8 aggravated the problem because of very heavy rates of house repossession in lower-income communities, notably heavily black inner-city areas where many homeowners could not keep up mortgage payments.

African Americans also lagged behind educationally. In 1999 almost twice as many whites (28 percent) had received a bachelor's degree than had blacks (15 percent). Among blacks, more women than men had earned at least a bachelor's degree—16 percent as opposed to 14 percent. For whites, this was reversed—more men (31 percent) possessed at least a bachelor's degree than women (25 percent).

Prison statistics reveal a tragic reality experienced by black male youth and young adults. African Americans have a six times greater chance of going to jail during their lifetime than whites and can expect to serve longer sentences for the same offenses. More than 28 percent of African American men can expect to be incarcerated at some juncture in their lifetime, while white males have only a 4 percent chance of imprisonment. In 1996, African Americans represented 30 percent of all convicted federal offenders despite the fact that they made up only 13 percent of the population. Between 1985 and 1995 the percentage of African Americans under correctional supervision increased 81 percent.[10] These figures have serious implications for black voting rights, especially those of African American men, for many states have laws barring ex-felons from suffrage. In effect, felon disfranchisement and measures for uniform voter identification cards have become the modern-day equivalent of the poll tax and other Jim Crow–era barriers to voting.

It is also evident that black politicians have fallen short of fulfilling the needs of their black constituents. Being a minority in most units of local government in the South, elected black officeholders have needed the support of white colleagues to deliver programmatic benefits. In places where they form a majority, mainly rural Black Belt areas, they lacked the fiscal and economic resources to better significantly the material conditions of their largely impoverished constituents. Even in the South's major cities, such as Atlanta, Birmingham, and New Orleans, where blacks have won election as mayor, economic power remained largely in white hands. "Blacks have the ballot box," an Atlanta editor admitted, "and whites have the money."[11] Moreover, the corruption of black officeholders in New Orleans, Birmingham, Baltimore, Detroit, and Jackson, Mississippi, indicated that some African American politicians have done no more than their white counterparts to transform the political system in pursuit of the ideal of full racial equality.

Meanwhile, African American capacity to elect candidates in "majority-minority" districts—or what historian J. Morgan Kousser more correctly labels "opportunity districts"—has probably reached its limit.[12] Even if the U.S. Supreme Court had not limited the possibilities for creating such districts, which it has done since the early 1990s, there are relatively few additional opportunity districts that could be drawn.[13] Given the political demography of the United States in which African Americans are a declining proportion of the population, the possibilities for the establishment of a substantial number of new congressional districts that favor the election of black candidates are limited. Though there may be further chances for expansion at the state and local levels, these too are restricted. Most of what can be done to create majority-minority districts has already been accomplished. It is evident that African American political strategists must explore new avenues for making progress. Outnumbered in every state and in the nation, they must figure out ways to establish meaningful coalitions and devise electoral techniques that link their constituencies with those sharing mutual interests.[14]

Four decades after the passage of the Voting Rights Act and the civil rights movement that spawned it, African Americans in the South have broken through the barriers of disfranchisement. However, the post-1960s development of the two-party system has not brought the expected reign of political liberalism. Instead, the conservative majority has been reconstituted thanks to the partisan realignment of the white South. Lyndon Johnson turned out to be an accurate prognosticator of the future of regional politics. After putting his signature on the Civil

Rights Act of 1964, which destroyed the legal foundations of Jim Crow segregation, the president confided to aides that he had just delivered the South to the Republicans "for your lifetime and mine."[15]

However, there have been signs of a genuine transformation of southern and national party politics emerging from the legacy of the civil rights movement. In the American political system, perhaps the ultimate measure of legitimacy comes in the presidential arena. In this respect, the campaigns of veteran civil rights campaigner and former King aide Jesse L. Jackson for the Democratic presidential nomination in 1984 and 1988, though increasingly forgotten in the popular memory of the early twenty-first century, indicated the arrival of blacks as active agents in national electoral politics. Never before had a black candidate mounted as strong a challenge for the top office in the land. Building upon a solid foundation of black votes, especially in the South, Jackson attempted to fashion what every national politician must ultimately create—a winning coalition. For him this meant an alliance with working-class and rural whites as well as with exploited minorities. Though Jackson's campaigns emerged from the tradition of protest and re-enfranchisement in the civil rights era South, they became part of the respectable electoral mainstream.

It should be remembered that in 1988 Jackson garnered some seven million primary votes, finishing second in the contest to Michael Dukakis, the eventual Democratic presidential nominee. He scored impressive victories in Alabama, Georgia, Louisiana, Mississippi, South Carolina, and Virginia, obtaining more than twelve hundred delegates. Capturing some 90 percent of the black Democratic electorate, Jackson managed to win only 10 percent of white voters, which doomed his candidacy. Despite his failure to secure the nomination, his campaign generated a significant expansion in black voter registration in the eleven former Confederate states (from 56.5 percent in 1982 to 66.2 percent in 1984). With more blacks registered to vote, the number of black elected officials underwent its greatest increase in nearly a decade (5.8 percent for men and 10.8 percent for women).[16]

Twenty years later, Senator Barack Obama of Illinois completed the quest started by Jackson. However, Obama differed from his fellow Prairie State resident in several critical ways. Most significantly, he belonged to the post–civil rights era generation of African American politicians. The middle-class black youths who led the sit-ins in 1960 attended segregated high schools and historically black colleges. The success of their movement opened the doors for the next generation of middle-class students to attend integrated institutions of higher education, including the most prestigious in the nation. Whereas the original sit-inners were more likely to attend Fisk and Howard, Obama graduated from Columbia and Harvard. As Congressman John Lewis acknowledged, "He doesn't have the scars of the movement, because of how he grew up." Nevertheless, the former sit-in and SNCC leader also observed, "Barack was born long before he could experience or understand the movement. He had to move *towards* it in his own time, but it is so clear that he digested it, the spirit and the language of the movement."[17]

Born in 1961 in Hawaii to a mixed-race family, Obama had a white mother who grew up in Kansas and an African-immigrant father from Kenya. Following his parents' divorce, his mother remarried and moved Barack to Indonesia. After four years in Jakarta, he returned to Hawaii and resumed living with his grandparents. The Aloha State had a mixed-race population but relatively few African Americans, leaving Obama feeling isolated and torn between the two cultural streams that flowed through his blood.

Receiving his undergraduate degree from Columbia University in 1983, Obama moved to Chicago in 1985 and became a community organizer, his first real opportunity to work closely in and identify with the African American community. For three years he strove to improve living conditions in the Altgeld Gardens housing projects, an impoverished neighborhood filled with crime and unemployment. From there he decided to attend Harvard Law School, becoming the first African American elected president of the prestigious *Harvard Law Review* and graduating in 1991. Obama learned, he later wrote, "to slip back and forth between my black and white worlds, convinced that with a bit of translation on my part the two worlds would eventually cohere."[18]

After serving in the Illinois State Senate for eight years, Obama won election to the U.S. Senate in 2004. Prior to this victory, he came to national prominence in that year's Democratic national convention in delivering a stirring keynote address that brought the delegates to their feet. Entitled "The Audacity of Hope," this speech recounted his life story, a child of black and white parents who gave him the African name, Barack, meaning "blessed," because they believed "that in a tolerant America your name is no barrier to success."[19] Binding together the American people in all their diversity into one shared community was his audacity of hope.

This speech reflected Obama's appreciation of what W.E.B. Du-Bois called "two-ness" or the double consciousness of hyphenated

Americanism, experienced by most inhabitants of the multi-ethnic United States.[20] Obama readily embraced his African roots as well as his blood connections to white America, optimistically believing that the two could be woven together in celebration of the nation's cultural diversity. However, he departed from many older black politicians, especially those that emerged from the civil rights generation like Jesse Jackson and John Lewis, preferring to speak in universalistic terms rather than in the language of identity politics.

Much had changed since 1960. The sit-ins had provided a major form of political expression in the South at a time when fewer than 30 percent of black adult residents of the region were permitted to vote. With passage of the Voting Rights Act of 1965 electoral politics became the dominant means of achieving the unfulfilled goals of the civil rights movement. Consequently, re-enfranchisement and political legitimacy diminished protest politics as the tactic of choice. The first generation of black politicians that emerged from the civil rights movement directly carried its legacy forward. Indeed, most black officeholders represented majority-black communities and operated on the local level. Not surprisingly, older politicians from the civil rights era like John Lewis were at first suspicious or at least wary of upstarts like Obama who had not paid their political dues.[21]

Obama learned some valuable political lessons in the two decades since Jackson campaigned unsuccessfully for the Democratic presidential nomination. Clearly, he was identified as an African American regardless of his biracial and foreign origins, but he had to run less as a black man than as the well-educated, extremely smart, and articulate person that he is. And given that his African roots only went back one generation rather than ten and that his father was a Muslim, candidate Obama had to prove that he is an American. In fact, Obama is part of a post–civil rights (but *not post-racial*) generation of successful and ambitious black politicians running in majority non-black municipal, state, and national arenas. This cohort also includes Deval Patrick of Massachusetts, Corey Booker of Newark, David Paterson of New York, and Harold Ford Jr. of Tennessee. As a matter of strategy if not predisposition, such politicians have to defuse hints of pro-black messages. Black politicians like Obama could never forget their racial heritage, but they sought to transcend it.

In 2008, Obama demonstrated that his appeal was much wider than that of the civil rights–identified politician, Jesse Jackson. Running for the Democratic presidential nomination, he won the Iowa caucus in a state where blacks constituted less than 5 percent of the population. He went on to place second in the New Hampshire primary, another state with a tiny African American electorate. On February 5, the hotly contested "Super Tuesday" races in twenty-two states, all of them with white-majority electorates, resulted in Obama and his chief rival, Senator Hillary Clinton of New York, splitting the delegates. Most established black politicians, including John Lewis, initially endorsed Clinton because of close ties formed during her husband's presidency.

Despite his impressive showing among younger, more affluent, and better-educated white voters, Obama's core strength rested with African Americans. In South Carolina, where blacks constituted 50 percent of the Democratic electorate, he won over 80 percent of their vote in the primary. Indeed, he captured most of the South with overwhelming support from African Americans in Mississippi, Alabama, Georgia, Louisiana, Virginia, North Carolina, and Texas. With black voters making their preference so clear, Lewis and his cohort moved away from Clinton to back Obama. Once again, as happened during the civil rights era, black leaders rushed to catch up to their grassroots constituencies. Congressman Lewis saw that history was yielding "to the forces" he had helped unleash, and he did not want to be "on the wrong side."[22] In contrast, Clinton drew her greatest strength from white women, many excited by the prospects of electing a woman to the White House for the first time in history. She also scored better than Obama with Latino and white working-class voters.

Race and gender played major roles in the campaign. The National Organization for Women and leading feminists, such as Gloria Steinem, enthusiastically backed Hillary Clinton. The contest between Clinton and Obama supporters about whether their candidate would achieve the distinction of being the first woman or African American to run as Democratic candidate for president turned into an argument over which group had suffered more historical oppression.

The attack on Obama by Geraldine Ferraro, previously the first female Democratic vice-presidential candidate in 1984, exacerbated these tensions. Now a Clinton fund-raiser, she declared. "If Obama was a white man, he would not be in this position. And if he was a woman, he would not be in this position. He happens to be very lucky to be who he is. And the country is caught up in the concept." The Illinois senator responded politely but firmly that being an "African American man named Barack Obama" was not a political asset. "Anybody who knows the history of this country," he asserted, "I think would not take too seriously the notion that this has been a huge advantage, but I don't think it's a disadvantage either."[23]

In fact, the increased focus on race appeared to hurt Obama. Faced with media revelations that his pastor, Jeremiah Wright, had made controversial remarks about America's fundamental racism from the pulpit of his predominantly black Trinity United Church of Christ in Chicago, Obama sought to quell this controversy. Speaking on March 18 in Philadelphia, the city where the Constitution was drafted, he used the occasion not only to place Wright's words in context but also asked Americans, black and white, to confront their own and their nation's racial history and prejudices. Rather than dwelling on past grievances, he urged all Americans to join together and create "the more perfect union" that the founding fathers had envisioned. This would mean using race not as a divisive issue but as an opportunity "to come together and solve challenges like health care, or education, or the need to find good jobs for every American."[24] He showed the kind of balancing skills and optimism that were his campaign hallmark. With the crisis behind him, however, Obama did not address the delicate matter of race again during the primary and presidential campaigns or following his victory.

Obama defied all expectations at the launch of his White House odyssey in winning the greatest prize in American politics. Although most of the South voted against him, he captured North Carolina, where the Greensboro sit-ins had taken place, as well as Virginia, and Florida thanks to enhanced support from white voters compared to the 2004 presidential election. As such, his success confirmed the historical reality that the Democrats have never been able to win the presidency without capturing any of the South's Electoral College votes. On the other hand, he lived up to a more recent trend that no post–World War II Democratic presidential candidate other than Lyndon Johnson in 1964 has won a majority of the votes cast by white Americans. Despite the economic conditions apparently favoring him, Obama's 43 percent share of the white vote nationwide was only 2 percent higher than John Kerry won in 2004 and well below Jimmy Carter's 47 percent in 1976.

Regardless of the historic nature of his victory, it was evident that the new president had his work cut out for him on several fronts. First, Obama would have to do more than other black political leaders who have become incorporated into the mainstream without making much of a difference in combating problems of urban decay and entrenched black poverty. His programs would need to help economically marginalized blacks rather than just middle-class members of the race. Moreover, he would have to do so in the face of the severest economic crisis since the 1930s.

Second, President Obama had to withstand the Republican Party and the associated conservative movement's attempts to delegitimize his election. Despite winning the presidency with the largest percentage of the popular vote since 1988, he faced attacks that queried his citizenship and his political orientation. The "birthers" questioned whether the president was actually born in the United States and therefore eligible to be president. In doing so, they emphasized Obama's "otherness," both as an African American and as a putative Muslim, a line of attack based on his African and Indonesian family connection. Proof such as an authorized birth certificate and contemporary newspaper birth announcements did not wholly satisfy such detractors.

Other critics decried Obama's ideology as alien and socialistic. The charge of liberalism was not sufficient to tarnish Obama's legitimacy as it was to defeat Michael Dukakis, Al Gore, and John Kerry and to hound Bill Clinton into impeachment. Owing to the ineffectiveness of the "l-word," right-wing critics have hurled the sobriquet of socialist at Obama (with the Cold War over, red-baiting political opponents as communist is old hat). After all, liberalism has its place in the American political lexicon along with conservatism, but socialism is a more suitable smear because it is identified, as Obama has been, with foreign countries and alien doctrine.

To overcome the conservative forces lined up against him, Obama faced a much tougher challenge than any previous Democratic president. The technological advances that turned twenty-four-hour cable television into the dominant form of communication meant that prime outlets such as Rupert Murdoch's Fox Television Network could reach and mobilize national audiences that in the past would have remained state or regional in operation. When Fox's Glenn Beck called Obama a racist in July 2009, he struck a chord with his target audience of conservative whites. By comparison, the Internet did the forty-fourth president less damage, despite being a hotbed for lies and nonsense. This is because Obama and his supporters understood how this technology works and put it to good use in support of their own purposes. Furthermore, unlike owning a television station, access to the World Wide Web is free.

Third, in evaluating Obama it is essential to understand that even the greatest presidents only made history to the extent that powerful, established institutions permitted them. Like other presidents before him, both liberal and conservative, he had to deal with a Congress that mirrored the preferences of those voters going to the polls, usually a relatively small number of those eligible to cast ballots in midterm elections. Moreover, the two-party system in the legislature had become increasingly partisan and polarized in the 1990s and beyond. This largely reflected the political transformation of the South from a conservative Democratic region into a conservative Republican one and the disappearance of moderate Republicans as a political grouping outside the South. Electoral defeat in 2008 did not produce a strategic reassessment within the GOP. Instead, the emergence of the Tea Party, supposedly a grassroots organization determined to save America from Obama's socialism, pushed it further rightward. Making the greatest midterm gains by any party since 1938, the GOP recaptured the House of Representatives and slashed the Democratic Senate majority in 2010 with a conservative campaign that capitalized on popular dissatisfaction with the limited recovery of the economy and continued high unemployment. Meanwhile, Obama inherited a conservative Supreme Court that was unsympathetic to the continued expansion of the political and social changes initiated by the civil rights organizations and other causes in the 1960s and 1970s.

Last but not least, in contrast to Abraham Lincoln, Franklin D. Roosevelt, and Lyndon B. Johnson, Obama lacked a necessary ingredient to pressure for progressive change and combat his challengers—the support of a mass, nationwide social movement. Lincoln had the abolitionists, Roosevelt had the labor unions, and Johnson had the civil rights movement. The 2008 electoral movement spurred on by young people and disseminated through grassroots organizing and the Internet showed no signs of developing into a sociopolitical movement of broader significance in the course of the next four years. History shows that progressive change is most likely when grassroots social movements and capable national leaders operate in tandem. Like fire and air, they need each other to burn through the timbers of resistance. At the time of the 2010 elections, Obama had yet to encounter his social movement—or create one, as Roosevelt's New Deal did the industrial labor unions. The ferment on the right that found expression in the emergence of the Tea Party was indicative of the wholly different political contexts of economic crisis in the early twenty-first century and the 1930s. Significantly, FDR had come under attack in his first term from populist organizations for not doing enough to help the common man.

In his perceptive biography, David Remnick portrays President Obama as the most successful member of the "Joshua generation," that group of black leaders who rose to power following the trail blazed by the "Moses generation" embodied by Martin Luther King, the sit-in demonstrators, and the early SNCC. Obama rarely made civil rights speeches or addressed the burdens of racism unless events forced him to do so, as with the campaign controversy over Jeremiah Wright's inflammatory remarks. In some of his best speeches and to mainly black audiences, Obama easily fell into the cadences of the church-flavored discourses of the civil rights era. However, much of the substance of that earlier period emphasizing white moral guilt and the need for economic and political regeneration was missing. The president did not discuss with any urgency what remains to be done with regard to reducing racial inequality. Instead, in pursuing economic and social reforms such as health care he recast the black freedom struggle into "an American freedom struggle."[25] Whether presenting the needs of disadvantaged blacks in universalistic rather than racially particularistic terms will be successful has yet to be demonstrated. Indeed, the early results were disappointing. Polls showed that Obama's election made African Americans feel better about their status, but the reality of their condition was very different. In the hard times of his first three years as president, the economic gap between whites and blacks widened, and black unemployment, poverty, and home foreclosures reached their highest levels since 2000.[26]

Celebration of the fiftieth anniversary of the sit-ins occurred at the outset of Obama's second year in office. Marking the occasion, the first African American president wrote a piece for the *Greensboro News-Record*. Reminding its readers that the sit-ins had begun in their city, he pointed out that the lunch-counter demonstrations had "reignited a movement for social justice that would forever change America," for which he was personally grateful. The president went on to tell how the sit-ins had placed in motion the forces leading to the Freedom Rides, the March on Washington, the Civil Rights Act of 1964, and the Voting Rights Act of 1965, giving all Americans "a fundamental right to share in the blessings of this country." Obama did not have to state the obvious—these sit-in inspired developments that laid the basis for his election to the White House, a milestone that three of the four original demonstrators would witness in their lifetime.[27]

Combining protest with electoral politics, the civil rights movement succeeded in transforming individuals and communities through collective struggle. Although Barack Obama lived far from the sit-ins and other momentous civil rights events in time and space, he carried on its legacy both by embracing its goals and transcending them. His 2008 campaign succeeded in expanding both African American and white political enthusiasm, especially that of the young. Yet enthusiasm could not reignite a genuine social movement to fulfill the unfinished agenda of the civil rights era. If history is any guide, presidential mobilization of grassroots support for social change represented the best hope of breaking the partisan stalemate that gripped Washington in the wake of the 2010 elections and meeting the enormous challenges that confronted the nation. This was a daunting task and one that mainly frustrated Obama during his term in office. It should be remembered, however, that the obstacles facing the young civil rights protesters who did so much to topple racial segregation and disfranchisement a half century earlier were even more formidable.

Notes

1. James W. Washington, ed., *Testament of Hope: The Essential Writings and Speeches of Martin Luther King, Jr.* (New York: HarperOne, 1991), 197–200.

2. Ella J. Baker, "Bigger than a Hamburger," in *The Eyes on the Prize Civil Rights Reader*, ed. Clayborne Carson et al. (New York: Penguin Books, 1991), 120.

3. For discussion see Clayborne Carson, *In Struggle: SNCC and the Black Awakening of the 1960s* (Cambridge: Harvard University Press, 1981), 38–42, 45–51, 74–81.

4. "Best Speeches of Barack Obama through His 2009 Inauguration," http://obamaspeeches.com/003-John-Lewis-65th-Birthday-Gala-Obama-Speech-htn; David Remnick, "The President's Hero," *New Yorker*, February 2, 2009, http:www.newyorkercom/talkcomment/2009/02/02/0902-taco-talk-remnick.

5. Steven F. Lawson, *Running for Freedom: Civil Rights and Black Politics in America since 1941*, 3rd ed. (Malden, Mass.: Wiley-Blackwell, 2009), 274.

6. Ibid., 292.

7. Ibid., 173.

8. Steven F. Lawson, *Black Ballots: Voting Rights in the South, 1944–1969*, reprint edition (Lanham, Md.: Lexington Books, 1999), 308.

9. Stephan Thernstrom and Abigail Thernstrom, *America in Black and White: One Nation Indivisible* (New York: Simon & Schuster, 1999), 288. Roland Burris of Illinois was appointed to replace Barack Obama after his election to the presidency. Burris did not run for a full term and was succeeded by a white Republican. Deval Patrick was elected governor of Massachusetts in 2007, and David Paterson, New York's lieutenant governor, became governor following the resignation of Eliot Spitzer in 2008. Paterson did not run for another term. As of June 2011, no African Americans held a Senate seat and only Patrick served as governor.

10. Lawson, *Running for Freedom*, 291, 339.

11. Ibid., 170.

12. J. Morgan Kousser, *Colorblind Injustice: Minority Voting Rights and the Undoing*

of the *Second Reconstruction* (Chapel Hill: University of North Carolina Press, 1999), chapter 5.

13. *Shaw v. Reno* 509 U.S. 630 (1993). Despite similar rulings in Georgia and Texas striking down additional "opportunity districts," the Supreme Court has not altogether eliminated race as a legitimate factor in legislative districting. In *Hunt [Easley] v. Cromartie* 121 S. Ct. 1452 (2001), it ruled that race was not an improper consideration as long as it was not the "dominant and controlling" one. The case involved the same district that North Carolina had tried to redraw several times. In a 5–4 opinion, Justice Stephen Breyer, a Clinton appointee, contended that the Democratic political affiliation of African Americans rather than race was the predominant concern in the minds of the Tar Heel legislators who created the challenged district. For analysis see Tinsley E. Yarsborough, *Race and Redistricting: The Shaw-Cromartie Cases* (Lawrence: University Press of Kansas, 2002); and Laughlin McDonald, *A Voting Rights Odyssey: Black Enfranchisement in Georgia* (Cambridge, U.K.: Cambridge University Press, 2003), chapter 17. For contrasting perspectives, see Carol M. Swain, *Black Faces, Black Interests: The Representation of African Americans in Congress* (Cambridge: Harvard University Press, 1993); and Ruth P. Morgan, *Governance by Decree: The Impact of the voting Rights Act in Dallas* (Lawrence: University Press of Kansas, 2004).

14. Some African Americans and their political allies have questioned whether creating more electoral districts for blacks to win will ultimately accomplish their progressive goals. They cite the inroads Republicans have made in southern congressional and state elections. These critics of majority-minority districts charge that drawing new boundary lines to create districts in favor of black candidates has come at the expense of moderate and liberal white Democrats, who are more likely than Republicans to support black goals. They ask whether African Americans will be better off if, electing a few more representatives of color, they find themselves part of an ineffectual minority political party. This is what Lani Guinier was advocating in 1993 when her nomination as assistant attorney general for civil rights was ambushed in Congress and withdrawn by President Bill Clinton. That an advocate of finding innovative ways of sharing political power across racial lines and becoming more inclusive with respect to electoral representation could be labeled a "quota queen" is a disturbing sign of how far racist discourse had once again infected the body politic. See Lani Guinier, *The Tyranny of the Majority: Fundamental Fairness in Representative Democracy* (New York: Free Press, 1994), chapter 4, and *Lift Every Voice: Turning a Civil Rights Setback into a New Vision of Social Justice* (New York: Simon & Schuster, 1997), chapter 10.

15. The aides were Bill Moyers and Harry McPherson. See http://www.masshumanities.org/?p=f04_rohm. For discussion, see Earl Black and Merle Black, *The Rise of Southern Republicans* (Cambridge: Harvard University Press, 2002); and Numan V. Bartley and Hugh D. Graham, *Southern Politics and the Second Reconstruction* (Baltimore: Johns Hopkins University Press, 1975).

16. Lawson, *Running for Freedom*, 223–35, 245–54.

17. Lewis quoted in "Remnick, "The President's Hero." For Obama and the politics of race, see Gwen Ifill, *The Breakthrough: Politics and Race in the Age of Obama* (New York: Doubleday, 2009); and Horace G. Campbell, *Barack Obama and Twenty-First Century Politics* (London: Pluto Press, 2011).

18. Barack Obama, *Dreams from My Father: A Story of Race and Inheritance* (New York: Cannongate, 2007), 82.

19. Lawson, *Running for Freedom*, 319.

20. W.E.B. DuBois, *The Souls of Black Folk* (New York: Signet, 1969), 45.

21. Matt Bai, "Is Obama the End of Black Politics?" *New York Times*, August 10, 2008, http://www.nytimes.com/2008/08/10/magazine/10politics-t.html.

22. Ibid.

23. Kathryn Q. Seeleye and Julie Bosman, "Ferraro's Remarks Become Talk of Campaign," *New York Times*, March 12, 2008, www.nytimes.com/2008/03/12; "Barack Obama Responds to Geraldine Ferraro," *ABC News*, March 12, 2008, www.youtube.com/watch?v=wYooyt13Tk4.

24. http://www.nytimes.com/2008/03/18/world/americas/18iht-18obamaspeech.11222332.html. For a very good journalistic history of the primary and general election campaign, see Mark Halperin and John Heileman, *Race of a Lifetime: How Obama Won the White House* (New York: Viking, 2010), which provides extensive discussion of the Wright controversy on pp. 234–39, 243–49.

25. David Remnick, *The Bridge: The Life and Rise of Barack Obama* (New York: Vintage, 2011), 494; emphasis in source.

26. Gary Younge, "Obama and Black Americans: The Paradox of Hope," *The Nation*, May 18, 2011, http://www.thenation.com/article/160782/obama-and-black-americans-paradox-hope.

27. http://www.news-record.com/content/2010/01/22/article/obama_greensboro_four_left_mark_on_nation. David Richmond died in 1990 at age forty-nine, survived by Franklin McCain, Joseph A. McNeil, and Jibreel Khazan (Ezell Blair Jr.).

Contributors

The Editors

Iwan Morgan is professor of U.S. studies and Commonwealth Fund Chair of American History at University of Collge London. He served as chair of the executive committee of the Historians of the Twentieth Century United States from 2007 to 2013. His book *The Age of Deficits: Presidents and Unbalanced Budgets from Jimmy Carter to George W. Bush* was awarded the American Politics Group's Richard E. Neustadt prize. His recent publications include *Broken Government? American Politics in the Obama Era* (coedited with Philip Davies); *Seeking a New Majority: the Republican Party and American Politics, 1960-1980* (coedited with Rober Mason); and *Reconfiguring the Union: Civil War Transformations* (coedited with Philip Davies).

Philip Davies is director of the British Library's Eccles Centre for American Studies. He is former chair of both the American Politics Group and the British Association of American Studies and is now chair of the European Association of American Studies. A specialist on U.S. elections, on which he has written numerous books, he has also coedited a number of studies with Iwan Morgan, including *America's Americans: Population Issues in U.S. Politics and Society*; *The Federal Nation: Perspectives on American Federalism*; and *Assessing George W. Bush's Legacy: The Right Man?*

The Contributors

Simon Hall is senior lecturer in American history at the University of Leeds and a former Fox International Fellow at Yale. A specialist on social movements, he has published three books: *Peace and Freedom: The Civil Rights and Antiwar Movements in the 1960s*; *American Patriotism, American Protest: Social Movements Since the Sixties*; and *Rethinking the American Anti-War Movement*.

John Kirk is Donaghey Professor of History and chair of the History Department at the University of Arkansas–Little Rock and was formerly professor of U.S. history at Royal Holloway, University of London. A prolific civil rights scholar, his publications include *Redefining the Color Line: Black Activism in Little Rock, 1940–1970*; *Martin Luther King Jr.*; and *Beyond Little Rock: The Origins and Legacies of the Central High Crisis*.

Steven F. Lawson is emeritus professor of history at Rutgers University, New Jersey. His publications include *Black Ballots: Voting Rights in the South, 1944–1969*; *In Pursuit of Power: Southern Blacks and Electoral Politics, 1965–1982*; *Running for Freedom: Civil Rights and Black Politics in America since 1941*; and *Civil Rights Crossroads: Nation, Community, and the Black Freedom Struggle*.

George Lewis is director of the Center for American Studies and reader in American history at the University of Leicester. A specialist on white response to racial change, he is the author of *The White South and the Red Menace: Segregationists, Anticommunism, and Massive Resistance, 1945–1965* and *Massive Resistance: The White Response to the Civil Rights Movement*.

Peter Ling is professor of American studies at the University of Nottingham. In addition to many articles on southern and civil rights history, his publications include *Martin Luther King Jr.* and (coedited with Sharon Monteith) *Gender and the Civil Rights Movement*. He is presently completing a study of the network of Southern Christian Leadership Conference financial donors.

Sharon Monteith is professor of American studies at the University of Nottingham. A cultural historian, her books include *Advancing Sisterhood? Interracial Friendships in Southern Fiction* and *American Culture in the 1960s*. She edited *The Cambridge Companion to the Literature of the American South* and co-edited *South to a New Place: Region, Literature, Culture* (with Suzanne Jones) and *The New Encyclopaedia of Southern Culture: Media* (with Allison Graham) among other collections. She is completing a book titled *SNCC's Stories: Narrative Culture and the Southern Freedom Struggle of the 1960s*.

Joe Street is senior lecturer in American history at Northumbria University. In addition to numerous scholarly articles, he has written *The*

Culture War in the Civil Rights Movement, also published by University Press of Florida. He is currently working on a study of the Black Panther Party.

Stephen Tuck is lecturer in American history at Oxford University. He is the author of *Beyond Atlanta: The Struggle for Racial Equality in Georgia, 1940–1980* and *We Ain't What We Ought to Be: The Black Freedom Struggle from Emancipation to Obama*, which won the American Politics Group's Richard E. Neustadt prize and the British Association of American Studies Book Prize.

Clive Webb is professor of American history at the University of Sussex. He is the author of *Fight against Fear: Southern Jews and Black Civil Rights*, which won the Southern Jewish History book prize; (with David Brown) *Race in the American South: From Slavery to Civil Rights*, which was a CHOICE Outstanding Academic Title in 2008; and *Rabble Rousers: The American Far Right in the Civil Rights Era*.

The University Press of Florida is the scholarly publishing agency for the State University System of Florida, comprising Florida A&M University, Florida Atlantic University, Florida Gulf Coast University, Florida International University, Florida State University, New College of Florida, University of Central Florida, University of Florida, University of North Florida, University of South Florida, and University of West Florida.

Index

Black Power and, 116, 125, 127, 166; British Friends of, 157, 168n28; Carmichael tour with, 141–42; Cold War imperialism critique by, 140–43; Cold War patriotism and, xi, 135–40, 143–44; communication department of, 157; community of, xi, 101–2, 116–18, 121–24, 128–29; conferences of, 87, *88*, 89–92; coordinating committee of, 92–93; cultural component of, 124; decline of, 117; fiction writing, 109; Forman and, 90, 93, 112; formation of, vii, 1–2, 9, 83, 138, 144; fragility of, 86–87; Freedom Rides and, 83, 90–92; goals of, 102, 104, 118–19; government, U.S., and, 143–44; group reports of, 119; growth of, 87; historical scholarship of, 83–84; identity of, 82, 86–87, 116; image of, 84–85; imagined community of, xi, 117, 124–29; integration of, 102, 120; intellectual transformation of, xi; on King, Mary, 6; leaders of, 88–89, 125–26, 146–47; Lewis, J., and, 83, 133n46; McDew election of, 17; membership of, x, 81–83, 90, 93, 95n18; mentors of, 81, 88; militant members of, 17; in Mississippi, x, 82; name of, 2; Nashville, 118–19; nomenclature of, x; nonviolence and, 42, 147–48; organizational structure of, 87, 93, 119, 123; organizers of, 98; philosophy of, 120; political ethos of, 103; principles of, 98; publicists of, 84–85; racial and class composition of, 123, 128, 131n32; racial policy of, 120; radicalism of, 103, 126, 129; reunion (1987), 104; second-anniversary conference, 18; segregation and, 171; Sellers on, 14, 119; sexism in, 85; staff of, viii, 109, 121, 127, 132n40; unofficial motto of, 14; Vietnam War and, 140–41, 144; volunteers, x, 86, 98, 121–22; Washington clique control of, xi; white members of, 16, 17, 34, 116, 120, 121–22, 128; women in, 92, 96n24

Student protests, 1–2; in Europe, 3, 19n7; growth of, 84–85; law enforcement and, 60–61; NAACP support of, 11; religion and, 65–69, 79n59; restaurant, 155; against Vietnam War, 2–3; violence and, 6, 20n14, 63. *See also* Student sit-ins; *specific types*

Students for a Democratic Society (SDS), 86

Student sit-ins, vii, 1–2; arrests, 25; Atlanta, 60; beginning of, 102–3; Bristol drink-in, 153–54; Cape Town, 155; Collins on, 76n4; court cases of, 34–35; demographics of, 15; Dienstfrey on, 17; family disapproval of, 4, 20n12; fines of, 7, 29–30; historians of, 23–24; Jackson campaign, 55n19; Jacksonville, 8, 42–44, 60–61; in jail, 6–7; Jim Crow ideology and, ix–x; justifiability of, 49; Knoxville, 68; Lawson on, 144–45; legal aspects of, 24; le sit-in, 156; Little Rock arrests, 25, 29–30; materialistic logic of, 15; McDew on, 17–18; media and, 72, 135; Nashville, 4, 41; outlawing of, 64; patriotism and, 137; peaceful activism of, 12; as psychological turning point in race relations, 53; religious institutional support of, 66–67; scope of, 5–6; Sitton on, 57n40; success of, 41–42; tactics, 50–51; at Toddle House eatery, 145; in UK, xii, 153–70; uniqueness of, 7–8; violence and, 20n14; white, 16, 17; white southerners reactions to, 58–59; Wilkins on, 135

The Student Voice, 104, 109–10, 111, 139

Sunday Times, 164

Supreme Court, U.S., 24, 30–31; Obama's inheritance of, 182; state action and, 33

Sweeny, Dennis, 114n37

Taboos, 4

Tampa Tribune, 61

Tea Party movement, 23, 182

Tear gas, 7

Teddy Boy hooligans, 162

Terrorism. *See* Racial terrorism

Thalhimers lunch counter protests, 51

Thelwell, Michael, x–xi, 98, 104, 105, 110, 114n29

"Thin White Line" (Forman), x, 98–101, 103

Thomas, Henry, 89, 91

Thompson, Allen, 45, 74

Thompson, Bennie, 172

Thompson, Ernest Trice, 66

Till, Emmett, 11, 102

Tillinghast, Muriel, 119

The Times, 154

Title II, 23, 33–34

Toddle House eatery protest, 145

Travis, Jimmie, 106

Trespassing, 45, 59–60

Trinity United Church of Christ, 180

Truman, Harry, 64, 136, 138